FAITH, GRACE AND HERESY

Best wishes!

Faith, Grace and Heresy

The Biography of Rev. Charles M. Jones

Mark Pryor

Writer's Showcase
San Jose New York Lincoln Shanghai

Faith, Grace and Heresy
The Biography of Rev. Charles M. Jones

Writer's Showcase
an imprint of iUniverse, Inc.

For information address:
iUniverse, Inc.
5220 S. 16th St., Suite 200
Lincoln, NE 68512
www.iuniverse.com

ISBN: 0-595-21718-4

Printed in the United States of America

I Corinthians—13

If I speak in the tongues of men and of angels, but have not love, I am a noisy gong or a clanging cymbal. And if I have prophetic powers, and understand all mysteries and all knowledge, and if I have all faith, so as to remove mountains, but have not love, I am nothing. If I give away all I have, and deliver my body to be burned, I gain nothing.

Love is patient and kind; love is not jealous or boastful; it is not arrogant or rude. Love does not insist on its own way; it is not irritable or resentful; it does not rejoice at wrong, but rejoices in the right. Love bears all things, hopes all things, endures all things.

Love never ends; as for tongues, they will cease; as for knowledge, it will pass away. For our knowledge is imperfect and our prophecy is imperfect; but when the time comes, the imperfect will pass away. When I was a child, I spoke like a child, I reasoned like a child; but when I became a man, I gave up childish ways. For now I see in a mirror dimly, but then face to face. Now I know in part; then I will know fully, even as I have been fully understood.

So faith, hope, love abide, these three; but the greatest of these is love.

Contents

Acknowledgments

This book would never have been written if not for the help and support of others. My few words of thanks here are poor offerings when compared to the enormity of the help I have received.

To the Snuffbuckets, an organization of academics, intellectuals, lunatics, and friends. Your polite but firm demands were the light at the end of this long tunnel, and your financial support was invaluable. Moreover, your love of, and loyalty to, my grandfather and grandmother have been as inspirational to me as the man himself. It is hard for me to resist thanking each one of you individually, but I shall try to do so. Let me just mention Charles McCoy and his unbounded optimism from across the country, Oliver Orr whose suggestions and offers of help were gratefully received and adopted, and John and Sibyl Barlow for their polite but pointed progress requests. Thanks also, to Dick and Lyn Griesemer for all their painstaking editing work, and also to Karen Abbotts and Harry Mihet for their creative input.

To my wife, Sarah, who made sure I understood how capable I was of doing this, and for giving me confidence and for urging me to finish my work and bring it into the world.

To my parents who read every word from the beginning, who gave honest criticism and invaluable suggestions, and who always encouraged me.

To my uncle Roy, who edited, suggested, read and reread whenever asked.

To my grandmother, without whom the great man would have been less great, and without whom the beauty of his story would have been tarnished. You kept his sermons, his newspaper articles, and his many attempts at writing his own life story. But most importantly, you remembered and shared the stories and memories of his childhood, and of your life together. Your only failing has been your lack of recognition of your own importance to his life, and his life's work.

Finally to my Aunt Beppie. Without you, this book would not have been started. Without you, if it had been started, it would still be ten years from completion. Without you, once near completion it would be less accurate, less interesting. You gave me the most encouragement of all, you pushed me when I needed to be pushed and understood when I left it alone. You showed me how to work hard on this book by working harder on it yourself. Everything I asked of you, no matter how small, you did with relish. I asked much, and you did it all, and then offered more. Often, I felt that it was 'our' book, but you always said it was mine. Your enthusiasm for this project, your vision, and your hard work and determination are all inspirations, and in this and in all things you are a credit to your father.

Thank you all.

Foreword—by William Friday

These pages record a turbulent, often trying, period of social history for this University town. It was an experience not unlike other southern communities feeling the stress and constructive tension of the integration of public schools and communities and the establishment of civil rights afforded each citizen under the Constitution of the United States. But there was one critical, powerful difference in Chapel Hill—his name was the Reverend Charles Jones.

Mark Pryor's extensive reporting of the events of the 50's and 60's is focused on the role and leadership Charles Jones exhibited as an active church leader in the South. How did he do it? His longtime friend and former University Law School Dean, Henry Brandis, put it this way:

"He put aside not only anger, but also irascibility; he eschewed cant, egocentric pride, pomposity, and sanctimony; he agreed to take seriously the most disturbingly difficult precepts of Jesus of Nazareth; and he embraced for the span of his life the fundamental simplicity of common decency."

And this is how he lived and moved among us, always bringing strength and encouragement to those challenging the status quo or seeking to make real the promise of personal freedom and a more joyful and useful life.

As I read these chapters, a flood of memories swept over me of times and events now decades old, yet still vivid. It is hard to read copies of words spoken and deeds done in the fierce passions of those times and not relive the pain, anger, frustration and disappointment. Yet, this modest, humble preacher worked among us counseling non-violence and charity at all times. His advocacy, which cost him his pastorate, prevailed, and the community moved forward in social relations.

I was privileged to be a friend of Charles Jones. My wife, Ida, was a founding member of the Community Church to which Reverend Jones was called to become its first minister. I attended services with her, because the sermons he preached taught the responsibilities of being a Christian as intensely personal obligations requiring commitment and personal action. I am profoundly grateful for these lessons which influenced my life.

Charles Jones died in April 1993 at age 87. James Shumaker, World War II prisoner of war and longtime editor of the Chapel Hill Newspaper, wrote:

"There might be another Charles Jones around here somewhere, but if there is, he has escaped notice so far."

It is worthy of note that the portrait of Charles Jones now hangs on the walls of the Chapel Hill Presbyterian Church along with other pastors who served this congregation. As is true of effective leaders, his work lives on in the lives of men and women and organizations to whom Charles Jones gave inspiration, courage, and faith to serve humanity as best they could.

For all of his adult years, and in all things, he was greatly blessed by the consistent presence and love of his dear wife Dorcas, who inspired him day by day.

Faith, Grace and Heresy will give you a deeper and wider understanding of America's struggle, yet ongoing, for social justice and an appreciation of the life and work of a good man who did his part to achieve that great good for all citizens.

Prelude

The life of Charles M. Jones was a story waiting to be told. From the months he spent as an inquisitive youth exploring the US to his decades-long socially active ministry in North Carolina, his life was one that touched people. Whether he was selling maps in Terre Haute, Indiana, or leading a civil rights demonstration in Chapel Hill, he sought to understand people and, perhaps more importantly, he endeavored to see that they understood each other. Working in car factories in Detroit, and playing manager, chef, and waiter in a small café in San Antonio taught him that the world of human experience was too wide to allow him to accept or understand only one set of moral or social norms. He made an effort to broaden his experience of people so that he could relate to all people, be they professors, waitresses, politicians or laborers. He knew, also, that both sides in any disagreement had something worth saying, and hearing—this is why he would rush home to turn on the radio and listen to his social nemesis Jesse Helms, then a conservative commentator. His ability to listen calmly and with an open mind was one of his greatest strengths, and meant that a difference of opinion with Charlie Jones would result in a dialogue, not a dispute.

Preacher, as he was known, was also one of life's optimists. When he sat down to talk a problem over with someone, he was sure they would listen to reason. Ironically perhaps, this may have been a weakness of sorts, resulting in his failure to see the darker motivations of the people that opposed him. Many of his frustrations arose out of his powerful faith in the Golden Rule, and his belief that man is capable of, and driven

1

to do, more good than evil. These occasional, if virtuous, blinders meant that Charlie sometimes failed to see that when confronting an issue as deeply ingrained as racism, reason was rarely a person's first recourse.

But Charlie's faith in human nature meant he attracted, and converted, many more people than he repelled. Almost a decade after his death, those who were his students in the 1940s, 1950s and 1960s still return every year or two to Chapel Hill to remember him and spend time with his wife, Dorcas. She was undoubtedly one of his earthly inspirations, and certainly the one person who in a practical sense allowed Charles Jones to become, as newspaper columnist and UNC journalism professor Jim Shumaker put it: "The Preacher who Raised Hell."

This book was written to honor his memory and to share his story, a story that is in large part the story of civil rights in Chapel Hill. It was written because there were many people, like Preacher, who fought against racism not because of a gradual realization that it was wrong, but because it offended them always. While he was one of the first to speak out, and one of the most active, they should all be remembered for their part in ending segregation.

I have pieced his life story together from a number of sources, many of which were incomplete in themselves. Memories fade, and I have had the same story told to me by three or four different people in three or four different ways. Needless to say, each teller was convinced his or her account was the correct one. Because much of this book details the unrecorded aspect of Preacher's life, all of these personal recollections have been invaluable. When presented with different accounts I have had to exercise the writer's prerogative and select the one that seemed most likely (or if nothing distinguished them, the one that made the best story!).

On a more personal level, it was during the last year of his life that I spent a great deal of time with my grandparents, Charlie and Dorcas Jones. Conversations would turn to past events, people loved, the good and bad of the Presbyterian church, the racial struggle. We looked at photographs, read old newspaper articles, and talked about those parts of Charlie's life, such as his childhood and his seminary days, about which no newspaper or magazine had written. I saw that his was a story with many dimensions that needed piecing together and just as I needed and wanted to see the whole picture, I knew it would contain memories and meaning for others.

Chapter One

The Early Years

"Life is going to ask more of us than counting the sunny hours. It will say, How much can you take? How long can you take it? How much strength, courage and patience have you? All this is to say, how deep are your roots? How strong are your foundations?"
- Charles Miles Jones.

In the beginning there was no Jones family - or so the story goes.

One version, the romantic, ignoble one, tells of a horse-thief named Jackie Dennis who lived in Knoxville, Tennessee, in the mid-1800s. Dennis was a shrewd operator and made a living out of his illegal activities for most of his adult life. But, as with most criminals, his luck eventually ran out, and with the law closing in he was forced to pack up a few belongings and flee 200 miles west to Nashville. There he adopted the inconspicuous name of Jones and a law-abiding lifestyle, using his ill-gotten knowledge of horses to set up a livery stable.

The second, and altogether more likely, story puts Jackie Dennis on the wrong side of public opinion and not the law, depicting him as a liberal and not a criminal.

It seems that Dennis, again the owner of a livery stable, was a small man who stood tall for what he believed and was not afraid to speak his mind. But his progressive views on race relations, at a time when discrimination, segregation and racism were considered neither problems nor even issues worthy of discussion, served only to make him unpopular. His refusal to accept blacks as second-class citizens, his refusal to call them 'niggers' and his inability to keep these views to himself, isolated him. Business dried up, and he was verbally abused in the street by former friends, acquaintances and customers who even threatened to torch his stables. Unwilling to endanger either his family or his livelihood further, Dennis eventually moved to Nashville, taking on, as in the first story, the name of Jones.

Toward the end of the 19th Century, Nashville, advertising itself as the 'Athens of the South', was home to 50,000 people. It was also home to a number of fine educational institutions, such as Vanderbilt University, Fiske University, the black college famed for its choir which performed worldwide, and the respected Meharry College.

It was in this seat of learning, amid such impressive educational influences, that William Bunyan Jones, Jackie's first son, managed to complete the third grade in the city's public school system. For his formative teenage years William traded the confines of the classroom for the streets of downtown Nashville, selling newspapers and working odd jobs to keep himself both busy and in pocket money. He was a smart boy and had no trouble reading, writing or making change for his customers. His friends were the other newsboys working the city streets and it was with them that he fostered a love of gambling he would never lose. In quiet moments they would gather and pitch pennies at a line drawn on the pavement, the closest coin winning the rest of the pot which was never more than just a few cents, as they played for fun not profit.

William's main paper stand was outside a three-story building occupied by several doctors and dentists, right in the center of Nashville. One of the dentists, a Dr. W.R. Chatham, took a special interest in

William and gave him the job of sweeping his office every morning so he could earn a few cents and stay off the streets, for at least a short time. It was the first of many acts of kindness Dr. Chatham would prove a loyal friend and generous benefactor over the years.

In fact Dr. Chatham's next good deed set the young newsboy on the path to a career, for he recommended William to his close friend, the portrait photographer A.J. Thuss, who was also in need of someone to do the cleaning up at his studio. William enjoyed working there and soon Thuss decided to take him on as an apprentice, part-time to begin with and later full-time. And with a regular income, William was able to enjoy gambling again, setting up a poker ring with friends and playing every week. But again, the betting was done with small amounts of money and purely for fun.

Such was William's lifestyle for fourteen years after he left school. He had no career and no real education, but his experiences on the streets as a child and working for Thuss and others gave him a basic knowledge of business and the ability to take care of himself.

It was while working for Thuss that William, at the age of 27, met, and fell in love with, Louise Virginia Koellein, the 24-year-old daughter of an immigrant German photographer. Louise was the second youngest of nine children, and was teaching in the public school system in Nashville when she met William. Her father had died some years before, leaving behind a protective mother who strongly objected to her daughter's suitor. The more she saw of William, the more Mrs. Koellein liked him, but she fiercely disapproved of his penchant for gambling and saw an educational and cultural gap too wide for any permanent union and she refused to give her daughter permission to marry. In November 1900, the young couple eloped anyway, were wed and did not return for six months. When they did it was at William's insistence, but Mrs. Koellein refused to let her new son-in-law into her home. It was only when William and Louise began their own family that she relented, with William ironically becoming a firm favorite.

After their wedding, William and Louise Jones moved into a four-roomed house, with no electricity or running water, in Treutland Street, Nashville, which they rented for $25 a month. They soon began to fill it with children of their own. Baby Louise Virginia was born in July 1901, and William Bunyon Jr., known throughout his life as Dub, was born in October 1903.

As the household started to grow, William decided to quit his job with A.J. Thuss and seek out better paid temporary work anywhere he could find it. Often he would be away from home for months at a time, sending back money orders when he could, or returning unannounced with wads of bills which he would present with a flourish to his wife and children.

One of these jaunts took him to Texas, after one of his poker playing friends sent him a postcard proclaiming excitedly that oil was "flowing like water", and assuring him of an abundance of high-paying, short-term jobs from which he could take his pick. As he always did, William followed up on this tip, and in the cold December of 1905 he left his two children and heavily pregnant wife and headed west.

And it was on the night of January 8, 1906, with his father a thousand miles away on an oil field near San Antonio, that Charles Miles Jones was born.

Charlie Jones' earliest memories actually begin with his father, a fitting reflection of the strong bond that would exist between them. Though William was often away from home in these early years, the Jones family stayed close-knit and supportive of each other until the head of the household returned. Louise would keep a calendar, counting down the days until her husband arrived home, telling the children the evening before his arrival and leaving them too excited to sleep. Every homecoming was a delight, for William often brought gifts as well as money. Once, he bade his children stand outside the house in preparation for their surprise. They did so, and were overjoyed to see a little brown puppy come bounding out from under the front porch as William whistled and called its name.

Even when he was home there was one family tradition he did not share in, for unlike his wife, William was a confirmed agnostic and he attended church just once a year, at Easter. While it was Louise, brought up a strict Presbyterian, who accompanied the children to church each week, it was William who took out their best shoes every Saturday and polished them up himself. He encouraged his children to go to church, and was always proud when the youngsters were awarded pins for their regular attendance.

After church, the family indulged in another Sunday tradition with their much loved grandfather, Jackie. Hitching up a young pony to his best Surrey buggy, he would take the older children, Dub, Louise and Charlie, for rides in the country. During the week, too, Charlie and Dub would often go over to spend time with their grandfather, or to play in the loft of his livery stable. On several occasions they discovered whisky bottles the old man had stashed away. They knew he drank too much, but they loved him and hated Grandmother Jones' incessant nagging about it, so they never disturbed the bottles nor gave him away. This drinking, a source of secret, childish excitement to Charlie and Dub, made a more serious impression on William, Sr. who remained a teetotaler all his life.

By 1912, there were five children and two adults living in the small, run-down house on Treutland Street. Two more boys, George Darnell and Otto Emil had been born. Living in such cramped conditions made having visitors almost impossible, and when Louise's brother Otto, known to the children as Uncle Dinky, came to stay while on furlough from the navy, he looked at the possibility of updating and extending the tiny property. He soon came to the conclusion this would be impractical and a waste of money, so he suggested to his sister they look elsewhere for a house to buy.

Louise wrote to her husband, who had again gone to Texas, and he hurried back, delighted with the idea. The three of them rented a buggy for a day and drove around looking for somewhere suitable. They found a house three miles away on Cleveland Street, and had the option of either renting or buying it. Uncle Dinky offered to pay for the house, and have them repay him at $25 a month. They jumped at the chance.

By the time they were ready to move, Uncle Dinky had returned to sea and William, Sr. was off chasing another once-in-a-lifetime opportunity. Louise placed an ad in the Nashville Tennessean, the local morning paper, to find someone to help them move. The next day Charlie was sitting under a tree in the front yard when a young black man came to the door and offered to do the job. Loading furniture and boxes onto his wagon, it was soon clear he would have to make two trips. Itching to see his new home, Charlie asked if he could go with the man and, promising to behave, climbed up beside him. To the six year old boy they seemed mighty high up, so he sat close to his new friend, enjoying every minute of the hour long ride.

Once at the house, the man, who had introduced himself as Sam, unloaded the flat-bed wagon while Charlie watched. They then sat together outside and shared Sam's lunch of sandwiches and cookies. And as Sam returned to Treutland Street, Charlie stayed to explore his new home.

The house itself had six rooms, three on each side of a long corridor. At the back of the property was a small barn filled with coal and kindling, and with hay in an upstairs loft. The house was in much better condition than their previous home, and once Uncle Dinky had installed running water and repainted it inside and out for them, it seemed positively luxurious. An added attraction for Louise was the Presbyterian church right across the street.

Also across the street, next to the church, was Glenn Elementary School, the two-story brick building where Charlie Jones began his schooling at the age of six. Unlike his brother, Dub, Charlie never distinguished himself in the classroom, except for a natural ability in spelling, and progressed through the school an average student.

As is often the case, school was the first place Charlie experienced a world outside his family and several of the teachers made lasting impressions on him. The most influential was the Principal Will Manlove, a fiery man who would decide on a course of action and then throw all his energies into accomplishing it. As America entered the First World War and food shortages began, he organized what he called his 'Army of the Furrows', using vacant lots as vegetable gardens for the children to cultivate. And it was Mr. Manlove who, recognizing the dangers of wounded pride, left anonymous food packages for the poor, an example that would be followed by the Reverend Charles Jones many years later.

Another not easily forgotten was the third grade teacher called Miss Annie. She suffered terribly from a guilt complex, bursting into tears at all times of the day as she agonized over the plight of dying African children who, not having been converted to Christianity, would be doomed in the hereafter. Her punishments were even more feared than Mr. Manlove's paddlings, for she would take the offender into the cloakroom and make him pray aloud for forgiveness as she wept openly. It was an embarrassment not many children were keen to endure.

His next year, fourth grade, Charles had to deal with the strange behavior of another teacher, Miss Eliza Arledge. She made it clear he was her favorite, and would often keep him behind after class to talk to him or give him little presents. One afternoon she asked him to sit on her lap. Stroking his hair, she told him what a special friend he was. Not fully understanding, just knowing something was happening that should not be, Charles later told his mother. She handled the matter discreetly, talking only to Miss Arledge who from then on treated Charles as just another pupil, much to his relief. It was only later he understood the import of Miss Arledge's behavior.

During Charles' final years at Glenn Elementary his father at last gave up his long-distance job hunts. When his friend and mentor A.J. Thuss died, William took over the Nashville photographic studio thanks to a loan from Dr. Chatham. He began to specialize, gaining a reputation for his top-quality children's portraits. In fact, his success enabled him to open a second studio in Memphis.

When not at school or doing other chores, Charles was an eager assistant, carrying equipment and mixing chemicals for his father. One Sunday afternoon, as the family was taking a nap, a young couple came to the house on Cleveland Street asking for William Sr.. Louise opened the door to them.

"We have a young child and we must have his picture taken today. We live two blocks over on Arrington Street, can Mr. Jones come over?"

A little disgruntled, William found his way to the house, taking Charles, now aged fourteen, to carry the photographic plates. A desperately sad-looking young woman opened the door to them, and said: "I'll take you to his room". She led them upstairs and into a bedroom where the lights had been dimmed and the curtains drawn. On the bed lay a baby boy, surrounded by flowers. On a trestle next to him was his coffin. There followed a bizarre scene in which the dead child was lifted into, and secured in, the casket. This was then stood on end and propped against Charlie's back, as he sat on the floor. Hiding his son under a black velvet cloth, William took several photographs of the boy.

Both father and son felt miserable for the couple and printed up the best pictures they could, took them to the house the next day and refused to accept any money for them. It was a gesture not forgotten: years later when William died they came by the house to bring a cake and express their sympathy to the family.

The same year he first encountered death, his final year at Glenn School, Charles also discovered the joys of puppy love.

Her name was Mary Jane Hardison, a tall, slender girl with curly dark hair and a slightly pointed nose. Each morning, many of the older pupils were apt to arrive early for school, lolling around the playground or the sidewalk in front of the premises. Charles and Mary Jane were no exception, and they would often exchange shy and embarrassed looks. One morning Mary Jane actually said "Hi", prompting a weak "Hello" in return from the timid Charles before he blushed and turned away. Nervous but encouraged, Charles volunteered for every trip to the grocer's store, giving him an excuse to pass Mary Jane's house. He also began sitting on the wall near her home, and one afternoon as he watched her walk down the street, she dropped her handkerchief. Not taking the hint, he sat there for a while before eventually deciding to pick it up. He did so, and when Mrs. Hardison answered his knock at the door he handed it to her with barely a word and headed straight for home, his good deed done.

Charles was very fond of Mary Jane's parents, kind people who also thought well of him. When they saw what was, or wasn't, happening, they began to invite him in for lemonade and cookies, and even took him to Huntsville, Alabama, when they went to visit relatives. Under such amused parental patronage, the two spent more time together and eventually mustered up the courage to hold hands. But these happy days were short-lived as they soon after graduated from elementary school, from whence Mary Jane was sent to a private school for girls while Charles began at Nashville's public Hume Fogg High School.

Around that time, the Jones family was put back in financial trouble when both of William's studios, and all his equipment, were destroyed in fires barely weeks apart. An investigation by the fire department concluded that in both cases chemicals in storage rooms had leaked, mixed together and somehow ignited. A good photographer and a hardworker, William had always been sloppy with his equipment and chemicals, as his family well knew.

Disheartened as he was, William saw photography as his only way to make a living, so he started to work out of his Cleveland Street home. He won a contract with the area's education superintendent and would travel around the county taking school and class pictures. It was a good enough job, but William had debts to pay following the fires and certain things, like pocket money for the children, became rare luxuries.

As a result, those old enough sought out part-time jobs to provide their own spending money. Charles spotted an ad in a drug store window for newspaper delivery boys, but before he could apply for the job he had to find himself a bicycle. Buying one was out of the question, so he went to the local cycle repair shop and started hunting through a pile of junk at the back. He found a bent and battered frame which the store owner let him keep, along with a second-hand wheel he needed. Having fixed it up, Charles went back to the drug store where he asked for, and was given, two delivery routes.

Every day he would be up at 4 am to meet the streetcar carrying his papers. One Saturday morning the headlines announced the arrival of the Barnum and Bailey Circus, and like many a young teenager before him he felt desperate to see the show. Not willing to ask his mother for the money they could ill afford, he decided to hide his papers under the house and be at the railway station by 4:30 am to see the circus unload. Enraptured, he watched the elephants carrying huge tent poles and pulling cages containing lions and monkeys, and he marveled at the organized chaos before him. As he soaked up the excitement of the scene, a bow-legged, wrinkled and roughly-dressed man approached him: "Say, kid, you wanna earn a dollar and a ticket to the show?"

Forgetting his paper route completely, he was thrilled: "I sure do."

He followed the man to a side-show tent, over which hung a sign: "Fattest Woman on Earth". He was shown two empty buckets and told to fill them from a nearby faucet and carry them back to the tent. Charles did so and was greeted by the most enormous woman he had ever seen. Folds of flab hung from her arms and legs and the young boy gave up trying to count her chins. She thanked him for the water, emptied it into her bathtub and sent him back for more. He made seven trips in all, each time staring open-mouthed at the obese woman.

This task finished, he was put to walking around the main tent, which was spread out on the ground, placing heavy iron pegs wherever the support ropes hung out. Two men followed close behind with a sledge hammer, banging them into the ground with a loud clanging that was music to the youngster's ears. When the three had finished setting up the pegs, Charlie was again treated to the sight of the elephants at work, as they carried the huge poles under the canvas and heaved them up and into place. When the tent was up, Charlie carried in boards for the seating until he thought he would drop. But eventually he was done, and he spent the next few hours wandering around eating pop corn and peanuts and watching the clowns, acrobats and other artists practice their tricks. Come show time he proudly presented his pass at the door and took his seat with everybody else.

On the way home, still buzzing with excitement, he remembered the stack of undelivered newspapers, a problem that called for some quick thinking and ingenuity.

In the morning he took the papers from under the house and started on his route. That day's paper he hurled onto porches and driveways as normal, while strategically throwing the previous day's paper under bushes and onto low roofs.

Not many customers complained when he went to collect for the week's delivery, but when someone did, he looked surprised, hunted around for a few minutes and came up triumphant with the missing paper, commenting on how foggy it had been that morning, and how difficult it had been to throw accurately. It was a lie he was not comfortable telling, and one he was very much afraid would be uncovered. And it was his mother's displeasure he was afraid of, not his employer's.

Through the family's ups and downs, in good times and bad, the church remained the one constant in their lives. Every Sunday, rain or shine, Louise would gather her six children together and they would all make their way first to Sunday School and then to the regular service.

Sunday School began at 9:15 am, and lasted an hour. It was organized into three departments: Primary, for six, seven and eight year-olds, Junior, for nine, ten and eleven year-olds, and Intermediate, for those up to age 14. Each department had separate classes for its age levels, and most were taught by older, very pious, dyed-in-the-wool Presbyterian women who had the best of intentions but poor communication skills. Like the religious routine itself, Charles accepted the weekly Bible readings and all he was taught at face value, unquestioning. To him it was much like ordinary school, where you went along, paid attention and went home again. And the amount of attention you paid depended on the class and the teacher. For Charles, a good lesson meant being allowed to talk about the day's Bible lesson, and a bad one meant sitting through a lecture on it. Except for the music, which he really enjoyed, he generally found the worship boring.

After Sunday School there was a brief break before the church service itself, for which the children would join their parents. It was in this break that any classroom boredom was exorcised, and the mischievous rituals of childhood were observed. For example, on his twelfth birthday Charles received his first suit of long pants, which he proudly wore for the first time to Sunday School, knowing full well the respect he would now enjoy. Sure enough, during the recess period he was surrounded and seized by a dozen of his young friends and stripped of his new pants. As was customary, they were hung high up on a nearby flag pole, which Charles had to climb to retrieve them. Naturally, the adults had long ago tried to end this practice, but by the time they reacted to the commotion outside the young victim was already on his way up the pole and the rest of the children were filing respectfully and innocently into church.

Every Easter a special effort was made to persuade people to join the church. The preceding Sunday an out-of-town minister would target those aged 14 and older, trying to convince them to "decide for Christ". When Charles' turn came he was put under additional pressure by his mother and his Sunday school teacher, who advised him to "think carefully" about what he would do - as if he had any choice in the matter. On Easter morning, then, with the choir and congregation singing "Why Do You Wait, Dear Brother, Why Do You Tarry So Long?", Charles watched as one brave youngster started for the front of the church. Others stood and moved forward and he joined them, feeling the eyes of his mother, friends and the minister upon him. He knew they were proud, but he felt nothing but embarrassment.

Again, apart from the music, Charles did not really enjoy church. He could seldom follow the long sermons - redemption, sanctification, predestination - and he was always glad for the final 'Amen' which signaled the end of the preacher's mystifying monologue. Even when he was older and understood more, Charles would often find these services uninteresting. But he never resented having to go, and not too much later he would come to feel that the church, unlike the public school system, was an institution that genuinely cared about his happiness and his future.

As a young member of the church he received certain privileges, like helping the deacons take the offerings on Sunday mornings and moving up a division in Sunday school. He was also eligible to be elected as a delegate to the Annual State Convention for young Presbyterians - an honor which befell him two years later, at the age of 16, when he was selected along with his brother Dub. The pair boarded a train, Charles for the first time, heading for Ovoca, Tennessee, 125 miles away where they joined a hundred other Southern Presbyterians their age.

A heavy schedule faced them; a short devotional in the morning, followed by group discussions on topics such as encouraging more teenagers to join the church. After lunch, served and eaten in a large open-sided shed, they were asked to rest in their bunks, which were arranged eight to a tent, for an hour. This gave them time to get to know each other and engage in normal, if somewhat muted, adolescent horseplay. The afternoons were devoted to talks by doctors, teachers and evangelists who had worked as missionaries abroad. Charles was enthralled by their tales, and absorbed more knowledge of geography here than he ever did in school. After these talks the youngsters were free to play ball, throw horseshoes or hike to the nearby waterfall with new-found friends. He enjoyed his week at the camp, and was surprised to find the stories, ideas and discussions that bored him in church and Sunday school could be made interesting and stimulating.

During the summer vacations, the church offered a two-week Bible School in addition to the regular Sunday School. Attendance was not forced on any of the Jones children, but because he liked many of the Bible stories, and because it meant he escaped garden chores at home, Charles liked to go.

Like the convention in Ovoca, it was a more relaxed environment, and he started to enjoy the tales of Samson, Jonah, and the other Old Testament figures, though he was never convinced of their historical accuracy. It was the New Testament, however, that really captured his interest, for he loved reading and hearing about Jesus.

Sixty years later, he would write of the influence these stories had on the way he interpreted the Bible and the Christian faith:

"From the stories I learned of Jesus I admired him as courageous, kind, and a fighter who helped poor people and all the lower classes. He seemed to be on our side, for we were poor.

"It seems clear to me that the man, Jesus, later became the basis for what I did and taught as a minister. Not Jesus who was born of a virgin, nor Jesus who changed water into wine, and walked on water...but Jesus, a simple, extraordinary man."

And, of course, there was the music. Always they were learning new hymns and gospel songs or belting out old favorites. Be it Sunday School, church or the vacation weeks, Charlie relished the opportunities to indulge his love for music. As his grandfather drank and his father gambled, singing was his addiction, and it too would last a lifetime.

Music played a major part in the Jones family right from the start. Louise taught piano to all her children, with Dub a natural talent, her daughter Louise a diligent student, and Charles, while not a pianist for long, a lover of music with a wonderful voice - both as a child and as an adult.

When in 1920 Charles entered Hume Fogg High School he felt as though he was six years old all over again. A new and huge building to map out, new faces everywhere and a whole new routine. He was anxious about getting there too, for instead of just crossing the street he had to pay a nickel and ride the trolley four miles into town.

Most of the classes he found to be harder than he was accustomed to. He saw the other students as more mature and quicker with their assignments than he. He passed all his classes with poor to fair grades, having to repeat one term of algebra. He got on well with most of the teachers, though he was frequently urged to study harder and often told he could 'do better'.

There was only one class he genuinely looked forward to. All students took vocational training, and Charles chose woodwork and carpentry. He learned to read blue-prints and use simple tools, making book shelves, a small stool and a table. In a school he found too large to make any real friends, his time in the workshop gave him a real sense of achievement.

In his first year at the school, along with every other fit and able boy, Charles underwent an hour's military training, three days a week. A regular army colonel, with the help of a couple of sergeants, ran the program.

The army outfitted the boys with a complete uniform, including two-inch strips of cloth for leggings. Few of the boys were skillful or careful enough to wrap them neatly and tightly and with these and their heavy-soled shoes, which were usually several sizes too large, the young privates looked like a rag-tag Confederate army retreating from battle.

Even so, they were taught the rudiments of marching in companies and regiments like the regular army. And for the second year students were issued wooden replica guns to carry on their marching formations.

At the beginning of the third year Charles' leadership qualities were recognized, and he was promoted to second-lieutenant, and put in command of four squads of eight men, with a sergeant under him. One summer's afternoon he was to lead his men, as they called each other, in a Merchants' Day parade along with the customary floats and marching bands. As happens with parades, it was late starting, and Charles and his group were left standing around in the blistering sun. The boys were hot and miserable in their heavy uniforms, so Charles let them go in pairs to use a water fountain just across the street. Unfortunately his commanding officer noticed these unofficial forays and collared the young second-lieutenant. At parade the next day Charles found himself once more a private, a situation he was not unhappy with.

This was not his only run-in with the program's authorities. His company captain, a student, was disliked by all the young cadets. He was arrogant, egotistical and enjoyed humiliating his charges. His 'men' managed to put up with him until he grew a wispy little mustache to further his image of himself as an officer. On a day when there were no drills or parades the captain, wearing full uniform as he had taken to doing, walked into an occupied restroom. After a brief huddle he was grabbed by four boys, one of whom was Charles, while a fifth stuck chewing gum onto his mustache. This had the desired effect - he had to shave it off completely - but it also landed them in hot water. They were told to report for extra drill the next day, at 7am, and were ordered to run around the gym. Charles was soon short of breath, and pulled up as the others ran on. He felt physically unable to continue and was sent to the colonel who demanded a doctor's certificate to say he was unfit for this punishment. Charles dutifully went along to the family doctor who discovered an enlargement of his thyroid gland which was pressing in on his wind-pipe. To his delight he was excused not only from the punishment drill, but from the entire military program. It was a happy day when he turned in his uniform and wooden gun. And while he underwent surgery the following summer, he never returned for his fourth year of military training. To make up the academic credits Charles took courses in typing, book-keeping, short-hand, and business arithmetic - subjects he found far more useful and practical than the mindless marching and parading.

Out of school, he continued working at odd-jobs. One afternoon, when he was fifteen, he spotted a sign in the window of Bell's Veterinary Hospital reading 'Boy Wanted'. Charles thought the building looked more like a converted garage, and once inside he saw he was right. In a partitioned-off corner a fat, thin-haired man in wrinkled trousers and a dirty white butcher's coat sat at a desk covered in magazines and pieces of paper. The youngster immediately had second thoughts, but the man, Mr. Bell, gave him no time to leave. He gave Charles two tasks: to dismantle cars he had collected in his back lot, and to help hold the animals during operations. He offered a weekly wage of $12, twice what Charles made delivering papers, so he accepted. It was a chance for the youngster to learn something about cars, and he enjoyed the work of taking them apart. He did not, however, enjoy helping with the operations - he hated to see the animals suffering and he did not like the blood. But he got on well with his new boss, and he was relieved to see the vet truly cared about the animals, talking to them and trying to reassure them as if they could understand. He worked there for one summer and a school year until Mr. Bell sold his auto-parts business and closed the animal hospital.

Attending the city's high school, Charles often found his schedule differed from those of the rural schools where his father traveled taking class photographs. Whenever he could William would take his son with him, to drive the horse and buggy rented from his own father, Jackie, and to carry equipment. Each of these trips into the countryside was an adventure for Charles, who loved to rattle along the dirt tracks, splash through flooded creeks and ride through uncharted and unknown back roads to the out-of-the-way schools.

In warm weather Charles and William would sleep out a short distance from the road, in a grove of trees or a soft green pasture. One night they settled for the night in a clearing in a wood, Charlie feeding and tying up the horse while his father built a fire and heated up their supper. They ate and then talked until they both became sleepy, drifting off under the stars. Suddenly Charles heard footsteps, opened his eyes and saw three men with guns walking towards them. One of them poked William with his boot and started asking him questions, while the other two messed up the buggy, apparently looking for something. The three men stood around the embers of the fire, and Charles, terrified and lying stock still under his blanket, finally realized they were policemen. One of them, the sheriff, told William a store nearby had been robbed and that it was not safe for them to be sleeping outdoors. The men left, but neither Charles nor his father slept well the rest of the night.

After four days on the road taking pictures, William would head home to spend Friday developing the plates and after supper the children would help print from the negatives. Newspaper would be spread throughout the house and the new photographs laid on them to dry. They would usually finish by about midnight, when William would fry up T-bone steaks for his helpers and serve ice-cream for dessert. After the feast he would give them each two dollars and rush them off to bed. The feeling, for Charles, was unbeatable: a full stomach, money in his pocket and all the pictures they had printed spread around the house, a testament to their work and his father's skill.

The next week William would travel the same route and deliver the pictures, coming home with a huge box filled with nickels, dimes, and quarters.

After months of traveling from school to school in a horse and buggy, William decided to buy a new piece of equipment to make his trips quicker and therefore more efficient - a model T Ford. He persuaded the

16 year-old Charles to learn to drive, saying he would do so himself later. So when his school schedule permitted, Charles would drive the car, with William continuing to use the buggy the rest of the time.

Once, when they had ten punctures in just four days, Charles asked his father for money to replace those tires beyond further repair. William refused, saying they needed all their spare money for supplies, and lost his temper when Charles started to argue. So the next Saturday Charles took money from his father's money-box and bought two new tires anyway, not saying anything until he had put them on the car. William almost blew a fuse when he heard, his face getting redder and redder as he stuttered, as he always did when angry. "You th-th-think I can't do without you? G-g-g-give me the keys, I can drive that car." He jumped into the driver's seat, Charles cranked the engine and William took off without waiting for instructions. Kangarooing all over the road, he finally got the car into high gear and drove around the block. Once. Twice. Charles was impressed his father had got the hang of it so quickly. He passed the house again. And again. Then, on his fifth passing, William shouted out to Charles: "Get in here and stop this God-damned thing, will you?" Charles jumped onto the running board, slipped behind the wheel and brought the car to a halt. Not another word was said about Charles' purchase of the tires. William did eventually learn to drive, badly, some months later. Always jealous for his side of the road he would drive down the center of the street to guard it. One night he turned up at home, battered, bruised and on foot, having rolled the Ford down a hill. He never went back for the car, saying it was "no good", and he never drove again.

When Charles graduated from high school in 1923, aged 17, he was back to job-hunting, only this time for a full-time, long-term job. There had never been any notion that he, or any of the other children, would go on to college simply because there was no way to pay for it, so he was not disappointed nor resentful at having to support himself. The courses in book-keeping and typing that had replaced his military training paid off when, within a week of graduating, he found a full-time job with an insurance firm. It felt good, at first, to be making his own way, earning $75 a month. From this he paid his mother $25 for room and board, covered all his own expenses and was able to save some. He liked his manageress, and she liked his work, but after three months he realized he had no intention of spending the rest of his life pounding keys in an office.

As his father had before him, Charles wanted to travel, to work in new places, see new things and meet new people. A week before Christmas he told his mother of his plans to leave Nashville come the New Year. She showed natural maternal concern, but Charles reminded her he had been finding jobs from the age of 12, and had $75 saved from his book-keeping job to get him started.

So, on Saturday January 8, 1924, his 18th birthday, Charles stood on the platform at Union Station waiting for the night train to St. Louis, Missouri. In one hand he carried a small tan grip with just a few changes of clothing, and in the other he held a light, and slightly too small, overcoat. Louise went with him to the station, carrying a paper sack containing sandwiches and cookies for his trip. As a final motherly gesture she pinned his money to the inside of his coat pocket to prevent it being stolen.

The dispatcher announced the arrival of his train, and after a quick hug Charles climbed on board. He felt suddenly alone and afraid, turning to face the window so his fellow passengers could not see his tears. Outside the conductor yelled "All aboard!", the train shuddered forward amid clouds of hissing steam, and soon the steady, rhythmic clackety-clack of the speeding wheels lulled the young traveler out of despondency and into sleep.

Chapter Two

Into the Great Wide Open

"No man's conscience is infallible. No man has a pipe-line to God that will give him final, complete and infallible answers to the most perplexing questions of conscience. Our conscience must grow; it must be educated and it must get its education, not from a single source, indeed from our experience in a real world."
- CMJ.

Charles slept well that night, and was awakened early in the morning as the conductor turned on all the corridor and coach lights, announcing loudly: "Next stop St. Louis. End of the line."

After a quick trip to the bathroom, Charles breakfasted on a sandwich saved from the previous evening. All feelings of despair had vanished, and he felt a surge of excitement and optimism as he waited impatiently for the train to pull into St Louis.

He had chosen this as his first stop because a former minister and scout leader, Harold Phillips, had moved there. Charles had not warned Mr. Phillips of his visit, planning instead to telephone him when he arrived. He was confident of a warm welcome, and thought he might stay a few days before traveling on to Chicago.

The train drew into the station at 6 am, and as it was too early to call his host, Charles bought a Sunday newspaper and spent the next few hours reading it and just wandering around. At nine o'clock he telephoned and Mrs. Phillips answered. She did not recognize his voice as he had hoped, and when he asked to speak to her husband he was stunned to hear her say Mr. Phillips was too busy to come to the phone. She added: "I'm afraid we were not expecting anyone for lunch and don't really have enough food. Will you call us tomorrow?" Terribly disappointed, Charles told her he was headed to Chicago that night and would let them know if he came back through St Louis. Hurt and angered by this rejection, he had no intention of contacting them again.

His train out of St. Louis did not leave until eight o'clock that evening, so he spent the day strolling through the city's parks and window shopping. He ate two hotdogs for lunch and killed time by talking to the vendor about how slow business was on Sundays. In the afternoon he walked down to the docks, enjoying the organized confusion as freight and passenger boats loaded and unloaded their cargoes.

He returned to the railway station with several hours to spare, tired and anxious about the next phase of his trip. Walking from platform to platform he amused himself watching people. An old man with wrinkled and slightly soiled clothes sat on the end of a bench, about four feet from a spittoon. He was chewing tobacco and every few minutes would take aim and let fly. He hit it, sometimes. Charles saw a clean-looking family, the three children perhaps eight, six and four - and marveled at their parent's accuracy in spacing them. And he enjoyed the smartly dressed young couple who stood oblivious to everyone else, their faces flushed with happiness. Newly-weds, he guessed. The man would steal a quick kiss now and then, and his bride would smile and squeeze his hand.

Eventually his sore feet led him to an empty bench. Giving in to tiredness, he lay down, resting his head on his grip, and started to doze. The next thing he knew, the dispatcher was calling "Train for Louisville, Indianapolis and Chicago now boarding on Track Three." He stood up, stretched, and again felt a surge of excitement, the thrill of being on the move, imagining himself a veteran traveler once more heading off into the unknown. The morning's disappointment was a world away and there was again a spring in his step as he made his way to the platform and climbed aboard a train much cleaner and more comfortable than the last. He watched a busboy in a smart uniform and polished shoes walk up and down the aisles selling drinks and snacks. Charles rented a small pillow from him and as they were about the same age they talked for a while. The busboy asked Charles about his brothers and sisters, and his plans for the future. He was unashamedly envious of the young traveler, as similar aspirations of his own had been limited by his parents to the job aboard the train. The young man moved on, returning a few minutes later to bid Charles farewell when his shift ended.

Fourteen hours after arriving in St. Louis, Charles was again on the move. It had been a far from successful visit and he was tired. But he was also happy and excited. He was constantly meeting new people and all of them seemed friendly. Now he watched the station lights flicker past his window as the train picked up speed, heading north. Settling in for the night, Charles munched his way through a boiled ham sandwich, drank a bottle of coke and for dessert ate a Hershey bar the busboy had given him. Then, with his head on his ten cent pillow, he quickly fell asleep.

It was still dark when the conductor came through announcing Chicago as the next stop and Charles noticed that the train was stationary. Several times it lurched forward and then stopped again. An old man wandered through the coach and, as he passed, Charles asked him if he knew what was causing the delay. The man told him a heavy snow fall had blocked the track but reassured him that though it was still coming down hard they should make it into Chicago before long.

They did and, following advice from the conductor who knew the young lad was in search of work, Charles headed for the business section, riding the elevated train around the 'Loop'. By the time he stepped onto the city's snow-laden sidewalks it was mid-afternoon and Charles decided his main priority was finding a bed for the night. He spotted a sign for a hotel and went inside, only to learn that rooms were three dollars a night, the money payable in advance. He decided to look else-where, and continued down the street. Half a block away he came across a sign outside an old shack: "Snow Shovellers Wanted", and he decided to apply. Inside a skinny old man sat behind a rickety desk, looking bored. The man was doubtful the young boy in front of him was up to the strenuous job, but he told Charles to report there at 8am the next day, warning: "It will be a long day, so don't shovel too fast."

Pleased to have already found a job, for the next few days at least, Charles continued his search for a cheap place to sleep. And not far from the office he found it. Nailed to the wall of a large building was a battered, hand-painted billboard that read: "Beds - 50 cents". An arrow pointed up some stairs, and Charles went up. He opened the door and saw not a corridor with more doors leading off it, but one huge room. Along all four walls neat, clean-looking cots were lined three feet apart, about 50 of them altogether. Charles had never slept in a room with so many people and had no desire to start now, but as he turned to leave a cheery, round-faced man appeared and asked if he wanted to rent one of the beds. Charles hesitated briefly before nodding, and the man puffed himself up and immediately launched into the conditions of res-idence: "You must be here by 10pm when the doors are locked. You will be woken at 7am and must be out by eight, when the doors are again locked until 5:30pm." His tone softened, and he asked: "Now, how does that sound?" A little perturbed by the man's manner, Charles conceded that the price was right and the conditions also suited him, so he said he would take it, and began to fill out a card. He paused, not sure what to write for his address and the man asked suddenly: "You're not running away from home? The police will check here as they do every night." It had never occurred to Charles people might think that he was a run-away and he quickly explained he was in Chicago looking for work, with his family's blessing. The man's attitude softened and the two talked for a while about finding jobs, looking through the want ads in the newspaper. Charles later went to nearby Thompson's Cafe to eat a large, but cheap, supper.

In the morning he reported on time for work. Snow-ploughs had cleared the roads overnight but in doing so had left huge piles of dirty snow on the sidewalks. Charles took his place among the other men at one such pile and started shoveling the heavy, wet snow into trucks that pulled up next to them. He was soon tired, his arms aching and his breath coming in short gasps. The foreman saw he was having trouble and gave him the job of directing traffic around the shoveling crew. Charles was relieved, as he knew he would not have lasted the whole day and he was grateful to the foreman for not patronizing or making fun of him for not keeping up.

At the end of the day he pocketed five dollars and returned to his dormitory where he slept like a baby, this time oblivious to the snoring and bed-creakings of his many roommates. In the morning he breakfasted at Thompson's Cafe before joining the snow crew again. The sun was shining and once more he was put to directing traffic and guiding the snow-bearing trucks into place. That and the next day passed quickly, with Charles collecting another five dollars at the end of each. The snow had melted after the third day, and though he was sorry to see the job end he had paid all his expenses and managed to save ten dollars.

Charles spent two days looking for another job, handicapped by his unfamiliarity with the city which often meant he arrived after a position had been taken. But on the third morning he was first in a line of about fifteen people at the Parke-Davis Pharmaceutical Supply Company, having seen an ad for a stock boy in the paper the previous evening. He was told the job would only last for six weeks, as the regular stock boy was taking time off and would be back. After a quick and easy math test Charles was offered, and accepted, the job, working ten hours a day

Monday to Friday and four hours on Saturday. He continued to sleep in his cheerful friend's dormitory and managed to save about $15 a week.

As the end of his stint drew near, a fellow worker at Parke-Davis told Charles that many of the car companies in Detroit were stepping up production and looking for more workers. This idea somehow appealed to Charles and the day after he finished at the drug company he said goodbye to his landlord and hopped aboard a bus to Detroit.

As soon as he arrived he knew he had made the right decision to leave Chicago and he was positively brimming with optimism. He rode the trolley out to Jefferson Street where many of the automobile factories were located and set about finding a place to live. He noticed a sign outside a large house that advertised room and board and he went up and knocked on the door. He was greeted by a motherly Polish woman who ushered him inside and showed him a good-sized room, fully-furnished and pleasantly decorated. The room, plus breakfast, a sandwich lunch and a full supper would cost $40 a month, and he took it immediately. He unpacked his few belongings and spent the afternoon sitting on the front porch reading through the want ads in the Detroit Free Press. There were a good many for delivery boys, typists, filing clerks and such like, but Charles was intent on working at one of the automobile factories. The supper bell rang at 6:30pm that evening and Charles discovered he had fifteen fellow boarders. He was not introduced to any of them and it took several days to learn their names. They were friendly people, many Polish themselves, and enjoyed his Southern accent without making fun of him. One of the men told him there were no jobs available at the car plants but the next morning Charles was up early and went to see for himself. The man was right, but undaunted Charles went back to the newspapers to continue his search.

Beginning to worry that he was spending and not earning, two days later he took a job with the Detroit Twist Drill Company which paid him fifty dollars a week, for 55 hours work. It was not a difficult job, and his sole responsibility was keeping various bins filled with the correct size drill bits. He was surprised by the size of the drills, some weighing up to 75 pounds, and was often exhausted from carrying them to and fro, but he was glad to be earning money and got on well with his boss.

These were happy days for Charles. The weather was warming up and in the evenings he would often sit on the porch with one of his fellow lodgers to play checkers or just talk. A card game would sometimes start, poker usually, and while he would watch them play Charles never joined in. He did not know how to play, and they did not offer to teach him - he assumed because they did not want to take his money. His mother and the church had taught him gambling and cursing were sins but while both were plentiful at the house on Jefferson Street, they did not seem sinful to him there. After a few weeks he even added the occasional 'damn' and 'hell' to his own vocabulary.

Weekends in Detroit were very special. One of Charles' favorite pastimes was riding the city's trolleys. In the summertime, when open cars were used, he would leap on and off the running boards while they were still moving, enjoying the feel of the wind in his face and watching the road flashing by beneath his feet.

And for the first time, he discovered the city's big movie houses. The Detroit theatres were as large as anything in Nashville, and far more opulent. Beautiful rugs for the floors, thick draperies on the stage and huge chandeliers to at first light the way and then slowly dim and leave the crowds in darkness. Charles was entranced by both the settings and the shows themselves and visited one or other of the theatres most Saturday afternoons.

On Sundays he would usually sleep through breakfast, but as he was the baby of the household his landlady always relented and gave him coffee, eggs and toast in the kitchen when he did get up. He would spend the remainder of the morning cleaning up his room, walking the tree-lined streets of the neighborhood or, very occasionally, writing letters. It was a truly peaceful day, differing enormously from the unrelenting religious activity of his Sundays at home in Nashville. Hours of church and Sunday School were replaced by time spent rocking gently on the porch swing, the fervent words of preachers and other religious teachers replaced by the silent, printed words of a newspaper. Mornings and evenings he could still hear, and enjoyed listening to, the pealing of church bells several streets away. The rhythmical chimes added to the peace and solemnity of the day, but Charles felt glad he could miss the church services themselves.

The focal point of the day was the fantastic, home-cooked lunch. The whole atmosphere of the house changed, with boarders donning their Sunday suits for the meal. Gone were the week-day gripes of lousy bosses and poor pay. The talk was not of strikes or disputes, but of plans for the afternoon, of visits to parents or cousins or friends.

Charles' Sunday afternoons were often spent on Belle Island, walking through the flower garden or the zoo, or watching youngsters playing in the park. One week he might take a short train trip out of Detroit, or maybe ride the ferry all the way across Lake St. Clair, the next he would just cross over the narrow stretch of water to the Canadian town of Windsor. There, he would sit in Windsor Park just watching people go by, occasionally striking up a conversation with a friendly passer-by. Invariably they would end up laughing about the other's strange accent.

It was not until Easter Sunday that Charles went back to church, spurred on by his fellow-boarders who themselves made ready for their own annual religious rites. The minister who had married his parents, Rev. Joseph Vance, now had the First Presbyterian Church in downtown Detroit, so Charles decided to go there. He arrived half an hour early, but already a line stretched out of the main doors and into the street. He started to wait, and once in the vestibule saw an immaculately printed sign in a brass frame which read: "Visitors will please be seated in the gallery or move into the hallway. You will be seated after the singing of the first hymn."

As he moved toward the hallway, an usher told him to wait where he was. Charles looked around him at the fancily dressed, bejeweled women and the men in their finely-tailored suits and suddenly felt unwanted and very out of place. He walked out of the church and went home. Dutifully he returned for the less busy evening service, finding himself on a cushioned pew which bore a shiny brass plaque saying: "The Dodge family". His first visit to church since leaving home was disappointing in almost every respect. He had felt unwelcome that morning, uncomfortable and out of place in someone else's plush pew in the evening, and he found the service itself mechanical and uninspiring.

Still wanting to work at one of the automobile plants, Charles always kept an eye on the newspaper ads hoping for an opening. It was in the papers that he began reading of the violence at the Ford motor plant. An attempt was being made by the employees to form a union, but it seemed the company had organized armed 'goon squads' and several workers had been killed in clashes there. Naturally, this became a major topic of discussion at mealtimes. Most of the boarders were in favor of unions and though Charles' own sympathies leaned that way, he felt he knew too little about the subject to express an opinion. But however much he wanted a job at one of the car factories, he decided to cut Ford from his list. The decision was born of both self-preservation and principle.

His fellow boarders, ever on the look-out for him, told him of expansion plans at the Hudson-Essex assembly plant, and suggested he inquire about work there. The next afternoon he walked to the employment office, but was surprised to find it closed. He was even more surprised when he saw a sign in the window saying: "Open 4am". It was odd but convenient, as he could go there before starting work for the day at the drill company. The next morning he arrived at the office 20 minutes early and was the first in a line of about 25 people also looking for work. The office door opened a few minutes after the hour, and a man behind a large desk took Charles' name, age, and address. He asked what kind of job he was looking for and Charles quickly told him of his high school qualifications and other work experience, saying he would take anything that fitted his training. The man then shook his head and said simply: "Sorry, nothing for you this morning."

Charles had been advised to be persistent and he went back every morning that week, only to be given the same negative response. The following Monday he went again. The man behind the desk looked surprised to see him back. He asked Charles if he knew how to read blueprints and use a micrometer. Charles assured him he could, though he had in fact never even heard of a micrometer. The man then asked if he could start that night and continue to work the 8pm to 4am shift. Charles readily agreed and was signed on as a parts inspector. He handed his notice in the same day at the Drill Company, explaining he was needed at Hudson-Essex immediately. He was relieved when his boss not only wished him well in his new job, but gave him the afternoon off to rest before starting work.

He arrived early for his first shift and was met by the employment manager, a man named Haskell. To begin with he was put to work in the stock room, sorting different automobile parts into large bins. It was much like his work at the drill company, and while it paid better, it was still not exactly what he had wanted to do, but he decided to bide his time and see what came up.

As the youngest in his section, and being from the South, Charles was teased and occasionally tested by his workmates. One day he was sent to fetch a left-handed wrench, which he did, pretending not to know any better. He brought back two wrenches and asked the prankster whether he wanted the left- or right-handed one. When the man asked for the left-handed one, Charles slowly held up the one in his right hand, smiled, and said: "Try this one, it should work just as well."

Watching this exchange was the assembly-line manager, a huge Polack named Mike Shammo. He laughed and said: "You-all, you're a smart one. How does a Southern guy know so much?"

"We're just born that way," Charles replied.

From then on, Mike Shammo took an interest in the young man from Tennessee, and the nickname 'You-all' stuck. They would sit together in their half-hour meal break and talk about the South. Shammo had never been anywhere but Detroit, and wanted to know if the tales of slavery he had heard were true. When Charles told him about segregation, about poor and non-existent education for blacks, and about their terrible living and social conditions, the big man would shake his head and ask why they had to live that way. For the first time Charles realized it was a situation he had more or less taken for granted throughout his life, and it was one he was at a loss to explain and could in no way justify.

But Detroit itself was not entirely free of racial tension. On weekends people, including many blacks, would take the ferry from Detroit to Belle Island, one of Charles favorite haunts. One Sunday two white men were waiting to board the ferry and, speaking intentionally loudly, agreed there were too many blacks on the island and that they should all be sent back to Mississippi. This remark was overheard and a fight broke out. The fight escalated as watchers and passers-by divided along racial lines, turning into a near riot and Charles could hear the police and ambulance sirens from the front porch of his Jefferson Street home as they sped to the dock. The National Guard was called out, and for the next few days they could be seen riding around in their jeeps, keeping a high profile in potential trouble spots.

After a few weeks working in the stock room, Mike Shammo offered Charles a place on the assembly line. Charles was thrilled, because not only was the pay an extra ten cents an hour, it was where he had wanted to work ever since he arrived in Detroit. Standing on a raised stage he would screw in spark plugs, or attach other parts to the car engines that would pass before him on a slow-moving platform.

He enjoyed the work, talking to those around him all the while, especially Mike Shammo. He even began to enjoy the unusual hours. When his shift ended he would walk the mile to his room along the empty, stone-paved streets as the sun painted the first glimmer of dawn on the horizon. The only sound would be his own foot-steps, save for the occasional clippity-clop of a horse pulling the early-morning milk wagon up the street. He felt far closer to God then than sitting on the plush Dodge family pew at the First Presbyterian Church, and from those days onward the silence and beauty of the early morning filled Charles with a special feeling of peace.

In June of 1924, after four months at the Hudson-Essex plant, Charles was laid off. The firm, like the other automobile plants, had manufactured as many cars as they expected to sell that year, and so once more he joined the ranks of the unemployed.

It was not long before he spotted his next opportunity for adventure and was again on the move. An ad in the Detroit Free Press promised students minimum earnings of $500 for the summer for anyone willing to "travel and hustle". A man named Claude Jones was holding interviews at the Michigan State University in Lansing, recruiting high school graduates and college students as sales representatives for the National Map Company. Charles thought it would be interesting work, so he boarded a bus and headed due west. A high school education and a pleasant manner were the only qualifications needed for the job, and Charles started immediately on a two-day training course prior to being assigned his sales territory.

It turned out he was to go to Indian Springs. The train from Detroit took him as far as Indianapolis, from where he rode the bus to the small town of Terre Haute. There, he spent half an hour walking in and around town until he found a small shed beside a railway track, where he bought his ticket to Indian Springs. It was a warm day, so he sat on the ground outside the shed, watching two men load supplies onto the back of a short railroad car, which, as well as the cargo area, had seating for about 15 people.

When it came time to leave, Charles presented his ticket, simply a piece of paper on which his destination was hand-written, and climbed aboard. The only other passenger was an old man who sat silently chewing tobacco and spitting into a tin can at his feet.

The rather singular vehicle eventually pulled out of the tiny station, and Charles settled back to enjoy the ride. A few miles out of town, they stopped to pick up two girls who went just as far as the next crossroads. There a man, one of the girls' fathers, Charles guessed, was waiting for them. Soon after, the car stopped, seemingly, in the middle of nowhere. The windows on either side of the carriage revealed nothing but fields and trees. No buildings or people, no station, and certainly no town of any sort. The driver told Charles this was his stop and only after he had alighted from the train did he spot an old man standing next to a motor car. The man introduced himself as John Martindale, proprietor of the only hotel in Indian Springs. He was there for potential customers and he asked Charles where he was headed, and if he needed a room. Charles explained his situation and asked if he could have the cheapest room available. Mr. Martindale nodded his agreement and on the short trip to Indian Springs he said he would lower the rate further if Charles took over the task of meeting the twice-daily train, at 9am and 6pm. He decided this would not interfere with his map selling and accepted the offer.

As they pulled up in front of the hotel, Charles looked around him with some trepidation. The town sat astride a wide dirt road. Next to the hotel was a large general store, and a little further down the street a livery stable. Neat, two-story houses dotted the road and nearby he noticed a small, one-room building with a lawyer's name stenciled on the window. Across the street was a solid-looking red-brick courthouse, to which the town jail was attached. He saw a few buggies and fewer motor cars, but hardly any people, and he began to wonder why he had been sent here, and to whom he would sell his maps. Mr. Martindale assured him the tourist season would soon be upon them (the town's main, and perhaps only, attractions were its springs, known for their healing qualities), but still Charles was unconvinced.

He was given a small, clean room at the back of the hotel on the second floor. It was furnished with a single bed, a rocking chair, and a battered table on which sat a bowl and pitcher for him to wash with. The bath and toilet, which he would share with other guests, were at the end of the hallway. Before supper, which he took with Mr. Martindale, Charles went for a walk through the town to get a better idea of where things, and people, might be. Behind the hotel he noticed a large meadow in which several horses were grazing. At one end of the field was an open-sided barn divided into stalls, and in one of these was what looked to Charles like a racing buggy. Further down the road was the regular livery stable and Charles realized this could prove useful for getting around the county once he had finished in Indian Springs itself.

The next morning he was up and ready to start selling. He had been taught to begin his campaign by securing the support of ministers, leading merchants and other prominent businessmen and citizens. With a little research he could easily identify such people and would be able to address each of them by name, a great advantage for the salesman, he had been told. This premise proved accurate, for in collecting names of those interested in buying his maps, about the only person to turn him down was the town's lawyer.

Next he needed to canvass nearby farms, a task he could not accomplish on foot. To this end he had struck another deal with Mr. Martindale who agreed to give Charles the use of his race-horses, for a better rate than the livery stable, because he said they needed exercising anyway.

So on his second day Charles took to the saddle, returning that evening very stiff and sore. The next time he went on one of his out-of-town sorties, Mr. Martindale suggested he use the two-wheeled racing buggy, a more comfortable option Charles welcomed. Mr. Martindale explained how to hitch the horse between the two wooden shafts, showed him how to sit on the bench between the wheels, and guided his feet into the stirrups in front of him. His final instructions were to use the reins with the lightest of touches to control the horse and leave the whip standing in its holder by his right hand. That first trip out was exhilarating for Charles, it was like riding a bicycle, but twice as fast and without having to pedal.

He made his first stop, wrapping the reins around the whip as he had been shown. When he returned, glowing with the success of another sale, he started to climb onto the buggy, putting one foot in a stirrup and picking up the reins. Doing so gave the well-trained horse the wrong message and he took off happily down the road, unaware that Charles was at first hopping furiously alongside trying to untangle himself, and then sprinting behind trying in vain to catch up. About fifteen minutes later a man on horseback directed Charles to where his runaway was now grazing quietly by the side of the road. He rested for a few minutes, catching his breath, before climbing carefully back onto the buggy, leaving the reins well alone until he was safely settled in.

After just three weeks Charles had nearly two hundred names in his order book, so the Map Company sent 250 maps for him to distribute. In that time he had started working two nights a week in the small movie house Mr. Martindale ran, as well as driving his 'taxi' every day. The theatre was in fact a recently repainted store, with a large canvas screen at one end. A young farmer operated the projector while Charles acted as ticket seller for the silent movies shown. And for 15 minutes before the start of the show, and during the changing of the reels, he cranked out tunes on an old hand-wound Victrola. Thus when the Map Company offered him an advance to pay for his living expenses he was able to refuse it - Mr. Martindale had decided he was earning his keep and no longer charged him for his room and board.

When the maps arrived he began the business of selling them to those who had placed orders. He was surprised, however, when many of them changed their minds and refused to pay. At first he was annoyed by this, but he soon realized that most people simply could not afford the maps so he never pressed them too hard. He eventually sold less than half the number he had anticipated and was naturally disappointed and a little worried about what his boss would say. But when he contacted Mr. Jones, he just offered Charles another patch, this time in Texas, his father's old stamping ground. And he told him because of the burgeoning oil industry there were people there with money to spend - an argument Charles had certainly heard before. The young man accepted the offer, mainly because he had no other options, but also because it meant he could visit his family in Nashville first. He wrote and told them of his plans to come home before moving on to Texas. They were excited to hear from him and looked forward to his return. But William Sr., from whom Charles had evidently inherited the adventurous side of his nature, had rather more traditional plans for his son.

So as the summer of 1924 began, Charles found himself back in Nashville. He was glad to be there, enjoying the security blanket of his family after being on his own and self-sufficient for the previous six months. And when his father offered him a deal to keep him in his hometown Charles did not have to think for long before accepting. William Sr. still had his contract with the county's education superintendent to take school photographs. And he needed an assistant for the summer. He told Charles that in return for his help over the next few months he would pay towards putting him through college. Charles accepted, and father and son worked closely together for the next 12 weeks, both putting money aside to enable Charles to attend college in the fall.

On September 3, 1924, Charles embarked on a new adventure, though this time he was not alone. Charles and his brother Dub went together to enroll at Maryville College, a Presbyterian Church College founded in 1819 in the town of Maryville, just south of Knoxville. Older by two years, Dub had left high school magna cum laude, and gone straight to work in the Tennessee Warehouse and Elevator Corporation. He had stayed there two years, which now made him a freshman along with his brother. Because they were brothers, and in the same year, Mama Jones told Dub she wanted them to room together. She wanted him to look after Charles, make sure he got to his classes and do both their laundry. She had added: "That way Charles won't get lonesome." But for the first time in his life, Dub flatly disobeyed his mother and the boys were assigned separate rooms on different floors. Charles was not sure whether Dub had done this because he did not want him tagging along, or because he felt his brother was old enough to look after himself and should be independent and make his own friends. Either way Charles was happy with the result. He was as tired of Dub telling him what to do as Dub was of telling him.

The registrar put Dub in with a young man from Chicago, Bob Harvey. Their interests were very different, Bob was the College's baseball pitcher and the starting half-back on the football team, whereas Dub's interests were more cerebral. But regardless of their differences the two were close friends from the start. They both joined the YMCA, Harvey being elected president and Dub vice-president.

Charles' roommate was a dark-skinned Syrian named Arthur Sargis. A few years older than Charles, he was on a scholarship from his church in South Philadelphia and was planning to join the Presbyterian ministry. It was with Art that Charles experienced blatant racism for the first time: some students and townspeople thought he was a "light-skinned Negro" and would have nothing to do with him and on several occasions the two friends would be turned away from restaurants.

At Maryville, as in high school, Charles was an average student. He majored in Chemistry and minored in Physics, finding the two subjects, his first in-depth look at the sciences, very stimulating, particularly enjoying the hands-on aspect of lab work. He also took a Bible course dealing with 'The Life of Jesus', which he conversely found dull and rather unsatisfying. The religion professor led the class verse by verse through the gospels tracing Jesus' journeys, lingering on his miracles. Occasionally students would notice, and ask about, a discrepancy or contradiction between the gospel stories, prompting the declaration that if they knew all the facts, which they didn't, then they'd be able to reconcile them. As well as taking religion classes, students had compulsory chapel each day, except for the weekend when they had to sign that they attended a church service in town. Although he never felt Maryville added to his store of biblical knowledge, nor strengthened any religious convictions, Charles was perfectly at home in the strong Presbyterian environment.

Bob Harvey, Dub's roommate, was fully expecting to graduate from Maryville and go and work in the slum sections of his home town of Chicago. Meanwhile there was a section of Maryville itself that he showed an interest in and both Dub and Charles often went with him. One block from Main Street, at the bottom of a hill and alongside a dirty stream, about a dozen families lived in overcrowded and ramshackle homes. None of the families had running water, just a shallow, dirty spring. They used the stream as a garbage dump and a toilet. No public services and no doctors served the people there. As part of their work for the 'Y', the three young men set up their own mission in the area, getting to know most of the inhabitants, and unofficially naming the area 'The Bottoms'. Convinced they could do something to improve living conditions, Bob Harvey and Dub prevailed upon the mayor to help them. They eventually persuaded him to dig a well deep enough to provide clean water and then build two outhouses, one for the men and one for the women.

As with all communities, The Bottoms had its unofficial leader, in this case a tough-minded, middle-aged widow. Four months after the young men started visiting the area she became ill, and was diagnosed as having breast cancer. They spent much time with her, taking turns to sit and talk, preparing her meals and doing what they could to make her last weeks comfortable. When she died she was given a pauper's burial by the city, while members of the 'Y' committee had their own small service, reading scriptures and saying a prayer for her.

A small boy from one of the slum houses also stood out, particularly catching Charles' attention. His name was Paul Garland, he was seven years old and as far as Charles could discover slept anywhere and everywhere around town. Every Sunday Charles would stage an informal ball game in The Bottoms. They had a soft old ball and used a plank for a bat, and despite being the smallest there, Paul was determined to take his turn with the rest. He was a bright, friendly and honest boy and Charles admired his spirit. When the weather was at its worst, and if they could find him, the young students would sneak Paul into their dormitory for the night, bringing him food and keeping him warm. More than 20 years later, when Charles was married and living in Chapel Hill, Paul paid him a visit - he was attending a convention in town and wanted to see his old friend.

Charles and Dub shared one other interest in college - debating. They both decided to try out for the school team, run by Dr. Hunter, head of the English department. An astute man, he soon spotted their strengths and thought they would do very well together. He told Dub that his logical approach would give them a sound, reasoned opening statement. Charles, on the other hand, would have the strength in rebuttal, using his gifts of eloquence and humor to poke fun at opponents and win over judges. As a team they traveled to many nearby colleges, their combined skills and complementary styles winning a large majority of their matches.

In the summer of 1927 Charles left Maryville College for good. He had studied there for slightly over three years, but not the four required to get his degree. Instead he enrolled for the summer at Columbia University in New York. Again he studied Chemistry and Physics and again he found it fascinating. He soon discovered, however, that teaching standards, subject matter and student requirements were far and beyond those he had known at Maryville. He enjoyed his time in New York very much, but at the end of the summer he found himself 21 years old, without a degree and once more looking for direction.

In fact it was an old path that led him to new pastures. He was toying with the idea of heading to Texas to sell maps again. But before making up his mind he spoke to his mother in Nashville who told him that his father was already in Texas, near San Antonio. Mama Jones said he had been there a while and had made enough money to buy half shares in a cafe, with a widow, Mrs. Ford. She said William Sr. had telephoned and asked whether Charles would go down and work with them. Charles told her he was considering going to Texas anyway and the idea of working with his father again appealed to him. So that night Charles telephoned Claude Jones, his friend and former employer at the National Map Company, and told him of his plans to help his father instead of selling maps as they had recently discussed. Mr. Jones was pleased Charles had found something he wanted to do and wished him well. He added that should the restaurant business not be to his liking, he would happily assign Charles an area in Texas, or anywhere else he wanted to go, to start selling maps again.

By the time Charles left New York there was only a month or so until Christmas and he decided he would spend it at home in Nashville. He spent the next four weeks around his old friends and family, enjoyed a traditional Christmas at home and once again kissed his mother good-bye at the train station. This time though, Mama Jones felt happier and more secure, knowing her son was going to be with his father, though at the time Charles knew she would rather have them both at home with her.

William Sr. was waiting when his son's train arrived at the railway station in San Antonio. They took a bus into town marked 'Austin Street' and at their stop they got off, suitcases in hand, and crossed the road to a two-story building. They climbed an outside staircase to the second floor and went through the screen door into the shabby two-room apartment they would share. The rooms were directly above the cafe, but soon after Charles arrived his father and Mrs. Ford sold it and bought another cafe some streets away, at 212 Broadway. They each took an initial from their names and called it the F&J Cafe. It was smaller than the Austin Street cafe, having 18 stools at a wood counter and just four tables that could each seat four people. The kitchen was at the far end of the narrow room with the cash register kept by the doorway.

It was in a good location, next to the classy Majestic Hotel and directly behind the press and printing works of the San Antonio Light Newspaper. They also had many Mexican customers who worked at a milk bottling station opposite the old Austin Street cafe. The Mexicans often came in without money, and William let them sign the backs of their checks after eating and pay him when they themselves were paid at the end of the week. This trust in them earned their respect, loyalty and honesty—not once did a meal go unpaid for. With a good many customers, business was good and Charles enjoyed his work, which was mainly waiting tables and cashiering. Charles also enjoyed being with his father again. In later years some of his most pleasant memories would be of their evenings spent alone together in the closed cafe, or at their digs. Charles would sit quietly, attentively and listen as his father talked for the first time of his own childhood and his early life in Tennessee. A contented father and son also passed many evening hours discussing the cafe, home and the future.

But despite the good trade and their renewed closeness, not all was well at the cafe. William Sr.'s relationship with Mrs. Ford was uncomfortable and occasionally bordered on hostile. Charles himself was having particular problems with Mrs. Ford's two teenage children. Both were at private Catholic schools and they began coming into the cafe during the busy lunch hour, demanding to be served immediately, insisting their orders be rushed ahead of other paying customers. This happened on a number of occasions and each time Charles told them they would have to wait their turn. Soon they went straight to the cook and gave him their order, and not willing to jeopardize his job, he complied. Charles felt this was selfish, arrogant and plain wrong. He spoke to the young Ford children and got short shrift. He then went to his father who in turn tried to speak to Mrs. Ford about the matter. This turned out to be one of their last arguments. She bristled at his suggestion her children should wait, saying they were in more of a hurry than most, and she reminded William she owned half of the cafe. A solution immediately presented itself: William would buy her out. For once the two partners were in accord and soon William Sr. was the sole owner of the cafe.

With just the two of them in charge, running things exactly the way they wanted, the cafe attracted even more customers and they soon started staying open all night. Late one evening William was having a cup of coffee with a passer-by, a salesman for a wholesale shoe company. The man told William about a small, forty-room hotel that was for sale in Cotulla, Texas, on the road midway between San Antonio and the border town of Laredo. William was interested, even excited, by the possibility of running his own hotel and went to investigate. When offered the place for just $15,000 he accepted. The cafe had been making good money and a down payment was made from its account, with the rest to be paid monthly. William started spending a lot of time in Cotulla, concentrating his efforts on making his new acquisition as profitable as he could. He saw that buses traveling between the two cities regularly stopped at the hotel for forty minutes giving passengers time for lunch there which provided a good many customers. However there was a cafe directly across the street which gave passengers an alternative. William offered the bus company about six square feet of space for a ticket booth in the hotel lobby and gave drivers their meals free of charge. Very soon he had all but monopolized the bus travelers' customers.

William looked for other ways to increase his business activity, and wanted to try one particular, and familiar, method - pool. As it was Cotulla had no pool hall, and though he had no extra room at his hotel he leased space in a building across the street and opened one. After two months of traveling back and forth William decided he should stay in

Cotulla and concentrate his time and efforts on running his two new businesses. He approached Charles about buying the cafe and taking it on himself. Charles was keen but did not have anything like the money to pay a fair price. His father just shrugged and smiled. He told him to pay what he could each month for a year and that would settle the matter.

Charles was delighted. The first thing he did was rename the place, painting a new sign and calling it 'The Charles Cafe'. He also took a look at the food they were serving and decided to make a few additions. The cafe's best sellers were chili and Irish stew. To them he added vegetable soup, corn bread he made himself, pork chops, hamburger steaks and T-bone steaks. Charles used a farmers' market less than a half-mile from the cafe, so vegetables were always fresh. He had once asked William why they did not serve sandwiches and was told they were far too time consuming and messy to make. He continued that policy. The Charles Cafe was now opening every day except Sunday, and on Saturday evenings Charles would often go to the Buck Horn Saloon. It sold no alcohol, but was decorated like an old-time saloon, deer antlers and other hunters' trophies adorning the walls. It also contained slot machines, the first Charles had seen. His interest in them was passing until he met Michael Brown, the man who owned them. Mr. Brown explained that he could set the machines to pay out at different rates, according to how the proprietor of the business leasing them wanted. He said for every dollar paid in, they usually paid out thirty cents. He and the leaser would split the profit. Charles decided to have one installed at the cafe. Every Saturday evening, just before closing, Mr. Brown would arrive, empty the machine and spread the dimes and quarters on the counter, carefully counting them out and stacking them in two equal piles. Customers approved of and enjoyed the machine. Two of his favorites, pressmen whom he knew as Sammy and Morino, gave up their lunchtime banter with Charles, cruising past him, dropping off their order and heading straight for the slot machine. Their change and many others' added a noticeable sum to the cafe's profits.

Running the business was easy enough for Charles, ordering supplies, fixing the menu, dealing with customers. But sometimes he came across situations he had not experienced before and he would often turn to his father for advice. A middle-aged Mexican named Manuel was his dishwasher, a hard working and friendly, if quiet, man. Over a period of a couple of weeks Charles had noticed that stocks of ham were continually low and often needed to be reordered. Too often, he thought. One of the pressmen who came in the back way for lunch one day told Charles he had seen Manuel put what looked like several pounds of ham in a plastic bag and carry it out to the large garbage can in the alley. Charles went out the back and checked for himself. Opening up a sack inside he saw a pile of ham steaks. He rewrapped it and left it there. That evening Manuel left for home, stooping by the garbage can and taking out the bag. Charles stopped him and asked, "What's in the bag, Manuel?"

Manuel did not try to lie or evade the question and replied simply: "It is ham. I have six children and my pay is not enough to buy food for them all. They cry. I am sorry."

Charles felt bad, not wanting to fire Manuel yet all too aware he had been stealing. He spoke to his father who told him: "You can't ask his children to pay for your profits. You must help him to feed them. Tell him that when he finishes his shift, anything in the refrigerator that is a day and a half old he can take home for his family, instead of you keeping it to determine the next day if it can be served. Buy two or three small containers for him to use. I think you will be able to trust him." Charles agreed with his father, did as was suggested and had no more problems with stealing.

But William was a smart as well as kind businessman and did not suffer people trying to take advantage of him, or his son. Charles had gotten to know one of his customers, a man named Fullerton. This man had been eating lunch every day at the cafe for some weeks, always signing his checks for payment later. Charles had no reason to doubt his word; the man had even introduced him to his two children who were about Charles' age. The three of them had gone for drives and to a church meeting together. But after more than three months and with a tab not far short of $100, Charles had yet to see money for the food he had supplied. Again he approached his father with the problem. William knew exactly what to do: "Cut the son of a bitch off. Serve him only for cash. If he stops coming in, which I think he will, you might as well tear up the checks." He was right. Mr. Fullerton stopped eating at the cafe and Charles never got a penny from him.

One Monday morning Charles went into the cafe early, planning to clean the kitchen before opening up. He had just finished when a middle-aged man came in and Charles took his order for hotcakes, shouting it back to the empty kitchen. Strolling back there he called out, in a different voice: "Three hotcakes it is!" The griddle was already hot so he put the batter on to cook and went back out front and set a knife, fork and syrup before the customer. Then back to the kitchen, saying he had to check on the hotcakes. Once there he flipped them over and sang a few bars of 'Texas Rose' as he watched them cook. When they were ready he served them up and left the man to eat. Half way through he looked up and asked: "These are good, did you make them?"

Charles smiled and said: "Yes. I thought I could fool you."

The man smiled. "And was that you singing back there?"

Charles nodded yes. The man then introduced himself as Mr. C.D. Johnston, a voice teacher. He said he was a soloist, singing at a local theatre, and that he also sang in a quartet at the Presbyterian Church. He liked Charles' voice very much and offered to give him singing lessons in exchange for food at the cafe. Charles was flattered and agreed. Charles made quick progress and Mr. Johnston soon suggested he join the large Presbyterian choir. The church operated an old-fashioned organ which needed to be pumped by hand, and at first Charles was assigned to this job, singing as he did so. The choir director soon promoted him to the choir. Charles was pleased at the opportunity and quickly found himself singing occasional solos as well as with the rest of the choir. He was thrilled by this, finding great satisfaction and enjoyment in both the gospel and more traditional church music. For the first time, he truly looked forward to going to church. For his lessons Charles provided Mr. Johnston with lunch and dinner several times a week. Setting him to work on semi-classical and more current, popular songs, Mr. Johnston also arranged for him to sing solo pieces at funerals at an undertaker's chapel nearby. For this he got paid $5 each time. He felt like a true professional. For a couple of weeks Charles also sang in the lobby of the Milam Hotel, with Mr. Johnston accompanying him on the piano, but the style and setting did not suit Charles and he decided to quit.

Local radio in San Antonio broadcast several of his solos, and his singing ability was soon matched by his interest in religious music, and he thought about somehow making a career of it. He was encouraged in that direction by both the choir director and the church minister. His voice teacher, Mr. Johnston, also agreed it would be a good idea, though he thought Charles should consider singing all types of music.

The next logical step for Charles, then, was to leave the cafe and his life in Texas and go back east. In September 1929 he enrolled at the Union Theological Seminary in Richmond, Virginia.

Charles arrived in Richmond at four o'clock in the afternoon, a Friday. Registration was not until Monday, but he wanted to look around campus and the town, not having been there before. Feeling lost, and just a little lonely, he spotted a policeman and asked directions to the Seminary.

"That's the preachers' school? Well, you need to go down Broad Street about eight blocks. You'll come to Adams Street and there is a hot-dog and hamburger joint. They sell them cheap there, but they're pretty good. Anyway, take a Chamberlayne Avenue bus and ask the driver to let you off at the Seminary. You'll be on the wrong side of the street, so be careful crossing. Good luck."

On entering the Seminary, Charles was met by a student who introduced himself and ensured the rather lost-looking newcomer was assigned a room and found some supper. The two young men got on well, so they ate together and sat up late talking, Charles learning as much as he could about the professors.

Unusually for Charles, he woke up late the next morning, around 10 am. He dressed and took a bus downtown. Sunday mornings in Texas, he often went to the Gunter Hotel where he bought the paper and ate at the coffee shop. He decided to do the same today, locating a large hotel, The Murphy, on Seventh Avenue. He bought a Richmond Times-Dispatch in the lobby and sat reading it for a few minutes before going into the restaurant for breakfast. He wandered through the town, taking in the sights, noticing the different churches and generally trying to learn his way around.

On Sunday night Charles had a chance to talk and listen to the students returning to the Seminary. He gathered that most had spent the summer working, some as assistants to ministers in larger churches and some supplying smaller churches when their ministers took vacations. Others had taken non-Seminary related work as carpenters, bricklayers, at grocery stores. However, they had one thing in common - all were glad to be back. At the time Charles was reminded of a large, welcoming, family reunion. There were 24 new students that year, one of whom was Charles' roommate. He was Frank Hall, a young man from Wilmington, North Carolina. Charles liked his friendly manner and admired his learning ability and the two got on well. Two other students, Jay Davis and Dewitt Helms, also became close friends.

Charles was at the Seminary to get what he called 'a religious background' to help develop his singing aspirations, not because he wanted to become a minister. However, he was obliged to take the same classes as the other students and these came as a considerable challenge, for until now most of his education, particularly in later years, had been science-based. Now he was tackling Hebrew and Greek, the ways and means of writing and delivering a sermon, the Bible. Many aspects of his new life were strange and a little trying. Every class opened with a prayer, though it seemed to him the morning prayer in chapel, which asked God for diligence and devotion to their studies, should have brought enough of both for the whole day.

Classes also proved tough for Charles because he was not used to accepting ideas on blind faith. When discussion was discouraged in a class he very soon lost interest and began to resent and even resist such methods of teaching. Dr. T.C. Johnson, a finicky and detail-oriented professor, presented his ideas as facts and gave his view of faith somewhat self-righteously, ridiculing students who either questioned or disagreed with him. He told students he refused to buy a Sunday newspaper or have one delivered because it involved a sin on the part of either the delivery boy or the store selling it. Seeing an opportunity to put one over on his professor, and being a little more than mischievous, Charles raised his hand and asked: "Dr. Johnson, does that mean you don't buy a paper on Monday as it is written and printed on a Sunday?" Charles never made a note of his reply.

Dr. Johnson was responsible for teaching the Presbyterian catechisms, which was done more or less by rote. This suited his dogmatic approach, while providing Charles with some of his gravest doubts about his faith and his presence at the Seminary. For example the question: "What rule hath God given to direct us how we may glorify Him and enjoy Him?" The answer: "The Word of God which is contained in the holy scriptures is the only infallible rule of faith and practice." So, Charles thought, the search for God and right and wrong is not only limited to the Bible, but the answer is infallible! That particular issue, the claim of the Bible's infallibility, would years later be something he would struggle with and cause Charles to question his own religious convictions. By trying to set religious answers in stone and promote unquestioning faith, his professors were achieving the exact opposite. Not able to discuss his fears and doubts, or anything else, openly, Charles started cutting Dr. Johnson's classes and barely squeaked through the course with a pass.

After three months at the Seminary, Charles was wondering if he had made a grave mistake. Other classes than Dr. Johnson's discouraged thinking and discussion and were equally frustrating. Hebrew and Greek came into this category, he saw them as pointless and irrelevant, so he went to the Seminary's President, Dr. Ben Lacey, to ask if he could drop them. Charles had always found him friendly and approachable, but this time Dr. Lacey was not supportive and tried hard to dissuade him. However Charles persisted and they eventually struck a deal - Charles could drop the two language classes but would receive a diploma instead of a degree at the end of his three years.

To make up the hours, Charles took two Bible study courses taught by Dr. Gray McAllister. He found them fairly easy but was still not happy with the teaching methods employed - solely from a Presbyterian perspective. Once when the class was asked to write a paper on Jonah, Charles went to the library, did some research and wrote his paper from a historical, non-religious perspective. Dr McAllister returned the paper with no grade; just a one-line comment: "This is not the Presbyterian position." Charles questioned him but he refused to grade the paper and Charles refused to write another one.

Dr. McAllister also taught Apologetics, the study of sermon-giving. He dealt with selecting a subject, writing an interesting and ear-catching introduction, outlining and writing the body of the sermon using logic and Biblical illustrations, ending with a conclusion that summarized the main points or issued a call to action. These classes Charles enjoyed and always looked forward to, giving him a chance to put into practice things he was being taught. Toward the end of the first semester Dr. McAllister asked the class for a term paper, a sermon from a topic of their choice utilizing the principles he had taught them.

Charles went to work with enthusiasm, enjoying the putting together of his sermon and pleased with it when he had finished. He was surprised and upset when it was returned with the comment: "A well thought-out and written sermon but it lacks Christian content." Of the two papers Charles had written for Dr. McAllister, one was not Presbyterian and the other was not Christian. Still the doubts piled up.

There were, however, a few glimmers of light. Two professors genuinely captured his interest and provoked serious and challenging thought within their classes. Dr. Ernest Trice Thompson taught a history of religions and the history of Christian doctrines. He traced the various creeds and beliefs from when they were known to have appeared, showing how they often grew out of the needs of the time, and followed changes and developments through the centuries until the present. He taught them about orthodox and unorthodox views on Christianity, about the differing ways people saw Jesus. Not once did Charles hear him emphasize: "This is the Presbyterian position." Dr. Thompson endured much criticism for his acceptance of other faiths and his failure to toe the Presbyterian line, particularly after one series of lectures at Yale Divinity School. But what the Presbyterian hierarchy saw as failings Charles knew were strengths and he admired his professor greatly.

Another favorite was Dr. W. Taliaferro 'Tolly' Thompson. Though unrelated to Dr. E.T. Thompson, the two men shared teaching methods and philosophies. Dr. W.T. Thompson taught Religious Education and had read extensively on the subject of child psychology and was applying these principles to Sunday school organization and instruction. His type of progressive thinking and Dr. Tolly Thompson's strong insistence on class participation endeared him to Charles. Lively discussion and a similar outlook drew the two men together and a strong bond of respect and friendship soon developed.

And Charles continued to sing. He took lessons at first from Earl Carbaugh, the voice teacher in charge of music at the Park Avenue

Presbyterian Church in Washington D.C. They got on well on a personal level and Charles progressed quickly, gaining confidence and ability all the time. In Charles' second semester, though, the number of students wanting voice lessons dwindled to just two, and Mr. Carbaugh decided it was no longer worth his time to travel to the Seminary. Still wanting tuition, Charles spotted a notice posted by a Mrs. Martin on a school noticeboard offering lessons at a good rate. He met with her for a few weeks but was disappointed by his lack of progress. She was about sixty years old, very fat and consistently sang off key. The few times they worked together she tried to get Charles to concentrate on getting his breathing right. While demonstrating the correct technique she made him put his hand on her stomach so he could feel where she was breathing from. Unfortunately all he could feel was a large roll of fat which wobbled as soon as she opened her mouth. He managed to corral his laughter but stopped his lessons with her after a month.

Along with his enjoyment of singing and the fascinating classes of the Drs. Thompson, Charles had another, very powerful, reason to stay on at the Seminary. He had met a girl.

He had been at the Seminary barely a week when one Friday he was looking at the notice board in the administration building and saw something that interested him - a small Methodist Church in need of a choir director. He was reading the note when a young man tapped him on the shoulder. "I just put that up. My name is Ben Persinger and I am pastoring a small church near Richmond. I would like to have someone direct our small choir as I can't sing a note, though I have no money to pay a director. But you will get some good experience and meet the finest people I know."

Ben was a fellow student at the Seminary, working at the church for experience, and he offered to come by and take Charles there on Sunday. Charles accepted. Arriving at the church, he was introduced to the pianists, Mrs. McKinney and her 20 year-old daughter Dorcas. Charles was struck by her immediately and spent that first Sunday afternoon with the McKinney family after sharing a grand lunch of chicken and vegetables that Mrs. McKinney produced. Charles agreed to take on the offered role of choir director, his mind made up long before he left the McKinney's home that day. Turning up at the church on Sunday mornings the small choir would sometimes practice before the service, but his leadership mainly consisted of performing the occasional solo and generally singing louder than everyone else.

Within two weeks he was an established figure at the church and looked to be a constant in the McKinney household. He started meeting Dorcas as she finished work at the Chesapeake and Ohio Railway office, riding home with her on the trolley. Their relationship developed quickly.

Years later he would write: "Dorc's spontaneous, warm nature and her considerate, thoughtful, caring ways surrounded me. I had a home! I knew I loved her within a few weeks. ...Those three years in the Seminary, that was my home and they my family. They were among the happiest I had known. In the midst of academic studies of tedious doctrines, extended theories concerning God and what being a Christian meant, Dorc in her quiet unpretentious ways exemplified the height, depth, length and breadth of love that is the very essence of Christianity. Amid all the theory I lived with, she brought reality."

Charles had made quite an impression on her, too. He was less conservative than most people she knew, and his intelligence and sense of humor also set him apart. She had not, in fact, wanted to be a preacher's wife, knowing one in the village (a Mrs. Jones, no less) whom she did not much care for.

On the afternoon of January 26, 1930, Charles and Dorcas went for a walk around Glenn Echo Circle where she lived and he proposed. It was two years before they got married, as Charles wanted first to finish at the Seminary. In the meantime she moved in with her bachelor uncle Bill Wysong, and they saw more and more of each other. Charles would still meet her after work and together they would walk several miles to the theatre. They could have ridden streetcars, but in nice weather they always chose to walk. After the movie they would head back down to their favorite restaurant, The Occidental, and eat dinner. The Occidental, on Seventh Street, was directly opposite the Murphy Hotel, where Charles ate a lonely breakfast his first morning in Richmond.

These were happy times for the young couple, their times together, and the small incidents that accompanied them, would provide memories to make them smile years later. For example, one night Dorcas waited for Charles on the street corner as he crossed over to mail a letter. Instead of going to the mailbox he went to a trash can and started walking around and around it, trying to find where to put the letter in. For some reason several people started walking around it with him. As Dorcas watched this farce unfold, a young serviceman approached her shyly and then propositioned her, thinking she was there to be picked up. When she explained she was waiting for her fiancée to post a letter, the young man apologized profusely and beat a hasty retreat.

Charles directed the Bishop Memorial Church choir for a year, until the start of his second year at the Seminary when Dr. W.T. Thompson offered him a Sunday preaching engagement in a small village called Cumberland, about 60 miles from Richmond. He accepted, seeing a chance to enjoy a rural community and make a much-needed $25 a week at the same time.

He drove there in a Model-T Ford he bought for $125, borrowing the money from Dorcas. The church seated about 100 people, and was a third full. He conducted the worship and preached. One family, the Danbys, introduced themselves afterwards and invited him to eat lunch with them, which he did. This became a twice monthly ritual for the two years he continued to minister at the church, with Dorcas often accompanying him to the service and then to lunch. The trip up there occasionally proved uncomfortable, as the front passenger window in the car was broken and on rainy days Dorcas had to hold cardboard over the gap to stay dry.

Charles' sermons at the church were simply stated and mostly drawn from characters in the Bible and the teachings of Jesus. He by-passed the stories of miracles—Jesus feeding the five thousand, Moses parting the Red Sea. He believed Jesus' words in the many day-to-day encounters provided material aplenty. He also avoided doctrinal sermons in the theological language widely used at the Seminary. In his two years preaching no one commented on these Biblical omissions; perhaps no one noticed.

In retrospect, he would feel the two years preaching at the Cumberland Church meant as much to him as the three years studying at the Seminary. He gained a new and working familiarity with the Bible, and learned how to make it more interesting and appealing to others by showing how it was relevant and applicable to their everyday lives. Of great personal value to Charles, was the congregation's acceptance and appreciation of his efforts which he felt invalidated his professors' judgements that his sermons were not Christian or Presbyterian enough. The doubts they had sown in his mind as to his understanding of Christianity soon faded.

Students at the Seminary were expected to do some form of summer work and this was always assigned by the Dean. Students with the highest grades, and those most favorably looked upon by the professors, were sent to work in the larger churches, as assistants to the minister. Charles received no such posting. He was to hold vacation Bible schools in six rural churches in Virginia. The minister of each church would advertise to get children to come, and secure volunteer teachers and other young people to help at play and meal times. Charles' tasks were to organize, direct the proceedings and teach. As a boy, he had attended such Bible schools, and he enjoyed utilizing the principles and techniques of teaching children learned at the Seminary, as well as the challenge of making them more interesting than those of his childhood.

The first was at the church of Dr. Garrison, the Home Mission Secretary for Orange County, Virginia. Charles stayed with Dr. Garrison at his home in Crozet, and was given one of the four upstairs bedrooms. Charles noted that Dr. Garrison slept in a bedroom at one end of the house and his wife in a bedroom at the other. He was puzzled at first, especially as the two rooms were not next to each other nor connected. But soon all became clear. Clear as a bell, in fact, as both of the Garrison's snored with considerable gusto, shattering any chance of sleep for the poor young preacher caught in the middle. He guessed that husband and wife both thought the other was the snorer, but either way the 'Good night' bid him each evening by his friendly hosts was quickly undone by their nocturnal duet.

The classes, though, went well. They ran for three hours a day, Monday to Friday, for two weeks, and consisted of an opening worship period, followed by Bible study, some memorizing of passages and simple crafts. Charles decided against organizing the play periods, letting them do pretty much as they pleased. He felt they appreciated this bit of freedom, and knew he would have done so at his Bible schools.

One little problem, however, did surface. Each day Dr. Garrison asked for twenty minutes before lunch to speak to the children. Initially, Charles wondered if the minister had the ability to hold their attention for that long, but as it was Dr. Garrison's church and he was in no position to refuse him, Charles acquiesced. His doubts were confirmed as he noticed the youngsters attention start to drift and saw young hands and feet begin to fidget. They were magnified, though, when Dr. Garrison sailed past the twenty minute mark and kept on talking. This happened again the next day, and Charles quickly settled on a way to enforce the agreed time-limit. He secreted an alarm clock on the bottom shelf of the pulpit, covering it with books and papers and making it virtually impossible to find. Set for 20 minutes, the alarm went off right on time, startling Dr. Garrison in mid-sentence. He looked around for Charles or one of the other aides to come to his rescue, but saw only blank, innocent faces, and the ringing continued until the clock wound down.

At supper that night he told his wife about the noisy clock, and with a smile she answered: "Dear, maybe that's a message from the Lord for you to finish up in 20 minutes and let the children get home in time for lunch. They will like that and so will their parents." And from then on, that's exactly what he did.

The final requirement to graduate the Seminary was to plan and conduct a complete service of worship, to which members of the community were invited. Many people did attend and the students were encouraged to make the services a proper worship experience rather than a classroom exercise.

The services usually began with an invocation or opening prayer, with the congregation joining in the Lord's Prayer, then a hymn and a scripture reading, on which the subsequent sermon was based. A short prayer and benediction closed the service.

Visitors usually left at that point, but the preacher for the evening and fellow students remained for a criticism of the worship service by professors. Often ten or twelve of them sat in a semi-circle in chairs placed around the pulpit, making comments. Charles later wrote that most of them, while not necessarily agreeing with each other, were gentle in their criticisms of students, always finding something to praise. He earned praise for his service—not the first or last time his sermon was excellent, and the professors also complimented him on his hymn selection and the relevancy of the Bible reading that led into his sermon.

On May 10, 1932, Charles Jones, with just his future wife Dorcas there to see it, collected his diploma and graduated from Richmond's Union Theological Seminary.

Chapter Three

The First Pastorate

*"When we deal with the physical world we grow great by the
things we master. We say to this material power, Do this...and it
does, and we grow powerful. But when we deal with the spiritual
world we grow great by the things that master us, by the goodness,
beauty and truth, and by the love, that lay hold on us and to which
we belong. That is worship." - CMJ.*

On November 21, 1932, Charles and Dorcas were married in a simple
7am service at the Seminary Chapel in Richmond. About 25 family and
friends were invited to the short, traditional, ceremony which was
jointly performed by Dwight Chalmers, a friend who ministered at a
large church in Charlottesville, and Seminary professor Dr. W.T.
Thompson. Immediately afterwards, the newly-weds drove for two
hours to their old friends the Danbys in Cumberland Courthouse for a
wedding breakfast.

The Jones' 10-day honeymoon began with a trip to Kingsport,
Tennessee, where they stayed at a hotel and spent several days exploring
the town, with their evenings devoted to eating out and going to the
movies. The first morning in Kingsport they started out quite late and

found themselves among the last to appear for breakfast. Charles was a little embarrassed and did not want people to know they were honeymooners, so that day, and the following morning, he made sure he carried his briefcase down to breakfast in the hope people would take him for a businessman instead of a bridegroom.

On leaving Kingsport they made for Charles' hometown of Nashville where Dorcas was to be introduced to her new family. Until then, she had only met Otto, Charles' younger brother. Otto had played the piano at an evangelistic meeting in Charlottesville, staged by well-known evangelist Gipsy Smith, for which Charles had organized the musical program in his last year at the Seminary. Meeting the rest of the Jones clan involved predictably nervous introductions, but there was, for Charles' family particularly, an added element of surprise. As Dorcas was introduced, one by one, each of Charles' relatives exclaimed to one another: "Why, she's not fat." After this happened three times, Dorcas was puzzled and quizzed Charles to know what they meant. Charles was also bemused, though on further investigation it was revealed that Otto had come home after his trip to Richmond and informed his family, "Charles is marrying a fat girl."

The final destination on their ten-day honeymoon was Chattanooga, where, quite by luck, they bumped into an uncle of Charles', Gideon Vivrette, at their hotel. The chance meeting took place in the hotel elevator and, on being introduced, a surprised Uncle Gid turned to Charles and exclaimed: "Why, she's not fat!"

With the honeymoon over, Charles' began his first full-time pastorate in Gordonsville, Virginia, in December 1932, a rural town just big enough to have its own elementary and high schools. His salary was set at $125 a month. The church itself was fairly traditional looking, constructed with red brick and fronted by large, wooden double doors. There were only about 20 members as the town had a church of each denomination catering to its 1000 inhabitants.

Though small, the church had a proud history, boasting that General Thomas J. "Stonewall" Jackson had worshipped there on several occasions during the Civil War. In fact, it was during a service at the church that Jackson received the summons to Richmond to act as General Robert E. Lee's right hand man.

The Home Mission Committee of the Orange Presbytery, which placed Charles, had linked the Gordonsville church with two others, South Plaines Presbyterian Church in Keswick 17 miles away and an even smaller church in the tiny community of Proffitt. Later a fourth church in the nearby village of Madison was added to his pastorate. Charles held regular Sunday morning services in the Gordonsville church, and afternoon services twice a month in the other three churches. The consistently high attendance at the little church in Proffitt once prompted Charles to offer his congregation more than the twice-monthly services. To his everlasting surprise they refused, and he could only assume they were accustomed to, and content with, the current routine.

Beginning his pastorate, Charles and Dorcas were due to live at the Manse beside the Gordonsville Church on Main Street but he arrived to find it was still leased to a widow, Mrs. Fitzhugh, and her teenage sons Norwood and Henry. It was decided he should move in with them for the first six months and he, as one friend put it, "kept the roads hot" between there and Richmond, where Dorcas remained with her family and continued working at the Chesapeake and Ohio Railway. In preparation for their life together she also kept busy buying and storing furniture and when the six months were up they moved everything into the Manse, left empty and spotless by Mrs. Fitzhugh.

They quickly became acquainted with their various neighbors and church members. One of these was a Miss Sampson who lived in a large house just down the street. Officially she was the Presbyterian church's choir director but because of the church's size there were never more than five or six choristers. Hence her role was more a practical one, distributing song books and ensuring people sat in the right places, than a musical one. On his first visit to her large home Charles was surprised to see a man's hat and coat hanging prominently on a hall tree. Assuming she had another visitor, he quickly apologized for intruding and said he would return later. She, in turn, hastily assured him she had no visitors and confided that, living alone, she was afraid someone might one day break in and harm her. The hat and coat, she said, were so any man forcing his way into the house would think a husband, brother or friend was there to protect her.

In the house diagonally across the street to the Manse lived a Baptist minister, Reverend James Cox and his five year old son Woodje. Almost every morning Woodje crossed the street to his new neighbors' where Dorcas would be waiting to give him a cookie. One morning Charles jokingly swapped the cookie for a dog biscuit, but Dorcas was accustomed to his jokes, practical and verbal, and on this occasion as on so many others, she was not to be taken in.

In any small town men with similar interests and personalities naturally attract one another, and Charles soon became friendly with Gordonsville's Episcopal minister, the Reverend A. Campbell Tucker. They were men of a similar intellect and enjoyed each other's company and friendship, passing many hours in the discussion of matters biblical and earthly. As a result of this friendship, Charles was once drafted to do what proved to be a rather unusual favor. Reverend Tucker had been asked by a US Senator to perform his wedding, but because the Senator was divorced the Episcopal minister could not. He asked Charles to help out, and they agreed Charles would officiate with Rev Tucker playing a supporting role. All was organized and the big day soon came. However, just before the ceremony both ministers became a little concerned. They had the impression that the Senator had been drinking as he seemed a little worse for wear, but after a short and muted conference they decided to proceed. All went well until the groom went to place the wedding band on his bride's finger. The Senator fumbled the ring and the church was silent as it dropped to the stone floor and started rolling.

Ever on his toes, Charles just managed to grab the ring before it fell through a heating grate, saving the day and the Senator's blushes.

Another character the Joneses came to know was old Mr. Stickney, who had lived in Gordonsville for a number of years. In his sixties, Mr. Stickney was small and slender, but with a full head of long hair, a well-kempt beard and a certain nobility of posture he cut a striking figure. He had once been a farmer in New Bedford, Massachusetts, but on contracting tuberculosis was advised by his doctor to move to a warmer climate so he up and sold his small farm and moved to Virginia.

Mr. Stickney had invested almost all of his money in an acre of land about a mile outside the town of Gordonsville, building himself a wooden, octagonal house with a large window in each wall. He told those who asked about the house's unusual shape that he wanted eight views of the beautiful woods that surrounded him, not four.

Sadly, the woods that gave Stickney his greatest pleasure in life were almost his undoing. One summer morning, in the very early hours, a freight train carrying lumber to the town's mill sent a shower of sparks into brush beside the track. In no time flames were rising, licking at the trees by the track and then, pushed by the wind, moving rapidly through the woods toward Stickney's house. The train driver saw the fire, and began blowing hard on his whistle, not letting up. Charles heard the racket and, even from his bedroom window, could see the orange glow spreading toward Stickney's place. He and others from the town raced out there as fast as they could. They arrived to find Stickney standing on the edge of his lot, just looking on as the fire consumed his home. Charles suggested they run for help, or try and fight the fire and save some part of his house but Stickney just shrugged and said it wouldn't do any good, that it would burn before any water was brought. And when a neighbor offered to take him away, back into town, he would not leave, saying simply: "I paid for it. I may as well watch it burn." The dignity of those few words, and more especially of the man himself, remained with Charles thereafter.

Stickney was an independent man and strong-willed. Even though he had suffered more than his share of knocks in life he was not one to accept charity, but he was also earning only a small wage as the high school's librarian, and could not afford to rebuild his house. Just as strong-willed was Mrs. Acree, wife of the owner of Gordonsville's grocery store where Stickney spent that first night after the fire. Without a word to him, Mrs. Acree arranged for the townspeople to come to Stickney's rescue. They began the Saturday after the fire, the men bringing materials and doing the labor, the women providing food and encouragement. Tradesmen, passers-by, even high school students were recruited, and within one week they had built the old man a new home. After this incident Charles and Dorcas continued to spend time with Stickney, having him over for dinner on many a Sunday, enjoying the man's great intelligence and his dry sense of humor.

Further down the street from the Jones, lived a Mrs. Bray who taught at a one-room school eight miles out of town. She had 18 pupils, all from poor rural families. She was not a Presbyterian, in fact she was not a member of any church, but she had heard about Charles, heard about the way he spoke and his way with people. She felt he might have something to offer her students and asked him to hold a devotional at the school. Charles was not keen on the idea. From his experience in teaching youngsters, and learning as a boy in Sunday Schools, he knew lecturing a group of restless children was rarely beneficial and quite often counter-productive. Instead, he suggested he come at recess, play some baseball with them and then tell them Bible stories, informally, afterward. Mrs. Bray agreed and that is what he did, winning their trust and respect and enjoying their attention as he told them tales of Joseph's treacherous brothers and Daniel's courage in the lion's den. He knew this was the way to capture their interest and imaginations as no sermon or lecture could have done.

On one of his visits to the school, Mrs. Bray expressed concern about three of her students, 12 year-old Cassie Lewis and her younger sisters

Lula and Mary. Mrs. Bray was fond of the girls and let Mary tag along with her elder sisters even though, at just five years old, she was really too young to attend school. Mrs. Bray told Charles that their father, an older man, was having difficulty supporting his daughters and had even taken them to a grocery store and made them steal fruit. They had been caught, she said, and now had to go to court. Charles obviously shared her concern and gave Mrs. Bray his full support when she went before the judge and argued that the three girls and their four-year-old brother Peter be taken away from John Lewis. The judge agreed and it was decided Charles and Dorcas would take them in, for a short while at least. The adults were aware a more permanent solution needed to be found quickly, one that would help the youngsters in the long term, and in seeking such a solution Charles turned to another member of the community, Mrs. Doris Neale. A member of the wealthy cereal-making Kellogg family, Mrs. Neale had previously talked with Charles of her desire to contribute to the community and, wanting to preserve her anonymity, she often donated money or clothing through Charles to those in need. After hearing about the problem and discussing it with Charles, she offered to pay for the two older girls, Cassie and Lula, to go to an Episcopalian boarding school nearby, while a family member from the children's mother's side took in 4-year-old Peter. That left little Mary, though deciding her future was relatively easy for Charles and Dorcas for in the time she had stayed at the manse, they had become very fond of the bright and pretty Mary. Thus in the Spring of 1933, less than six months after they were married, the Reverend and Mrs. Jones had their first child, a 5-year-old girl.

In late 1934 Charles and Dorcas moved within the same pastorate to the tiny and somewhat more rural village of Keswick, into the manse beside their church. Their friend Dwight Chalmers had helped persuade the Orange Presbytery to fix up the large, four-bedroom house and the idea was for Charles to spend more time in the small town so he could serve more people directly and encourage more people to join the small South Plaines Presbyterian Church.

It was in Keswick that Charles and Dorcas began two practices that would become almost traditions for them, lasting for many many years.

The first was keeping an open house, welcoming strangers that were passing through the area and needed somewhere to sleep or a hot meal. These were the years of the Great Depression when poverty had forced so many out of their homes and onto the street. Many people, tramps or those just temporarily down on their luck, passed through town on the railway and these unfortunates often found a safe and nourishing haven at the Presbyterian manse. Years later, as they moved into the relative affluence of a liberal college town, Charles and Dorcas would put up and feed students and faculty at the drop of a hat. They would even leave their doors unlocked while away on holiday so anyone who wanted to could drop by and use their pool table or a spare bed. This open house tradition was utilized and appreciated by many over the years, but probably never more so than by those whose hunger and genuine need prompted the custom.

The second lasting legacy of these early years of hospitality was the practice of taking in lodgers. The first of many was Keswick's old postmaster, Mr. Watkins. During the summer he lived with his well-off sister but each winter she closed up her house and went to Florida, leaving old Mr. Watkins homeless. Already a friend of the Jones, he was invited to move into the manse while his sister was away, paying a small amount of rent. All three were great music lovers and together they would drive to Richmond to listen to tenor Richard Crooks, or attend operas at Richmond's Mosque, a magnificent and slightly bizarre looking building built in 1927 as a lavish replica of a Muslim temple. (These trips were made in their new car, an acquisition that had come as something of a surprise to Dorcas. Charles had been to Charlottesville on church business one day the previous year and crashed their old car. It was pretty well beyond repair so he arrived back in Gordonsville with a brand new one.) The three of them also enjoyed listening to opera on the radio, broadcast from New York every Saturday afternoon. On those days Mr. Watkins would hurriedly close up the post office after lunch, dash home, pour himself a bourbon and settle in with his landlords just before the music began.

Church life in Keswick was as quiet as it had been in Gordonsville, with Charles holding Sunday services and making himself ever available to his congregation. This tended to be made up of working men and women, the laborers and foreman of the neighboring farms. Grace and Will Drumwright were one such couple, owning a small farm nearby. While not being educated people they were intelligent, articulate and had a grace and charm common to the people of the area. They also had a touch of originality in their love for things agricultural - particularly animals, of which they had several trained to perform households functions for them and tricks for visiting friends. Every morning their dog would trot across the field to fetch their morning paper while Mrs. Drumwright's canary would, at the words "Now perform for Preacher", hop onto its perch and then gracefully loosen its grip until it was hanging upside down. There were many such characters that Charles and Dorcas enjoyed spending time with and visiting and it was big news in the small community when Dorcas announced that she was to provide a sibling for little Mary.

And so it was, at 2 am on February 11, 1935, with snow draping a soft white blanket around the manse and the surrounding countryside, that Charles and Dorcas readied themselves for the drive to the hospital in Charlottesville. Just as they were about to leave they heard a knock at the door. Charles opened it and welcomed inside a man, cold and tired and looking for shelter while making his way to Charlottesville where, he told them, he had relatives who might take him in. With Dorcas about to give birth to her first child, Charles knew he had but one possible course of action. He helped his wife and the tramp into the car and drove them both to the city, dropping off the tramp before taking

Dorcas on to the hospital. Later that morning she gave birth to a healthy baby girl, Bettie Miles Jones.

In January, 1937, Charles and Dorcas moved to Brevard, North Carolina, on the advice of Dr. Tolly Thompson, Charles' former and favorite professor at the Seminary. Dr. Thompson was a frequent visitor to Brevard and thought it would be a wonderful career move and a fine place for the Joneses to live, so when he heard of a vacancy at the Presbyterian church he recommended Charles for the position and his application was readily accepted.

Brevard was a larger town than any of those they had served in Virginia. Being a tourist town they found it a more interesting place to live, with visiting families augmenting the usual 100-strong congregation during the summer months. Charles and Dorcas were keen for Mary to attend one of the area's children's camps and because they could not afford to pay the fees, Charles offered his services in exchange for her attendance at Camp Ilahee. One such service was to take the girls canoeing in the French Broad River, not the safest activity for a man whose strongest, and only, stroke was the doggy-paddle.

Charles himself often took advantage of Brevard's location deep in the Blue Ridge mountains. He would often go off to explore the stunning trails, hiking deep into the woods for hours on end. Even when it snowed Charles would jump into his car and drive as far up Mount Pisgah as he could, just so he could be on it, watching the soft flakes falling over his beloved mountains.

And it was here in Brevard that he began following other new paths, ones that led from religion into social issues.

One of the issues that arose involved the education of local children, in which Charles took an immediate interest. In Brevard there was a high school for white children but not for blacks which meant they were being bussed to the nearest school in Hendersonville, twenty miles away. Charles met several times with leaders of the black community to try and work out ways to improve both this situation and the overall living conditions of the economically and socially oppressed black population in Brevard. One such meeting took place at a small elementary school in Brevard, a poor, run-down and completely inadequate excuse for an education facility, but the only school the black community had. After hearing about the condition of the building, and on seeing it for himself, Charles commented half-jokingly that they could do little unless the whole place burnt down. His joke turned into prophesy, for just a few nights later exactly that happened. There was never any question of arson, however, as an investigation revealed that the blaze was started accidentally by children who had been smoking beside the building.

Such was Charles' obvious interest in helping that one of the preachers of a white church in Hendersonville heard about him and objected quite strongly. (He even, when Charles moved on to Chapel Hill, sent a letter to the Presbytery warning them of Charles' liberal leanings.)

Toward the end of Charles and Dorcas' first week in Brevard the organist from the local Baptist church came by and introduced himself, wanting, he confessed, to see what the new Presbyterian preacher was like. The Jones' and Alvin Moore instantly became friends and Alvin would appear at their home most Sunday evenings to play the piano while Charles sang. One day Alvin decided they should do their duet at the elementary school where he taught music. Charles met the principal, John E. Rufty, a large, fastidious man who liked to exert his control over the children by snapping his fingers and fixing them with his most terrifying look. Standing before the whole school Mr. Rufty introduced Charles and then went to sit down. He missed his chair entirely and as Charles, Alvin and the whole school dissolved into laughter, Mr. Rufty sprang from the floor, eyes spinning and fingers snapping wildly, all in vain.

The Sunday evening recitals at the Jones' house made them another friend for life, their 16-year-old baby-sitter Janet Jenkins, whose family belonged to the Presbyterian church. After her baby-sitting duties were over, Janet would often stay behind to listen to the music and if it went on too late she would even end up spending the night there.

Alvin had already admitted to Charles and Dorcas that he was not really a Baptist at all and that he just went to church there so he could play in front of an audience. The Baptists, he had told them, preferred short and simple services with no final hymn at the end, as some denominations did. This meant he would usually try and sneak out early, a move that required his creeping past the baptismal. After making it out safely and arriving at the Jones' house one night he laughingly told his friends, "I was so afraid I was going to fall in and get all those sins on me."

Alvin, like Charles, loved to spend hours at a time hiking through the woods, following trails new or familiar, and enjoying North Carolina's great outdoors. It was on one such trip that Alvin made an unusual friend, one whom he would later introduce to Charles. She was called Queen Hester and she lived in an old log cabin with a dirt floor, stuck on the side of a hill a few miles outside of Brevard. She managed to eke out a living by growing a small amount of tobacco, for which purpose she kept a large ox corralled behind her shack. Even though Alvin had never heard of her, Hester had built herself something of a reputation in the area and there were many stories about her and her family's wild ways. Her father, so the story goes, caught her mother in bed with another man and told people later, "Right then an' thar I suspicioned summin was wrong." Hester had once had a husband of her own who, soon after the wedding, took to drinking. As a result, she took to the bottle herself and out-drank her husband into his grave. When she was not tending her tobacco plants Hester kept faithful to her husband's addiction, if not him—her two favorite pastimes were entertaining men and emptying bottles. Her infamy was such that it even had her featured in a local newspaper once, an article chanced upon by a determined missionary from Texas who made the trip to North Carolina only to be thrown out on his ear with Hester's assurance that she did not want to be saved. But Alvin took a liking to her, and she to him, and he and Charles occasionally made the trip to her cabin to spend an hour just talking with her. Charles' friendship was recognized and honored by her pasting a picture of him, cut from a newspaper, onto a wall of her cabin.

Charles continued to minister to his congregation in much the same manner as he had in Virginia. He stressed the importance of biblical messages rather than claiming infallibility for the Bible itself, and he referenced social issues and day-to-day matters to make Christianity relevant to everyone's lives. He made it plain that Christianity was more than appearing just once a week for a Sunday morning refreshment of faith; rather it involved practicing Christian values to your neighbors, your work colleagues and through all walks of daily life. And this, he emphasized, included those who walked different paths—people of different beliefs, different social status and different races. He did not speak much in church on the race issue, however, keeping his sermons general and allowing for his congregation to glean for themselves his meaning.

As in Virginia, Charles did not make regular house calls in Brevard for the simple reason that he did not wish to intrude on people's lives, rather trusting them to call upon him when they needed to, and for any kind of advice or consultation he made sure people knew he was always available. For him, the importance of being a minister lay not just in the few minutes each week he had to preach to his congregation, but in the open front door of his house and in the hours he could spend talking with them about matters great and small. His nature was to be social, not aloof, and he wanted to be a part of their everyday lives, not just see them once a week and then retire to the Manse for the next six days. Everywhere they lived Charles and Dorcas made genuine friends, earning respect for who they were rather than for the positions they held. The fact that they stayed friends with so many people for so long was proof that their love was sincere, and it was very much reciprocated.

This was never more true than for two freshmen at the Methodist affiliated Brevard College, Wayne Kernodle and Bill Dunnagan. The two young men had become upset at what they saw as the autocratic and heavy-handed college authorities. Faced with strict rules on dating, restrictions on leaving campus and a host of other seemingly pointless regulations the two friends were chafing at the bit. They had no sympathetic ear within the college itself but had heard Charles preach there and knew of his reputation, so they decided a visit to see him might help.

They walked from the college up to the Manse and knocked on the door. After a minute it opened and both men were stopped in their tracks by two simultaneous and strong sensations: the first was the smell of freshly baked cinnamon bread that hit them the moment the door was opened. The second was when they saw the beautiful young Dorcas Jones in the doorway. Right then and there, both fell head-over-heels in love!

Dorcas asked them in and they explained why they had come. Her husband was busy right then, she told them, but she offered coffee and a sampling of the cinnamon rolls just baked, if they wanted to wait a few minutes. They accepted her hospitality, enjoying the food along with the singing and piano music that was playing in another room. Then, after a few minutes, the music suddenly stopped and Charles and Alvin Moore appeared to greet the young visitors, apologizing for keeping them waiting while they finished their music practice. Alvin left and Charles took the two young men into his study and heard them out. By talking to them, by calming them down and giving his advice, Charles had begun a journey that would take him into the lives of hundreds of students, a journey that would last through his time in Brevard and become even more important in his later ministry in Chapel Hill.

From then on both Wayne Kernodle and Bill Dunnagan became de facto Presbyterians, appearing regularly at his Sunday services and calling upon Charles and Dorcas whenever they had problems they wanted to discuss, and quite often for no particular reason at all. For so many young people Charles and Dorcas would be more than just advisors in times of crises, they would be a potent mixture of friend, parent and teacher. Thus Dunnagan and Kernodle would spend Sunday morning listening to Charles at church and then skip a class or two on Monday to go hiking or camping with Charles and Alvin Moore.

After they had been in Brevard for some time, Charles and Dorcas decided it was time their old friend Mr. Stickney paid them a visit. Knowing he was unable to afford the train fare and would be too proud to accept it directly from them, they sent the money to Mrs. Acree who bought the ticket and took Mr. Stickney to the station. Stickney then went to great pains to choose his train. He took the slowest one he could and traveled all day. Then he got off and spent the night in a cheap hotel and boarded the slow train again in the morning. When asked why he didn't try and get to Brevard as quickly as possible he pointed out that he would probably never get that way again and so wanted to see as much of the countryside as possible.

Charles was also getting to see the countryside, though his interest lay as much with the lives of rural people as with the beauty of the land itself. One friend was Dr. Charles Newland, a medical doctor who was often called to work in the small rural hamlets around Brevard. Charles spent many hours riding with him, enjoying the man's company and learning more about the people and the conditions in which they lived.

Another good friend of the Jones' was Phillips Verner, a former schoolteacher who had retired to Brevard. He would often dine with Charles and Dorcas and would occasionally invite them to his house. As an intellectual man they enjoyed his company but equally as delightful, for Charles especially, was the fact that Verner kept a cow which meant frequent donations of fresh buttermilk. One morning, early in 1941, Charles received a call from Verner and accepted an invitation to have lunch with him and to meet his cousin who was visiting. The cousin was Phillips Russell, a highly respected newspaperman turned professor who taught first in the English department and then in the journalism school at the University of North Carolina at Chapel Hill. Russell was something of a teaching legend and was well-known for holding his classes out of doors, under the large trees that shaded the UNC campus. (His writing class was described by the Atlantic Monthly magazine as one of the four best in the country.)

Phillips Russell told Charles that the Chapel Hill Presbyterian Church was currently looking for a minister and asked if he would be interested. Charles said he would be very interested, and on his return to Chapel Hill, on the strength of that one meeting, Phillips Russell had no hesitation in recommending Charles for the position, and in turn, his recommendation was accepted by the Presbytery.

Jones handed in his resignation, which was "received with deep regret" by the Committee of the Congregation of the Brevard Presbyterian Church.[1] After considering the resignation, the committee issued a report praising Jones and wishing him well for the future. Sad to see him leave, the elders were grateful for all he had done during his four-year pastorate, and also for the man himself.

"In the pulpit, in Sunday School, and the midweek meetings, and on other occasions, Mr. Jones has shown himself highly progressive without departing from the basic elements of the religion of Jesus Christ; of broad and deep scholarship, intellectual and moral independence, and profound sympathy…. Mr. Jones' chief asset, both as a man and a minister, is a combination of a broadly charitable and kindly disposition with a keenly analytical mind. He is

---

[1] Report of the Congregational Committee, Brevard-Davidson River Presbyterian Church. April, 1941.

happily free from narrowly dogmatic contention, but at the same time strongly appreciative of the need in the present perilous time for the deepest consecration to the promotion of the Kingdom of God as proclaimed by the great Founder of the Christian Church."[2]

This summation of Jones' personality and his ministerial abilities is clear and early evidence that his beliefs were rooted in a practical desire to practice what he preached, and that he saw himself first as a Christian, and secondly as a Presbyterian. It was a belief system that would become even more apparent in Chapel Hill, where it would also be put to the fiercest of tests.

---

[2] Ibid.

<u>Above</u>: 'Mama' Jones holding baby Charles Miles.

<u>Below</u>: Jones siblings—l to r: Charles Miles, Otto, Louise, Mary Catherine ('Tootie'), George, William Bunyon ('Dub').

Above: Charles Jones while at the Seminary in Virginia.

Right: Charles and Dorcas Jones, at the Seminary, soon after their wedding.

Above: Charlie and the car he used to travel between his Virginia churches.

Above: Charlie, Dorcas and Mary at their home in Keswick, just after Mary's adoption.

Below: Charlie, Dorcas, Mary, and newly arrived Bettie Miles, Winter 1935.

Above: Brevard Church, North Carolina.

Below: Charlie holds baby Ginnia and Bettie Miles, flanked by Dorcas and Mary.

Chapter Four

The Southern Part of Heaven

"The similarity of the ethical teachings of the various great religious faiths is impressive not alone in the literature of the religions of the world but in the persons who come to us from these religions. We see this daily on our campus: loving, gentle, wise and friendly souls." - CMJ.

The cornerstone of the University of North Carolina at Chapel Hill, America's first state university, was dropped into place on October 12, 1793. North Carolina Grand Master William Davie, assisted by six other Masonic officials, laid the stone on the southeast corner of what was to become the building known as Old East, in the very heart of the new campus. The Rev. Dr. Samuel Eusebius McCorkle gave an address during the ceremony, setting high goals for the University by saying: "May this hill be for religion as the ancient hill of Zion; and for literature and the muses, may it surpass the ancient Parnassus!"[3] And for Chapel Hill itself, he declared: "Ere long we hope to see it adorned with an elegant

---

[3] Vickers, James, et al. Chapel Hill: An Illustrated History. Barclay Publishers, Chapel Hill. 1985. (p22)

village, accommodated with all the necessaries and conveniences of civilized society."[4]

But it was not until 16 months later, on February 12, 1795, that the first student came to Chapel Hill. Custom has it that 18-year-old Hinton James walked the 150 miles from Wilmington to Chapel Hill to be that first student, arriving tired but happy, and living alone in Old East for two weeks until his fellow students arrived. One of those students was named John Taylor, and 150 years after Taylor came to Chapel Hill, his great-grandson, Louis Graves, would write about the changes in the town, the changes so earnestly hoped for by the Rev. McCorkle. Graves, who founded the Chapel Hill Weekly, wrote: "Though there are a few buildings that give Chapel Hill the flavor of being old, and a few old dodos walking around the streets who contribute to the same illusion, Chapel Hill is really a new village. It's growth has created for it new and troublesome problems. And more growth is in prospect, with more problems."[5]

Chapel Hill came to the attention of writer David L. Cohn, who described it for readers of the Atlantic Monthly in the March issue, 1941.

> "Chapel Hill is a one-street village entirely surrounded by the
> University of North Carolina. Its main thoroughfare, whose
> merchants, movies and restaurants cater alike to town and
> gown, is perhaps typical of all the village-college main streets

---

[4] Ibid.
[5] Ibid.

of the country. Here is the local store of the A&P, where professors' wives, overalled tobacco farmers, and students in search of the makings of a midnight feed, shop from the same shelves; the social-center drugstores, where gossip, banana splits and medicines for the dying are dispensed at the same time; the barbershops, on whose floors mingle the shorn locks of freshman and the thin gray hairs of village elders; the secondhand bookshops, awhirl with cyclonic activity at the beginning of the semesters and moribund during the long intervals; the schizophrenic clothing stores, half rural and half collegiate; the restaurants that serve corn flakes with one hand while cashing two-dollar checks with the other.

"Across the street, lost amid oaks, hollies, cedars, redbud, dogwood, and flowering fruit trees, stand the buildings of the University, ranging from the first structure completed in 1794 to the last dormitory built with the assistance of PWA [Public Works Administration] funds in 1940."[6]

Charles and Dorcas arrived in Chapel Hill three months after this article appeared, in June of 1941, just as the growth Thomas Wolfe feared, and Louis Graves seemed to lament, was in full swing. The population of the University town had more than doubled, increasing from 1,438 people in 1920 to 3,654 people in 1940. And those people brought to Chapel Hill the high levels of academic achievement that became,

---

[6] Cohn, David, L. Chapel Hill. Atlantic Monthly (March, 1941).

and remained, the hallmark of the town: in 1940, the 2,155 Chapel Hillians over the age of 25 possessed an average of 13.7 years of education, compared to 12.5 at Palo Alto and 12.3 at Berkeley, California. To accommodate the influx of people, the town was improved and enlarged. Streets that were once dirt roads were paved and residential expansion grew through the 1920s into the 1930s, grinding to a near standstill through the Depression years, and being revived only after the New Deal had come into effect.

Into this academic and progressive town, came Rev. Jones and his family. They moved straight into the Presbyterian Manse, just a short walk from the Chapel Hill Presbyterian Church on East Franklin Street where Charles was to take up office. The church itself had been rebuilt in 1920 directly on the foundations of the old one, far larger and taller, in order to accommodate its growing congregation. In fact, a number of churches had sprung up in the 1920s as a result of the town's burgeoning population—so many that Louis Graves was prompted to make a wry comment in his newspaper on the proliferation of religion, and religions: "About the only thing the Fundamentalists and the Modernists agree on as essential to Religion is the regular collection."[7]

The Presbyterian Manse itself was built in 1836 by Professor Deniston Olmstead for his own use, but when he accepted a chair at Yale he sold it to Charles Phillips, then a tutor of mathematics at University of North Carolina. It remained in the Phillips family until 1899 when the house was sold to the Presbyterian Church for use as a

---

[7] Vickers, James, et al. Chapel Hill: An Illustrated History. Barclay Publishers, Chapel Hill. 1985.

Manse. The following is taken from an article written for the Chapel Hill Weekly newspaper in 1934 by Lucy Phillips Russell, the daughter of Charles Phillips, describing the house as she remembered it from her childhood.

"The exterior of the small house has changed but little and the interior has been improved by the necessary adjustments to modern ideas of comfort. My father's study was on the right as one enters, a book-lined room that always smelled of tobacco and ancient tomes of Hebrew theology, but its atmosphere was permeated by the radiant personality of the man who occupied it. Scholar, teacher, preacher, he drew all to his side that was best in the life of the community. Back of the study was the nursery that later became the boys' room. Across the hall was the parlor with Chinese matting on the floor and horsehair furniture, both sleek and cold and prickly. Back of that was grandmother's room, she who had been "Pretty Polly Johnston" of Edgecombe County. The narrow hall was lighted by a wrought-iron lantern with crimson glass sides, and through a door on the right, one plunged down deep steps into the basement where the dining room was always the warmest place in the winter and the coolest in the summer, and where many good things to eat were piled on the table by dark hands that knew how to cook.

"In a small recess near the low west window was a small stand bearing the family Bible and eight hymn books bound in brown leather for use at family prayers. These were pre-historic days when every well-regulated family began the day on its knees and every member of the family was present at the breakfast table with no excuse accepted, except sickness. Even yet I can hear my father's sonorous voice leading his restless brood: "O Thou from whom all goodness flows I lift my soul to Thee."

"The other room in the basement was the pantry with a long recess that kept the milk and butter cool. On the second story were two bedrooms, one with a huge family bedstead of cherry under which a trundle bed slid easily for knee-age children, the other furnished in pale green and rose for the oldest daughter. Half-way up the stairs was a small closet under the sloping roof where trunks and feather beds and extra pillows were stored, the hottest place to be found, but a joy to the children who made dollhouses there and were safe from intrusion.

"The kitchen was out in the yard lest delicate nostrils of those who dwelt in the big house be offended by the odors of the cooking. A crane of pots hung in the ample chimney, and the hearth was cluttered with skillets, and spiders, and trivets and pot hooks now beloved by antique hunters. These were replaced by a wood-burning stove, one of the first to reach the town, by no means welcomed by her whom it was meant to relieve. "Aunt Jinny" never thought stove biscuits as sweet as those baked in a skillet with live coals above and below. Also in the yard was the smoke house, holding hams cured with hickory chips, and other heavy groceries, a barrel of molasses, one of corned beef, a bin of corn to be ground in to meal at Millett's mill whose ancient wheel still stands on the bank of Bolin's creek.

"The well-house also stood in the yard, containing a primitive bath tub with a still more primitive shower attached, both being filled on demand by ice-cold water drawn from the 60-feet-deep well.... Behind these buildings stood a row of apple trees (rusticoats, red June apples, sweet'nings) and below them stretched the garden, where the home of Mrs. J.M. Bell and another faculty house now stand. It was a noble garden, with box-bordered beds and fig bushes, green gage plums and black heart cherries, red raspberries and currants, and on one side a large cedar tree whose branches laden with honey-suckle made an excellent hiding place for one with a forbidden story book.

"The rose bush planted by my mother's hand eighty-six years ago still stands at the end of the front porch and bears small white roses as fragrant as her memory.

"....If all houses in which men have lived and died are 'haunted', then surely some gentle ghosts may linger under the great hickory that is a golden torch when November frosts fall and that was a slender sapling when the first bride walked under its branches."

The elegantly appointed and prayer-filled house described by Lucy Russell was in for something of a shock at the hands of the new minister's family. Jones moved his books into the room used as a study 50 years before by Charles Phillips. Soon, though, the comings and goings of his children, and countless students and visitors, forced Jones to abandon the idea of having a study at home, and he retired instead to his office at the church on the rare occasions that he needed to get away from people and work in peace. Moreover, had he wanted to make a return to his home study, it was soon made impossible by the pool table he purchased from the University and placed in the room that for Lucy Russell had been such a shrine to academic and intellectual power.

The basement, formerly the dining room, was taken over by Bettie and little Virginia, known as Ginnia, who would invite their new friends over to hold secret meetings of their secret clubs. They were forced to relocate when Dean Winn, a medical student at the University, moved into the house. He made his home in the small closet halfway up the stairs, used in Lucy Russell's day as a storage area for trunks and spare pillows, and described by her as the hottest place in the house. Dean and Preacher, as the students had begun calling Jones, decided they would raise chickens. After the U.S. became involved in World War II, meat and eggs were rationed and a measure of self-sufficiency seemed like a good idea, so Jones and Dean Winn built raised wire cages in the basement, and two dozen chickens were moved in—and Bettie and Ginnia moved out. However, the chickens didn't stay long. The renovation of the house had seen a hot-air furnace put in the basement, and as the chickens fouled the earth floor beneath them, the furnace efficiently circulated the rather ungodly smell throughout the Manse. Not surprisingly, Dorcas had something to say about this and just as the Phillips family years before had had their smoke house in the back yard, so Preacher and Dean Winn soon built themselves their very own chicken house there.

A principal feature of the Jones Manse, one that distinguished it from that known by Lucy Phillips Russell, was the kitchen that had been built onto the back of the house. Whereas the Phillips family had their kitchen in the back yard "lest delicate nostrils...be offended by the odors of cooking", family, students and other friends gravitated towards the Jones' kitchen, relishing the rich aromas of home cooking that transformed the Manse, for so many young people, into a home away from home. All meals, except Sunday lunch, were taken at the long table in the kitchen, a table long enough to seat the multitudes that would descend on the Manse, usually unannounced, just in time for breakfast, lunch, or dinner.

Immediately popular, there was little time for the family to settle in and adapt quietly to their new surroundings. Charles now had a church with 171 members, and a host of church activities to arrange and coordinate. Meanwhile Dorcas faithfully joined the various women's groups, attending functions with more regularity than enthusiasm. That summer, Charles also got a call from the University asking him to participate in orientation for students in the Fall, which he agreed to do. This parish was by far his largest yet, but he was keen to expand it further, and particularly keen to engage the minds and hearts of the younger people, including students. Being away from home and challenged at a new intellectual level, these young adults, he felt, might need both spiritual sustenance and moral guidance from the church. Letters from grateful parents reflected his success in this endeavor. The Rev. W.A. Lynch, a retired Methodist minister from Bridgewater, Virginia, wrote to thank the Joneses for making their daughter feel so welcome in Chapel Hill, and in their home. "I think it is grand that you can be a friend to these students and that they may be made to feel that the church and religion have a part in their lives."[8] B.J. Caldwell, in charge of the circulation department at UNC's library, wrote Jones also, noting his minister's ability to touch all the members of his congregation with the same words. "Just an informal note to tell you how much I enjoyed your sermon last Sunday. Anyone who can occupy the minds of girl scouts and college professors at the same time, deserves no small amount of merit."[9] A similar sentiment was expressed by James Tippett:

"Your sermon last Sunday was so perfect that I want to tell you how much I enjoyed it. It seems to me that you will be of invaluable encouragement to the young people if you can help them resolve their probable doubts so understandingly. I thought you delivered a masterpiece in language that anyone could follow. Thank you for doing it just as you did. And on the Sunday before I enjoyed equally what you did. It is no

[8] Lynch, Rev. W.A. Letter to Charles Jones. March 9, 1943.
[9] Caldwell, B.J. Letter to Charles Jones. October 28, 1941.

easy task to talk to children and university professors, in such a way that both will profit. You did it to my admiration. I hope you won't mind getting this bit of fan mail. Mrs. Tippett joins me in the sentiments it expresses. You needn't take the time to thank us for the letter. We have been thanked by your sermons."[10]

As well as affecting young people with his words, Jones welcomed them into his home. And that was true for everyone. Professors and students, professionals and passers-by, all would stop in without notice to discuss matters of great importance, and of minor interest, with the new Reverend. One of the church members who would often stop by to talk was Frank Porter Graham, the University's President since 1930. Graham was a tiny man, just 5'3" tall and weighing 125 pounds. But the force of his personality and intellect made him a giant, and immensely popular, in Chapel Hill.

Charles himself became popular very quickly, also. His relaxed and approachable manner, his beautiful singing voice and his persuasive speaking skills all drew people to him. But he became best known for his innovation at the church, a direction that brought him many new church members—membership broke the 200 mark in 1943. Under his leadership, the Chapel Hill Presbyterian Church became more identified with the University than with other Presbyterian churches in the area. He changed the emphasis of the services, preaching on the human condition, stressing the social gospel more than traditional piety. He also stopped holding communion at the 11 am service, limiting it to the

[10] Tippett, James S. Letter to Charles Jones. November 6, 1941.

9:30 am service. Students, who tended to come to the 11 am service, he said, were less interested in that type of worship. These students, as well as many professors and townspeople, came to hear Charles talk about issues affecting the community, and this included the race issue. From his first day at the church, Charles had maintained an open door policy, welcoming people from all walks of life, from every social and educational level, and this included blacks. It was a policy rooted in his egalitarian ideology, and he was not shy in expressing his views to his congregation, nor acting on his principles. For example, Charles had begun a discussion group that met every Sunday morning over breakfast. In the early part of 1942, at one of these breakfasts, the suggestion was made by some of the students present that some friends from the North Carolina College for Negroes in Durham be invited to breakfast and to the morning worship afterwards. Jones agreed, and the following week five black students and one black professor accepted the invitation and came to Chapel Hill. Breakfast was served and they attended church with no special seating arrangements. The friendships between black and white students strengthened over the months and these contacts were repeated at various intervals.[11]

On November 27, 1942, there was a move to solidify the fight against racism when thirty people gathered for an evening meeting in the St. Paul's A.M.E. Church of Chapel Hill. At the start of the proceedings, Rev. Charlie Jones was elected chairman of the group, and he began the meeting by explaining that they were there to consider and take appropriate

---

[11] Anon. A Consideration of the Church and the Racial Problem by the Elders, March-June, 1944. July 22, 1944.

action on the problem of alleged mistreatment of black prisoners by the local police, as revealed by the Daily Tar Heel. After some discussion, Rev. J.M. Culbreth moved that a resolution be sent to Chapel Hill Mayor R.W. Madry to "enlarge the committee of investigation by the appointment of four additional members, half of whom shall be colored and half white." The motion passed unanimously, as did the second motion: that the new group call itself the Chapel Hill Interracial Committee.[12]

The meetings between the races continued, with Jones usually either organizing them, coordinating them, or at the very least present. Jones was a member of the Fellowship of Southern Churchmen, an interdenominational network of black and white Christians across the South. The group had been founded in 1934 and was active in promoting racial and social justice, and by 1943, Charlie Jones was a member of the FSC's executive committee. In January of that year, there was an interdenominational event in which white ministers and members of the Baptist, Methodist, Episcopal, Presbyterian and Jewish religious groups came together with the black churches in Chapel Hill. Seating at the service was handled by black and white ushers, again with no special seating arrangements. The speaker was Dr. Howard Thurman, the black Dean of the School of Religion at Howard University.[13] This was perhaps the first integrated public meeting in Chapel Hill.

In a church as large as the Presbyterian Church, and with so diverse a congregation, it was hardly surprising when some members began to express dissatisfaction with the leanings of their new minister. For the

---

[12] Minutes of meeting of Chapel Hill Interracial Committee. November 27, 1942.

[13] Anon. A Consideration of the Church and the Racial Problem by the Elders, March-June, 1944. July 22, 1944

first few years, these rumblings remained below the surface, but eventually, in the Spring of 1944, the dissension began to show.

A letter quoting an unhappy church member was sent to the Rev. E.E. Gillespie in Greensboro, a member of Orange Presbytery. The letter, sent by Fayetteville attorney Charles G. Rose on May 26, 1944, quoted, but did not reveal the identity of, the church member. Rose did state, however, that the writer was "born and reared in a Scotch Presbyterian Church, in the upper Cape Fear Section." Rose added: "You have probably had complaints of this kind before, but it seems that, if this church is still under the jurisdiction of the Home Mission Committee, something definite ought to be done." He then quotes the letter he received from the unnamed church member.

"If you go to the General Assembly, or know anyone going, please put in a word for this poor little Chapel Hill Church. It is going from bad to worse under our present pastor, who wants social equality among the races. The officers who stand by him weren't brought up Presbyterians, nor in the South. What worries me is the fact that the real Presbyterians are leaving the church, and <u>some</u> taking their membership. I don't understand why Synod doesn't look into our state of affairs, nor why they pay part of the man's salary under the head of 'Christian Higher Education.' Surely would hate to have people in the State know what goes on here in our church. We need a <u>pastor</u>, not a fanatic on Negro question. He has them in his home (for meals), [then] says he doesn't visit congregation because he is too busy. I really <u>hate</u> for my grandchildren to be brought up in such a church. It's too soon to ram down our throats with this question. I like Negroes, but why neglect your own flock for them, when <u>they aren't interested in church.</u> We have one ardent Presbyterian, who has written members of Orange Presbytery, but they seem to think the officers should take a stand, but, unfortunately, the majority of them (officers) believe in letting Mr. Jones run the church. If you know <u>anything</u> to do, please help us!"[14]

Then, in early June of 1944, a member of the Chapel Hill Presbyterian Church approached elders to protest the occasional attendance of blacks at morning worship services and some student meetings. Jones called a meeting with the elders to consider the protest. In fact, there were a total of three such meetings, each one attended by Jones and all of the elders.[15] Afterwards, the Church released a statement addressing this 'racial problem'. In it they stated:

> "Negroes have been in attendance on Church worship services not more than five times in the past two years. Negro attendance at student Friday evening meetings has been more often, probably at one fourth of the meetings (about twice since last March).

> "Mr. Jones reported that he had received little adverse criticism. No students had objected and they seemed to be helped by the experience. Three adults had expressed disapproval to him, only one of whom seemed to feel very deeply about the matter. He reported a number of people had expressed approval of this policy, but he felt that the vast majority had no deep feelings either way.

---

[14] Unknown to Charles G. Rose. May 26, 1944.

[15] Statement by elders of the Presbyterian Church. <u>A Consideration of the Church and the Racial Problem by the Elders, March-June, 1944.</u> July 22, 1944.

"Mr. Jones stated to the officers that he felt the Church would
not be true to the teachings of Jesus if it should let color, creed,
or race bar anyone from its fellowship."[16]

In the three meetings of the elders, there was considerable debate on
how to tackle the issue, or whether it was even a matter for the Session
to deal with. "It was felt by some that the present problem was not one
of false doctrine or immorality and that it might be neither wise nor
right for the elders to legislate as to who should attend the Church and
seating arrangements for those who did attend."[17]

However, the elders did decide to consider the matter, using as their
reasoning a number of historical and current trends relating to racial
relations. For example, the Presbyterian Church in the United States
(Southern), in its first General Assemblies, had besought the emanci-
pated blacks to remain members of the then existing churches and not
set up separate churches. It was also noted by the elders that blacks were
members of the General Assembly of the southern Presbyterian Church
and had full privileges of the Assembly. And a decision by the North
Carolina Council of Churches to invite black churches to join the
Council on a basis of full equality was seen by the elders as an example
of the awakening of the conscience of the church on this matter. During
one of the meetings, Jones was asked what he thought the church's policy on race ought to be, and in response he wrote and delivered the following statement:

---

[16] Ibid.
[17] Ibid.

"It was the faith of Jesus that all persons are the children of God and that God's love and concern extend to every person. In His fellowship Jesus transcended the barriers of race, color, creed or social position. The Christian Church, looking to Jesus for its faith and practice, should in like manner transcend these barriers.

"There is an honest difference of opinion among sincere Christians as to how to apply the teachings and spirit of Jesus to our day. But believing that the Christian Church unites in fellowship all who accept Christ and His gospel, we declare it to be the policy of this Church to welcome any who wish to have a part in its life and program."[18]

On June 7, 1944, Church elder Francis Bradshaw presented three motions in support of Jones. The elders had, he said, taken into consideration all views on the matter, examined the laws of the church, and looked at the "recent decisions of representative churches, church courts, and the North Carolina Council of Churches." His motion went on to declare:

"In the light of these discussions and our efforts to approach a common point of view, we entrust the matter to the conscience and judgment of the minister, who has heard all the discussion sympathetically.

---

[18] Ibid.

"We report to those who have raised the question that we have analyzed this matter together carefully, that the minister is fully aware of the factors involved in the situation, and that we trust ourselves to his informed and conscientious leadership."[19]

The motion was adopted by a 5-2 vote, with Jones, as moderator of the session, not voting. The officers voting in favor of the motion were: the University's President Frank Porter Graham, philosophy Professor Francis Bradshaw, former Chapel Hill mayor John Foushee, Professor Floyd Edmister and Professor Paul Wager. Those voting against it were Professor Reece Berryhill, the Dean of UNC's Medical School, and long-time Chapel Hillian Alf Pickard. In their statement published in July, elders said the vote was the result of "this mutually patient effort to deal harmoniously with a complex and important situation which without some compromise and much patience could lead to bitter and possibly permanent dissension."[20]

This, however, was far from the end of the matter. Between the time members passed this resolution supporting Jones and its publication in mid-July, there was an incident that upset and shocked many people, from the church, from the town of Chapel Hill and across the state. Ironically, it stemmed from a mixed-race, and coed, picnic that was held while Charles was away at a ministers' conference in Montreat, North Carolina, on Sunday July 2, 1944. But the incident crystallized the fears of many in that community that he was increasingly oblivious to the

---

[19] Ibid.
[20] Ibid.

sensitivities of whites in the town and treating blacks a little too much like equals. In reality, the picnic was no more than a quiet, two-hour event at Battle Park. It had been arranged by a group of students who called themselves the Snuffbuckets. The origin of the name is much debated, but one story has it that the name came from an old Red Skelton sketch. Another story tells it this way: several young people were taking Dean Francis Bradshaw's class in "Ethics and Civilization" at the University, and were discussing the class in the lounge in the basement of the Presbyterian Church, while also being entertained by the antics of Wayne Kernodle and Bill Dunnagan, the two young men who had known Preacher in Brevard, and were now graduate students in Chapel Hill. The two had a routine they would perform to amuse their fellow students, about spitting at, and missing, a snuffbucket. One Sunday evening, Dean Bradshaw, who was an elder in the Presbyterian Church, invited those who were in his class and active in the supper-discussions at the church to his house. The Bradshaw's daughter, in high school at the time, was involved in a school production of Gilbert and Sullivan where she was to sing "I'm called Buttercup, dear little Buttercup." To amuse Dean Bradshaw, Charles McCoy altered the words of the song: "We're called Snuffbuckets, dear little Snuffbuckets, Study and work is our rule. And if you want Snuffbuckets, call for us Snuffbuckets, we'll be at Jones' playing pool...." The young students sang it for the Bradshaws who loved it, and the name Snuffbuckets stuck with the group—for the next 60 years. Those who made up the group became ardent supporters and loyal followers of Charlie Jones, believers in his progressive views on social issues, including race. In fact, some of the Snuffbuckets had befriended members of the all-black band that was a part of the Navy's preflight school that had moved onto the University's campus in 1942—it was the presence of four of these black musicians at the picnic that so riled some church members and others.

Dorcas and her two youngest daughters, Bettie and Virginia, along with student Miriam Williams, were already at Battle Park when the young white and black people met at the Presbyterian Church, mid-afternoon. The plan was to walk the few hundred yards to the picnic grounds, though some members were worried about being seen walking through town together. However, they set off along Franklin Street, and according to an account written three weeks later by the Snuffbuckets, the group began to string out somewhat with people walking in pairs down the street. All told, there were 12 people who walked to the picnic, including the Jones' oldest daughter, 17-year-old Mary, and there were about 20 people at the picnic. As well as the black band members, the group included two black females and one black male from the North Carolina College for Negroes. The Snuffbuckets' written account says: "Once arrived at the picnic grounds the group had a good time. Supper was being served by 6:30. The group stuck very close to the fireplace throughout the evening. After supper the group talked and sang and played charades." The bandsmen, it explains, had to be home by 8pm, and after walking to Preacher's car, Dean Winn drove them back to their quarters at the Negro Community Center in Carrboro, built by the Navy.[21]

The storm broke after several Chapel Hillians saw the group of black and white people walking together down Franklin Street, and an elderly woman complained to the University. Word of the event spread through the town and University immediately after the picnic, even making it as far as the University newspaper, The Tar Heel, which decried the "juvenility" of those spreading the "vicious rumors that have run rampant

---

[21] Taken from The Snuffbucket Picnic of July 2, 1944. Author(s) unknown. July 31, 1944.

about Chapel Hill during the past two weeks."[22] The newspaper detailed the exaggerations: "Taking full advantage of the Leap Year privileges, six coeds from the University recently 'dated up' six members of the Pre-Flight band here for an afternoon picnic. Anyway, it seems the picnic was held, and later during the afternoon the young people divided up into couples, with each couple heading for the darkest and best-hidden spot available." The article goes on to reassure readers that the truth of the matter was entirely "uninteresting and dull" and that "…the whole afternoon, the group stayed together on the picnic grounds."[23]

Whatever the truth or lies, the incident undoubtedly further alienated those seeking to bring whites and blacks together, and those fighting to maintain a distance between the races. Sensing this, Jones and three other ministers active in promoting racial equality wrote to the Chapel Hill Weekly. Their letter began: "In view of the misunderstood intentions and erroneous reports of Christian inter-racial activities in our community, we, the undersigned ministers of Chapel Hill, desire to make the following statement:

"It is a fundamental principle of Christian progress that the spiritual growth and the social well-being of a community are the result of group co-operation and individual initiative. The following statement is the reasoned opinion of the ministers whose names appear below, with the understanding that each in his own way is free to carry out the spirit and intent of the declaration."[24]

---

[22] Hill, Kat. Free Press section of The Tar Heel. July 18, 1944.

[23] Ibid.

[24] Barnett, Das Kelley. Gribbin, Emmet. Jones, Charles M. Culbreth, J.M. A Statement from Four Ministers. Chapel Hill Weekly. July 21, 1944.

The letter makes four points. The first stressed the need for Christians to emulate Jesus who "transcended the fetishes of race and color and the man-made barriers of creed and social position." The second acknowledges the failure to apply this principle in a world that made doing so difficult. "Nevertheless, this failure does not absolve us from the continual effort to apply these principles in the Chapel Hill area."[25]

The third enumerated point stated: "In pursuing this aim, it is not the purpose of the Church to provide for, or to promote, social intercourse, as such, between the races, but simply to affirm and seek to apply the obligation of Christian brotherhood and service."[26] The fourth and last point stated: "It is regrettable that some citizens of Chapel Hill have permitted themselves to be victimized by rumor-mongering. Certain recent incidents, judged to be of an objectionable character, have been exaggerated and distorted in such a way as to confuse them with measures, acknowledged to be wholesome and innocent, which the Churches have sought to employ wisely and constructively."[27]

Jones authored a second letter a week later, when the statement affirming the Chapel Hill Presbyterian Church's official support for Jones was released. He had a copy of the letter and the statement sent to each and every member of the church. The letter began:

> "The racial problem is most acute in our day. Organizations and institutions all the way from political parties to churches are confronted with it.

---

[25] Ibid.
[26] Ibid.
[27] Ibid

"In the natural course of events we are confronted with this problem in the life of our Church. I know that every member of our Church has nothing but good will for other races and we all desire to see some significant progress made toward a Christian solution of these problems. There is naturally a wide divergence of views as to just how to meet these problems in a Christian way."[28]

He then offered to hold a series of congregational meetings to discuss the issue of race, asking members to respond if such a meeting might prove useful. He added that he would also be willing to meet individually with members if they so desired.

Reaction to the letter and the elders' report was immediate, and it seems for the first time church members felt they could express their unhappiness, and in some cases outrage, at Jones, his supporters and the path the Chapel Hill Presbyterian Church was taking. A number of people called for his immediate resignation. One of the briefest, and most pointed, responses came from Mittie Pickard, daughter of church officer Alf Pickard who had voted against Jones. "To improve the work of the church you should resign as pastor."[29] Another member wrote: "The Negro's needs, about which all Christians must be concerned, do not include any Christian imperative for social intercourse on the level commonly understood as social equality. The many good Negro friends I have had all my life are only embarrassed and led into difficulty by such practices. As you well know I have protested your actions from my

---

[28] Jones, Charles M. Letter to church members. July 27, 1944.

[29] Pickard, Mittie. Letter to Charles Jones. July 29, 1944.

first knowledge of them, and I now find myself more than greatly shocked at your methods of meeting justifiable criticism based on these activities and attitudes."[30]

This paternalistic view was common. Many of Jones' church members, like so many people throughout the South, were sincere in their belief that blacks were happy with their lot, and to interfere would do nothing but hurt them. Norma Berryhill, the wife of church elder Dr. Reece Berryhill, wrote to Jones.

> "Many of us in this community have been aware of the problems of the Negro race. Many of us have nursed them-fed them-clothed them-bought coal and wood for them-put them in jail-gone to court for them-gone into their homes to prevent installment furniture dealers from denuding their homes-worked with the school encouraging their leaders in tangible and intangible ways.

> "Most of us believe you have been seriously unwise in the way you have attempted to help the Negro. Many of us are concerned because we believe the Negro will suffer because of the things you have done in the community."[31]

The battle lines had formed, and former friends and colleagues were preparing to fight as the great sincerity and strength of feeling on both sides of the race issue pushed those with opposing views further and further apart. Dr. Berryhill himself wrote to Jones in response to an

---

[30] Comer, Jane White. Letter to Charles Jones. July 30. 1944.

[31] Berryhill, Norma. Letter to Charles Jones. August 4, 1944.

invitation to attend a student reception in September of 1944. After thanking Jones for the invitation, he continued: "Since I spend six days weekly in intimate contact with students and since your duties are apparently full time with this group, I feel that on the seventh day I must devote all the time possible to my children and other members of the Presbyterian community in a feeble attempt to make amends for what you and your church have failed to do for them."[32]

The letter that appeared in the Chapel Hill Weekly from the four ministers garnered some attention of its own. One response came from W.C. George, Professor of Anatomy at UNC's Medical School.

"The white people of Chapel Hill desire to live in peace and harmony with the colored neighbors on a basis of mutual consideration and friendliness but social separateness. This basis is approved, I believe, by the majority of our sober colored people, and peace and harmony have prevailed." Jones, he goes on to say, was the principal agent in a "widespread effort to stir up the Negroes", for political reasons. "I do not know that the other ministers [who signed the statement] have done anything to stir up racial discord and I regret to see them involved in seeming to support essentially evil enterprises which are given a false atmosphere of holiness through the unrighteous use of Christian phraseology in an unworthy cause."

He accused Jones of "plastering over radical proposals with quasi-religious statements," confusing adolescent minds and misleading them as to the real issues. He went on:

---

[32] Berryhill, W.R. Letter to Charles Jones. September 21, 1944.

"The race problem is not a religious one; it is social-biological. Fundamentally there is one issue, and that issue is: Are we going to maintain the white race in this country, or are we going to allow the population of America to be converted into a mulatto race?... The race problem being what it is, the essentially evil implications of recent inter-racial goings-on are recognized and deplored by many of our people, although one may recognize the probability that their promotion may have been prompted by Christian intent in a zealous but befuddled mind."[33]

Other members, however, wrote to Jones to lend their support. James Tippett wrote again on behalf of himself and his wife, applauding Jones, commending the elders for giving him the latitude to run the church as he saw fit, and voicing his support for the group of people speaking out on behalf of blacks. "Our own sympathy lies entirely with the group, which seems to be in the majority, that distinctions because of race, color, creed or economic or social status have no place in modern, cooperative, community life. If we can serve that cause in any way, we shall be delighted to be asked to do so."[34]

Jones had also received a letter of support from a group of black ministers in and around Chapel Hill. The letter followed a meeting between the ministers and Jones, and conveys a definite message to those whites in Chapel Hill frightened that social interaction with blacks might be dangerous.

"We would like to make it plain that Negroes do not wish to promiscuously invade the privacy of the homes, clubs, churches or any other

---

[33] George, W.C. Letter to Chapel Hill Weekly. July 25, 1944.
[34] Tippett, James S. Letter to Charles Jones. July 29, 1944.

institution, or to force themselves on people who do not [want to be] with them. Most of us would like to only be looked upon as members of the human race, and accepted with a natural freedom into the life of our churches and nation on this basis and not on any basis of race."[35]

While he welcomed the letters of support, and while his resolve was never weakened by those who spoke out against him, Jones sought to bring both sides closer together, to replace hostility with understanding. He did not want a pro- and anti- black war in his church or in Chapel Hill, and he did not want a church split along opposing theological and moral lines, forcing a confrontation that could only end with winners and losers. Instead he sought to talk with those who attacked him. He invited them to meet with him at his office, or to come to the church meetings where all those involved in the rapidly escalating controversy would be gathered together. Rather than draw his supporters around him and close ranks, he sought to diffuse his congregants anger through reason and discussion.

Interestingly, the open manner which allowed Jones to face the most controversial of issues head on and without artifice, also brought him to the attention of those in more clandestine circles. In August of that year, the War Department prepared a confidential memorandum entitled: "Commingling of Whites and Negroes at Chapel Hill, N.C."[36] It was written by the Fourth Service Command in Atlanta, Georgia, and forwarded to Intelligence personnel after both the source and the information were evaluated as "credible." While the informant was not named

[35] Troublefield, G.W., Stanford, J.R. et al. Letter to Charles Jones. July 22, 1944.

[36] War Department memorandum, Fourth Service Command, Atlanta, Georgia. Dated 19 August, 1944.

in the memo, his or her information came directly from police sources—specifically Police Chief W.T. Sloan. Two other police officers also spoke to the informant, giving inaccurate accounts of happenings in Chapel Hill, and making it clear that the police were spreading false rumors about Jones and his church. The report also named University President Frank Porter Graham and Dean of Students Francis Bradshaw, saying with sinister vagueness that it was "interesting to note" that the two men were supportive of Jones. As to specifics, the report referenced the welcoming by Jones of "some members of the Navy Band (Negroes) at his church, along with some coeds of the University of North Carolina, (white, of course)." Moreover, "the coeds and negroes were seen walking side by side on the streets of Chapel Hill on this particular day." The report stated that this and other similar incidents had caused great consternation in the town, and warned that "serious trouble could develop" as a result of this behavior. According to the memo, the only way to resolve the situation was to see Jones "dismissed at once."

The tension between Jones and his supporters, and those who thought he was abusing his position as minister, did not ease after this initial flurry of letter and article writing. Despite the criticism, Jones was unwilling, and unable, to resist leading the fight for social equality. In May 1944, Jones had helped the executive committee of the FSC to choose Nelle Morton as the organization's new General Secretary. She arrived in Chapel Hill in 1945, to spend three-quarters of her time leading the FSC, and the remaining quarter as Director of Christian Education at the Presbyterian Church. She remained as the head of the FSC for almost five years, working closely with Jones to arrange interracial meetings and activities on college campuses across the South. One major event was staged at Memorial Hall, on UNC's campus in 1945. Jones was friends with a New York minister named Shelby Rooks who was the husband of the black singer Dorothy Maynor. She agreed to come to Chapel Hill to perform and raise money for the FSC. But she would come on one condition: that the concert be unsegregated. President Frank Porter Graham agreed to this condition readily, and on the evening of the concert, the first such unsegregated event on the campus, every seat was taken. Graham, however, was unable to provide Maynor with a place to stay at the University-owned and segregated Carolina Inn—that was beyond his control. So the soprano ended up staying at the one place in Chapel Hill where blacks and whites were allowed, welcomed, together: at the Manse with Charles and Dorcas Jones.

As the interracial meetings continued and as Jones' words and deeds continued to show him up as an advocate for blacks' rights, so he continued to alienate an increasingly active proportion of his own congregation.

In the summer of 1945, a strongly-worded petition began circulating amongst some of these church members, and was presented to the Church elders. It called for nothing less than the removal of Charlie Jones as pastor of the Presbyterian Church. It read:

> "The problem of the dissention and confusion among the membership of the Chapel Hill Presbyterian Church in regard to certain views and practices of our present pastor has for some time been a topic of general discussion and concern throughout our community as well as within our own church. We, the undersigned, are increasingly distressed over the situation because of the low state of effectiveness and spiritual vitality to which this has reduced our church in its service to the membership and its rightful place of religious leadership in the community. Repeated efforts to improve the situation through the regular administrative channels of the session have failed to produce results satisfactory to us, and some of our regular members are now seeking elsewhere the spiritual nourishment and satisfaction denied them in their own church.

> "We wholeheartedly approve as a pastor for our church one whose views and convictions are sufficiently progressive and

broad to make him an able and worthy leader of religious and spiritual thought in this university community. At the same time we disapprove of a pastor whose convictions and views do not hold due reverence for, and appreciation of, the accepted and long established spiritual principles and tenets of our denomination—principles and tenets from which social conscience and Christian social action flow.

"Perhaps we cannot hope to have a pastor who represents in full degree all that is desired in academic and intellectual reaches and who at the same time reaches perfection in the spiritual and religious realm, for he is certainly subject to human limitations as we all are. We do hope, however, to have a pastor who will meet as many of these essential qualifications as is humanly possible.

"It is our firm conviction that the church membership will continue to disintegrate and the church's usefulness decline so long as we continue under the restricted concepts and ideas of service of our present spiritual leader. When there are glaring omissions of emphasis in some of the important areas which we believe are vital to the spiritual health of the church and when there is an overplayed emphasis on one or two social applications, it leaves us definitely undernourished in both our spiritual and social needs.

"We would gladly accord the pastor the right to a place of service and leadership in the field of his dominant interest and convictions, but if leadership in this cause is more important to him than spiritual and pastoral service to the membership of our church then we believe he should enter specialized service in this field. We do not believe the area of his dominant interest is the special need of our membership and of our church at the present time—nor does it seem likely that a pastor with such restricted interest in and interpretation of religious objectives can fill the needs of our church.

"We believe that the primary need of our church at this time is for a pastor who can first of all heal the wounds and bridge the deep gap that exists between members of the congregation to the end that a united church with the confidence in its spiritual leader may go forward in the religious life of the community. In order to achieve this there is a need for an emphasis upon pastoral service to the membership, upon visits to and communion with the sick and distressed as well as a better acquaintance with and feeling toward the well; emphasis upon a sincere interest in and proper regard for such rites of the church as Baptism, preparation and reception of members— children and adult, and the Sacrament of the Lord's Supper. It seems to us that our pastor's interest in these important areas of the church's responsibilities is sadly lacking.

"We appreciate the difficulties of the situation and the factors involved. But with all due regard for the pastor's sincerity in the field of his chief interest and for the position of the Session, we believe the future welfare of the church organization as a whole is paramount. We regret to ask the Session for a change in pastors and would not but for the fact that other methods to improve conditions have failed and it is our conviction that the situation has now reached such an impasse as to require a change in leadership for the good of the church."[37]

---

[37] Pickard, B. Pickard M. et al. Petition to the Session of the Chapel Hill Presbyterian Church. 1945.

The petition was signed by 41 people, including former elders Alf Pickard and Dr. Reece Berryhill.

On September 24, the Session issued a four-page response, sent to every church member. In full, it read:

> "In view of the fact that there has been expressed, orally and in writing, criticism of the pastor of the Presbyterian Church, the Session wishes to reply, not in any spirit of controversy but with a desire to subordinate differences through agreement on fundamental purposes and thereby to establish a working harmony. It earnestly hopes that the members of the church will cooperate in the efforts of the Session to carry out the aims and ideals implicit in the Christian faith.

> "If members of a church petition for a change of pastorate, it is the duty of the Session to consider carefully the reasons advanced for requesting the change. And if criticism of the pastor's work and behavior seems to be based on insufficient information, it is likewise its duty to try to present the facts.

> "The petition refers to 'the low state of effectiveness and spiritual vitality' of the Church. With regard to this point, it would appear that the continued large attendance at Sunday morning worship suggests a healthy condition. While this does not in itself prove spiritual vitality, the composition of the congregation, the quality of the service, and the atmosphere of reverence which prevails do not indicate a lack of it. It is true that some members of the Church have ceased to attend, but it is doubtful if many preachers could have produced more consistently fresh, vigorous, soul-stirring sermons than have come from the pulpit in Chapel Hill in the last four years.

> "It may be that preaching is not the most important element of a pastor's work. The Synod gives emphasis to other elements

and contributes to the Church for student work. In former times, a full-time assistant aided the pastor in carrying on this activity, but since Mr. Jones has been here, he, with the help of his untiring wife, has met this responsibility alone or with part-time assistants. Moreover, the volume and importance of the work has increased because of the presence of hundreds of servicemen. The Manse has been an open house for these young men day and night.

"Each Friday evening a group of young people have been meeting at the Church for forty-five minutes of Bible study. This study period has been preceded by a supper and a fellowship period. From contacts made here, students troubled in mind and spirit have sought out the pastor in his study and laid their problems before him. Only those who have intimate contact with young people know the strain under which they lived in wartime. Some have had brothers killed in the service; some were approaching their own induction confused and worried. Young people in such a state cannot be given advice and sent away; they must have constant attention. At all times of the day or night such calls have come, and they have been met with sympathy and understanding. These ministrations drew heavily on the time and energy of the pastor, but surely no one would have wanted him to curtail them.

"Due to the abnormal demands of youth in wartime, the pastor has spent less time in visitation among members of the Church than would have been desirable. Possibly some newcomers, some elderly people, and some sick persons failed to receive the attention they should have received. The pastor is aware and regrets it. While there may have been oversights, wherever he has known of sickness, he has visited these homes and ministered unto these people. If some have failed to receive the pastoral attention to which they were entitled, it has not been due to a lack of willingness on the part of the pastor.

"The petition refers to the disintegration of the Church membership. When the present pastorate began in July 1941 the Church had a membership, active and inactive, of 171. Since then, 46 persons have come into the Church on confession of faith and 47 by letter. The loss by death or dismissal to other churches has been 32; therefore the present membership is 242. During Mr. Jones' pastorate there have been five adult baptisms and fourteen infant baptisms. During this period the general revenue of the church has grown, and the benevolences have increased threefold. For the first two years a communion service was held only twice a year. This was because the service was held irregularly while the church was without a pastor and the Session had failed to reestablish it promptly on a quarterly basis. However, two years ago the quarterly communion was resumed and has been held regularly since.

"There has been some criticism to the effect that the children of the Church have been neglected. For years prior to Mr. Jones coming the Sunday school was small, in spite of the great loyalty and devotion of Mr. Foushee, Mr. Gwynn, Mrs. Saunders, and others. At the present time (when school is in session) the Sunday School has an attendance of 60-75, and there are twelve teachers. An educational committee, appointed by the Session, with Mrs. L.M. Brooks as Chairman, has given much constructive thought to the educational work of the Church with most encouraging results. The Church has been fortunate in having the services of two trained workers in the field—Miss Aline McKenzie and Miss Nelle Morton. As a result of the educational programs many boys and girls are coming into the Church for week-day activities.

"When Mr. Jones assumed the pastorate, no work was being done in the Church for the youth of high school age. Now the church unites with other denominations in a religious meeting every Sunday night and often in a mid-week activity. Of the 45 persons received into the Church in the last four years on confession of faith, 15 were young people of high school age from families in the Church. Preliminary to joining, every one of these young people went through a period of study and preparation with the minister. So far as has been discovered, no one in the Church has reached college age during the present pastorate without having participated in such a class and without having joined the Church. Six other young people who have come into the Church from the Church family were above high school age before joining. In each instance they joined after personal consultation with the minister. With so many transients among the population of this war period, it is probable that there have been both young people and older people with Presbyterian background who have not been personally invited by the minister to join the Church. But if this has been true, it is only because their identity has not been discovered. No one who has manifested to the minister or to the Session a desire to affiliate with the Church has failed to receive a cordial invitation to do so.

"For the past three summers the Church has united with one or more other churches in conducting a two-weeks vacation Bible School. This summer all five churches cooperated, and the school had an enrollment of nearly 200. Mr. Jones taught a class each morning.

"There has been less visitation among members of the church than there ought to be. But it is the officers of the Church who have been more derelict in calling on new members; they have not called on the sick and troubled as much as the true spirit of Christian fellowship implies, they have tended to place too much of this responsibility on the pastor. And if he has failed fully to meet all the heavy demands upon him, the blame is not solely his.

"Attention has been called to what was said to be 'an over-played emphasis on one or two social implications' of the teachings of Jesus. Mr. Jones would not be in the ministry if he did not believe it his duty to call attention to some reluctance on the part of the church to translate the teachings of Jesus into social action. With dignity and logic, in simple straight-forward terms, he has shown what these teachings imply in personal and social behavior. This kind of preaching is disturbing.

"The position of the Session, adopted after many hours of deliberation, sometimes in joint session with the deacons, was stated in a memorandum which was circulated among the membership of the Church a year ago. It is as follows:

1. We agree that the pastor in order to serve effectively must have freedom of conscientious judgment and action in attempting to respond in the spirit of Christ to the concrete situations which confront him as he goes about his sacred calling.

2. We agree that this Church should not fail to manifest a vocal and active concern and leadership in behalf of justice and goodwill in the relations between all the races, creeds, and classes of mankind. This obligation is especially binding in regard to the inter-racial relations of our own community and doubly imperative in these years of racial persecutions and racial tensions.

This Church has not and does not encourage Negroes to desert their own churches for membership or worship in this Church. On the other hand we do not close our doors or discriminate against or receive with aught but the spirit of Christian brotherhood any sincere worshipper who may present himself.

3. The officers of this Church openly acknowledge the responsibility of the Church to stand for the economic, educational, political, social and religious progress of all peoples regardless of race, color or creed. As law-abiding citizens we have due regard for the laws of the State and the public policies of the people. We are conscious of the need for intelligent, gradual adjustments to new situations. We do have a long-range sense of the responsibility of the Christian Church for leading the people in a gradually widening communion of the Church Universal. We pray God for the wisdom and the spirit which in these perplexing times will not alienate but win people.

4. There has been opposition to Mr. Jones because of a social application of the Christian message. Other pastors might have approached the task differently. But so long as Mr. Jones' preaching and conduct are worthy and true to the teachings of Jesus, it is the responsibility of the Church to support him.

"'A city that is set on a hill cannot be hid.' A church in Chapel Hill cannot enjoy seclusion. Its location subjects it to the crossfire of a state-wide public opinion. It will be praised and blamed for what it does and for what it fails to do. It should not attempt to avoid attack by taking a neutral position. Its policy must be dictated by what is intrinsically Christian.

Prudence is always in order, but the Christian Church will command respect only when it tries to be true to the word and spirit of Jesus. The Church is dedicated to the advancement of truth and justice. It seeks to be faithful to the teachings of Jesus and to be courageous in their support. Its flag has been planted on the high ground of His teaching; it must not be hauled down."[38]

The document was signed by Floyd Edmister, Frank Porter Graham, Franz Gutmann, Sturgis E. Leavitt, Ernest L. Mackie, W.T. Mattox and Paul Wager.

This response from the Session was an unequivocal message of support for Jones, the first but by no means the last vote of confidence he would receive from his church's elders. As a result, Jones not only kept his position as pastor, but was strengthened, both personally and publicly, by the stand taken by the Session. However, the issues raised in the petition were not destined to die quietly. Questions about Jones' dedication to the Presbyterian doctrine and his regard for the rites of this denomination would be raised again, and there would be echoes of the petitioners claim that he was too concerned and too active in "the field of his dominant interest."

---

[38] Statement to members of the Chapel Hill Presbyterian Church. September 24, 1945.

Chapter Five

Trouble in Paradise

"The best social conscience of our time is concentrated on the re-formation of the social order which, if successful, will make our present injustices and inequities impossible. When it comes to building such a social order we of the churches should be there." - CMJ.

On June 3, 1946, the Supreme Court of the United States handed down its decision in the case of Irene Morgan versus the Commonwealth of Virginia. State laws requiring segregation of interstate passengers on motor carriers was henceforth unconstitutional, for such segregation of passengers crossing state lines was declared an "undue burden on inter-state commerce".[39] This decision was later interpreted by justices in the Court of Appeals for the District of Columbia to apply to interstate train travel as well as bus travel.

---

[39] *Morgan v Commonwealth of Virginia*, 328 U.S. 373, 66 Sup. Ct. 1050, 90 L. Ed. 1317 (1946).

These judgments were early and significant victories for the civil rights movement that was emerging in the South. The practice of making blacks sit in the backs of buses had long been a powerful symbol of prejudice, and was one of the principal humiliations forced upon them daily. In the wake of the decisions, two civil rights groups decided to organize a 'Journey of Reconciliation' through the upper South to determine whether the bus companies were recognizing and abiding by the Morgan decision. The groups also wanted to see how bus drivers, other passengers and the police would react towards those who non-violently and persistently challenged newly illegal racist laws.

One of the groups was the Fellowship of Reconciliation, which described itself as a Christian organization, "composed of men and women of many races and nations who recognize and practice the unity of all men. Members of the FOR believe that depressions, dictatorships, and war are caused by our political, economic, social, and moral maladjustments. FOR members face these problems by a flat refusal to participate in war and by an attempt to use non-violence in all personal relationships.... They believe in facing injustice and dictatorship wherever it is found—at home and abroad—by non-violent resistance."[40] The other group was the Congress of Racial Equality, otherwise known as CORE.

Sixteen people took part in the rides, all were men, eight of them black and eight white. On each trip, between eight and ten of them would board a bus, with the white members usually heading for the back while the black members sat at the front. On the trains the black and white friends sat together in the cars previously designated for whites only. The first bus ride was from Washington, D.C., to Richmond, Virginia, and took place on April 9, 1947. The last ride was two weeks later, on April 23, and was from Charlottesville, VA, to Washington, D.C. In all there were twenty-six rides, taking the protestors through Virginia, North Carolina, Tennessee and Kentucky. As well as testing the Morgan decision, the riders used their time traveling across the upper South to arrange speaking engagements at meetings of the National Association for the Advancement of Colored People (NAACP), churches, and colleges. At each, the Morgan ruling was explained, and reports given on what was happening on the buses and trains as a result of this decision.

For the first two days, the bus rides were uneventful. Then as the travelers tried to move out of Virginia into North Carolina, the first arrests were made. Many of the buses were delayed as drivers and passengers tried to persuade the riders to move to the 'proper' seating, and then delayed further while officials decided what to do when the riders politely refused. In some cases, as noted by the report, oftentimes it was blacks who remonstrated with the riders. When a bus was delayed at Oxford, N.C., for example, a black school teacher was allowed to board to plead with Bayard Rustin, a black man and one of the leaders of the Journey of Reconciliation. The teacher told Rustin, "Please move. Don't do this. You'll reach your destination either in front or in back. What difference does it make?"[41] Another time, when Conrad Lynn, a black New York attorney, refused to move from the front of a bus, the passengers waited patiently for two hours while a warrant was sought for his arrest. The only fuss came from a black porter who boarded the bus and saw Lynn. He was surprised at what was causing the delay and said: "What's the matter with him? He's crazy. Where does he think he is? We know how to deal with him. We ought to drag him off."[42] Meanwhile, on different occasions and in different places, white passengers voiced

---

40 Houser, George. Rustin, Bayard. We Challenged Jim Crow! A Report on the Journey of Reconciliation. April, 1947. (2).

41 Houser, George. Rustin, Bayard. We Challenged Jim Crow! A Report on the Journey of Reconciliation. April, 1947. (4).

their support for the interracial groups, and in Tennessee, a white woman berated one bus driver when he threatened to have two riders arrested.

There were two principal reactions to the travelers, as noted in the report following the rides. The first was confusion. "Persons taking part in the psychological struggle in the buses and trains either did not know of the Morgan decision or, if they did, possessed no clear understanding of it. Thus when police officers and bus drivers in authority took a stand, they tended to act on the basis of what they knew—the state Jim Crow law. In the South, where the caste system is rigidly defined, this confusion is extremely dangerous, leading to frustration, usually followed by aggression in some form."[43] The second reaction was apathy. "The great majority of the passengers were apathetic and did not register their feelings even in situations where it was apparent from facial expressions that they were for or against the action which the group was taking."[44] However, the riders did notice that while other black passengers seemed at first worried by the black riders sitting at the fronts of the buses, when the protestors were left alone and unmolested, they often moved from the rear of the bus towards the front. The report also noted that there were no incidents of "police inconsideration," with officers remaining polite and calm in every case. However, according to the report, the bus companies were "attempting to circumvent the intentions of the Supreme Court in the Irene Morgan decision by

42 Ibid.
43 Ibid.
44 Ibid.

reliance on state Jim Crow Laws, by company regulations, and by subtle pressures."[45]

The report also addressed the issue of violence on the rides. While noting that there was little physical violence, it was also observed that the strongest aggression was reserved for the white participants. And the chief danger, it stated, came when there were crowds present. This observation was made chiefly as a result of the ride scheduled from Chapel Hill to Greensboro, on April 13.

The morning of that trip, six members of the Reconciliation group arrived at the Presbyterian Manse, in Chapel Hill, and were welcomed by Rev. Jones. The group then had lunch with Preacher and his family, after which Jones drove them to the bus station on Rosemary Street.

Andrew Johnson, a black student from Cincinnati, and Joseph Felmet, a white member of the Southern Workers Defense League, boarded the bus. They sat three rows from the front, and were immediately asked by the driver, Ned Leonard, of the Carolina Coach Company, to move to the back of the bus.[46] When they refused, the police were called and the men arrested. Felmet, slow in rising to go with the police officer, was in fact pulled bodily out of his seat and shoved from the bus. The driver then began handing witness cards to passengers, at which point a young white girl told him: "You don't want me to sign one of those. I'm a damn Yankee and I think this is an outrage."[47] Once Johnson and Felmet were off the bus, Bayard Rustin and Igal Roodenko, a white man from New York, moved from the back of

---

[45] Ibid.

[46] Bus Incident Culminating in Arrest of Four Men May Develop into Test Case for 'Jim Crow' Law. Greensboro Daily News. April 15, 1947.

[47] Houser, George. Rustin, Bayard. We Challenged Jim Crow! A Report on the Journey of Reconciliation. April, 1947. (5).

the bus and took up seats at the front. When the driver returned, he summoned the police again, and Roodenko and Rustin were also arrested. The charge was disorderly conduct and obstructing police officers.[48] The incident caused the bus to be delayed about two hours, during which time a crowd had begun to assemble, watching the protests and the comings and goings of the police. Many of the observers were local taxi drivers, as the town's main taxi stand was directly opposite the bus station. One of the cabbies recognized two other riders that were at the bus station, though not on the bus. They were George Houser, the executive director of CORE, and James Peck, editor of the Workers Defense League *News Bulletin*. It was the latter, James Peck, who bore the brunt of the taxi driver's ire, a single, hard blow to the side of the head.[49]

As the crowd had been gathering, Hilton Seals, Charlie Jones' assistant in charge of student work, happened to drive past. He realized the potential danger of the situation and called Jones. Meanwhile, Peck and Rustin made their way to the courthouse across the street from the bus station, and paid the $50 bond for each of the four men arrested. As the men were being released, Jones also arrived at the courthouse. He piled the men into his car and sped off towards the Manse, but not before being spotted by two cabs filled with taximen. The cabbies gave chase, and Jones darted down side streets, heading to the Manse the quickest way he knew, arriving just a few moments before his pursuers. As Jones and the bus protestors made it to the safety of the house, the taxi drivers

---

[48] 4 Men Testing Law Against Segregation Placed under Arrest. Chapel Hill Weekly. April 18, 1947.

[49] Houser, George. Rustin, Bayard. We Challenged Jim Crow! A Report on the Journey of Reconciliation. April, 1947. (10).

jumped out of their cars, brandishing sticks and rocks, but staying at the curb. Jones called the police, but was told that there were no officers that could be sent to help. He called back three more times and was told the same thing each time. On his fifth call, Jones told the officer on the other end of the phone that a group of students at the Manse were going to go outside and confront the taxi drivers, and that any blood spilled would be on the hands of the police. Shortly afterwards, two officers arrived and sent the taxi drivers on their way. As soon as it was safe to do so, Jones arranged to have the group driven to Durham, and then on to Greensboro, where they had planned a speaking engagement for that evening. But that was not the end of the incident, for the same evening, there were several threatening phone calls made to the Jones residence, threats to kill and to burn the house down. Worried about their children and their own safety, Charles and Dorcas Jones decided to go away for a few days. They waited until it was dark, put their children and a few bags in the car and drove across town to the house of their friends, sociology professor Lee Brooks and his wife Evelyn. They stayed the night there, and then set off the following evening for Greensboro, where they spent the night in a tourist home, before heading up to the familiarity, and safety, of Brevard where they were welcomed by concerned friends, Hal and Hester Hart. Dorcas and the children stayed there for a week, but Jones wanted to be back in Chapel Hill. He knew his family was safe in Brevard, and felt that his place was in Chapel Hill where he could continue his work. Although he never said so, it is also possible he was concerned about the students who had offered to stay in the house while he and his family were away. He was responsible for their safety, but also wanted to ensure they would put into practice the doctrine of non-violence that he had espoused, and that they had embraced, in the face of even the most direct physical threat.

The students had decided to stay at the house to ensure none of the threats of violence were carried out, and also to keep a log of all telephone calls. The students spread themselves throughout the house, each responsible for a particular room. After an early incident, in which someone hurled a stone towards Hilton Seals as he walked outside the Manse, the night passed quietly. The second night also seemed likely to prove uneventful, until just before dawn one of the students in an upstairs bedroom heard a car motor running slowly. He looked out and saw someone standing at the curb where the taxi drivers had been. He saw a man standing by a car with his arm upraised, about to hurl an object towards the house. The student jumped out of the window onto the roof and, using none too delicate language, demanded to know what the man was doing. An indignant voice came up from the curb-side. "Mister, I'm just delivering the newspaper."[50]

The incident at the Chapel Hill bus station was instant news all over the state, and for his part in the events, Preacher Jones became big news too. The interracial picnic at Battle Park had angered enough people to put his name in the editorial and news pages of the Chapel Hill papers, but now, for the first time, the large media organizations across North Carolina, and even further afield, were starting to sit up and take notice of what was happening in Chapel Hill. Most of these papers told the story of the incident at the bus station by giving purely factual accounts of the events at the bus station. But in describing Jones and his role, and his position in the community, sometimes the words assumed an air of subtle, but definite, commentary. The Greensboro Daily News described him as "pastor of the local Presbyterian Church, who has caused a split in the membership of his church as a result of his attitude on the race

---

[50] Notes written by Dorcas Jones. Undated.

question."[51] The somewhat more liberal <u>Raleigh News and Observer</u> noted the sharpened racial tension in Chapel Hill, and while mentioning Jones in the second paragraph of the story, resisted the temptation to editorialize and described him as "the Rev. Charles M. Jones, who asked for police protection for the four arrested men."[52] The <u>Chapel Hill Weekly</u> described him as the Presbyterian minister "whose advocacy of the mingling of the races at gatherings has caused a division in his church and has been the subject of spirited discussion among the people of the town".[53] Soon, though, the real editorial writers weighed in. The <u>Greensboro Daily News</u> was none too happy to see in action this "fresh crop of martyrs", and seemed more concerned with keeping the peace, and maintaining the status quo, than with taking any moral stance. "Above all, it is to be hoped that none of our own residents who invite this sort of seemingly unnecessary embroilment upon us will be permitted to use it for purposes of personal exploitation."[54] The <u>Atlanta Constitution</u> was less restrained. "An Example of 'Commies' at Work" a headline declared. After claiming that "in the Deep South States…the biracial problem is less by virtue of less Negro population". The protest riders, the newspaper claimed, were in fact out to worsen race relations, and embarrass those who really were trying to improve things. "Southern police forces and communities will do well to expect other such demonstrations. They will know in advance not to consider them local disturbances, but, in the 'Commie' manner, seeking to disturb local

[51] Bus Incident Culminating in Arrest of Four Men May Develop into Test Case for 'Jim Crow' Law. Greensboro Daily News. April 15, 1947.

[52] Racial Tension Mounts after Chapel Hill Incident. Raleigh News and Observer. April 15, 1947.

[53] 4 Men Testing Law Against Segregation Placed under Arrest. Chapel Hill Weekly. April 18, 1947.

[54] North Carolina Can Take It. Greensboro Daily News. April 16, 1947.

relationships."[55] Prophetically, Raleigh's <u>News and Observer</u> published a story that had come from a reporter at Glade Valley High School, in Allegheny County, where the Orange Presbytery was meeting jointly with the Winston-Salem Presbytery. The story quoted Dr. T. Henry Patterson, the executive secretary of the Orange Presbytery, as saying "no action is scheduled" for the meetings in regard to Jones and his activities in Chapel Hill. However, Patterson added: "You can never tell, though, what extra business might come up during the business portion of the meeting."[56] The <u>Charlotte News</u> also doubted the value of the Journey of Reconciliation, and the worth of other types of "agitation". "We seriously question whether this action, as one of a series, will have the beneficial effects its authors intended." The editorial piece ended with this quotation from Chapel Hill Police Chief W.T. Sloan. "We are going to give protection to everybody who needs it, to the limit of our ability. I think it is only fair to ask that people help us all they can by trying to refrain from doing things that stir up bad feeling."[57]

One more incident at the Chapel Hill bus station increased tension in the town. The <u>Durham Sun</u> reported that in the aftermath of the initial furor at the bus station, Martin Walker, a white World War Two veteran and student at UNC, was attacked by three taxi drivers when they saw him talking to a black woman at the station. The newspaper said that one of the taxi drivers, Mickey Merritt of Carrboro, had admitted hitting Walker, and quoted police as saying there would be several arrests "soon."[58]

---

[55] An Example of 'Commies' at Work. Atlanta Constitution. April 20, 1947.

[56] No Action Now Scheduled on Chapel Hill Minister. Raleigh News and Observer. April 16, 1947.

[57] A Remedy Becomes an Irritant. Charlotte News. April 21, 1947.

[58] Vet Attacked for Talking to Negro at Chapel Hill. Durham Sun. April 16, 1947.

On April 17, four days after the bus station incident, the <u>Daily Tar Heel</u> urged all students, faculty members and townspeople to attend an afternoon meeting on campus.

> "The purpose of this meeting will be to present complete facts and details as to what actually happened concerning disorders, violence, and threats which have characterized the local scene during the past few days. It is hoped that the air may be cleared somewhat, and the rumor-mongering in the community aborted."[59]

Jones continued to press for equal rights for blacks, speaking eloquently from the pulpit and working actively in the community. And as described by the church elders in 1945, Jones put much of his energy into attracting young people to the church. His eloquence and progressive views on social conditions also made him attractive to other communities and he was frequently invited to speak and attend conferences in North Carolina and in other states. He was particularly busy speaking at college campuses across the South. Many schools held Religious Emphasis Weeks, when ministers and other well-known moral or spiritual leaders would come and lead discussions or give talks. Jones was frequently asked to attend these religious events and he would go whenever he could. His popularity earned him visits to black universities like Morehouse College in Atlanta, women's colleges like Randolph-Macon in Lynchburg, Virginia, and even some of the more traditionally conservative schools. His popular appeal sprung from

---

[59] Drama of Racial Violence Invokes Mass Meeting Today. Daily Tar Heel. April 17, 1947.

the innate simplicity of his message, as much as from the way he delivered it. Even when not discussing race, his emphasis was always on applying Christian principles to everyday living, in relating Jesus' teachings to the current issues of the day. This manner won him many accolades from his parishioners, but also served him well in his dealings with young people. In the summer of 1948 he led a conference for the Board of Christian Education of the Moravian Church in America, in Winston-Salem. Afterwards he received a letter from John Fulton, Secretary of the Board. "A large number of our young people personally expressed to me their delight in your work with them as conference leader and I believe that you made a contribution at camp which has not been made in a long time in dealing with the subject of personal Christian living."[60] To encourage religious education, Jones would also invite groups to meet at his church, and attend church services while in town. After arranging one such meeting at the church, Sara Little, the assistant director of the Synod's Office of Religious Education, in Charlotte, joined members of her group for a service there. She later wrote to Jones thanking him for his hospitality. She went on: "And then let me add this personal note of thanks for your sermon this morning. In these days when my dissatisfaction with the church is growing, most sermons are only words; yours was food. Thank you."[61] His relaxed and friendly manner combined with his obvious sincerity made his sermons nothing short of legendary. As early as 1944, Frank Porter Graham had been quoted in the Tar Heel as saying Jones was "the only preacher he knew who never preached a bad sermon."[62] Even the

---

[60] Fulton, John W. Letter to Charles Jones. September 14, 1948.

[61] Little, Sara. Letter to Charles Jones. February 15, 1948.

[62] Editorial. The Tar Heel. June 20, 1944.

church's older members had been impressed. Parkhill Jarvis had left Chapel Hill and moved to New Bern, NC, and returned to the Presbyterian Church where he had been accustomed to hearing one of Jones' predecessors, the Rev. William D. Moss, speak. Parson Moss, as he was known, was a Canadian who came to Chapel Hill in 1912. Like Jones, he was somewhat unorthodox in his ministry, and also like Jones Parson Moss was an intellectual yet charismatic man who appealed particularly to the young. It was under Parson Moss that the church's membership first broke one hundred. With Parson Moss in mind, Jarvis wrote to Jones:

> "During the pre-cellophane era I was a great admirer of Parson Moss and usually when I left the church I would tell him, 'that was a damn good sermon.' Yesterday my wife and I attended your church and enjoyed the services very much. I didn't take the opportunity of coming up front to tell you too... "that was a damn good sermon". If you have a copy I would like to have one. I have always been very much interested in your church and I hear that you are doing a swell job. I feel that you are a worthy successor to the Parson and that is definitely a compliment from a member of the class of 1919."[63]

While most people acknowledged that Jones was a good man and a gifted speaker, there were still people at the Church who did not believe Jones was a true Presbyterian, and that his ministry was more attuned

---

[63] Jarvis, Parkhill O. Letter to Charles Jones. April 29, 1946.

to the needs of blacks in the community than to his own congregation. His personality, beliefs and leadership had won over the majority of his Church members, but there was an increasingly vocal minority who, while not disliking Jones personally, wanted to see a more traditional Presbyterian ministry in Chapel Hill. Since the Session's affirmation of support for Jones in 1945 these feelings had remained somewhat hidden, but they resurfaced in 1951. In the fall of that year, some members gathered to discuss the need for a second Presbyterian Church. By December they had organized to petition Orange Presbytery to start another church in Chapel Hill. The group consisted of about 20 people, including faculty members and businessmen, one physician, and several graduate students.[64]

One couple that helped to organize the petitioners was Dr. and Mrs. Bernard Boyd. He had come to UNC in 1950 as the James A. Gray Professor of Biblical Literature, from Davidson College where he had been a member of the Bible Department. As Presbyterians they had attended Jones' church and found him "very personable both in the pulpit and out," and the Chapel Hill congregation "a very friendly, warm group."[65] But they did not find the church at all Presbyterian as they had been used to, or understood it should be. They visited other churches in town, but still longed for a Presbyterian Church with which they could truly identify. The petition for a new church was a reflection of their needs, and the needs of other similarly dissatisfied members.

---

[64] Johnston, Rev. Edward. The Controversy Between Charles Miles Jones and Orange Presbytery, 1952-53. Thesis for M.A. Degree. University of Virginia. 1973.

[65] Ibid.

The petitioners formally addressed themselves to the Council of Orange Presbytery in March, 1952, stating that a second church was needed "in order to meet more adequately the spiritual and pastoral needs of our community."[66] The petitioners were not concerned with Jones' social views or his stance on the race issue. Their plan was not to oust Jones from his church, but to bring to Chapel Hill a Presbyterian church that was more traditional in its ministry.

However, it seems clear that the Council of Presbytery, to whom the petition was presented, was very much concerned with Jones' activities as they related to race. The Council's executive chairman, T. Henry Patterson was a conservative man, and did not welcome all of the people, nor all of the publicity, that Jones had brought to the Chapel Hill Presbyterian Church. Patterson admitted in an interview some years later that he was keen to see Jones out of the church, believing he had been there too long and that both Jones and his congregation were ripe for a change.[67]

So by the spring of 1952, there were two groups hoping for a pastoral change at the Chapel Hill Presbyterian Church. Both favored a return to a more traditional ministry, but it seems the similarity ended there. While the petitioners sought an entirely new Church for Chapel Hill, the Council of Presbytery saw no need for that, and instead sought to keep the existing one—minus the Reverend Charles Jones. Thus the petition, when placed before them, gave Council members a reason to investigate Jones, gave them an entry into his ministry whereupon they

---

[66] Unsigned letter dated March, 1952. Minutes of the Presbytery of Orange, CLXXXIII No.2, p.7.

[67] Interview with T. Henry Patterson by Rev. Edward Thompson. For Masters Thesis, University of Virginia. 1971.

could seek reasons to at first encourage, and then later, pressure, him to resign.

Patterson began by inviting Jones to Greensboro to meet with a group composed of members from Orange Presbytery's Commission on the Minister and His Work, and from the Council of Presbytery. In all there were ten men who met with Jones at the First Presbyterian Church of Greensboro, in April of 1952. Patterson opened the meeting by stating they were there "to talk with [Jones] as brethren and friends about the Chapel Hill Church."[68] He said that the Council had received complaints about Jones ministry from around the Synod and that there were a number of rumors that needed to be explained. Accusations were leveled at Jones, for example, that he was the president of the Chapel Hill chapter of the NAACP. In truth, Jones had not even joined the organization, saying that he would prefer to be a member of an association that stood for the Advancement of All People. It was put to him that in a sermon he had called the first communion of Christ with the Apostles a 'cocktail party,' that he did not believe in the divinity of Jesus or in the Atonement; and that when officers of his church disagreed with him, they were forced out.[69]

Jones spoke to each of these issues, trying to assure and reassure those in front of him. Though they appeared to listen, as the meeting progressed several people present expressed the opinion "that the truth or falsity of the rumors was of no consequence as far as people they talked to were concerned. These people believed them."[70] This made

---

[68] Complaint to the Synod of North Carolina by the Chapel Hill Presbyterian Church, Exhibit No. 3.

[69] Ibid.

[70] Ibid.

plain, then, the chief reason for the meeting—not to discuss and resolve problems, but instead to remove Jones from the ministry.

The Council then presented Jones with prepared questions relating to his theological beliefs. They wanted to know his views on the Bible, Jesus Christ, the Virgin Birth, the Atonement, and the bodily resurrection of Christ.[71] It was immediately obvious that a great theological gap existed between Jones and his questioners. The answers they sought were exact and definite responses according to Presbyterian theology, answers from the Westminster Confession of Faith, literally interpreted and precisely rendered. They were not prepared to accept the latitude and imprecision of Jones' own views, just as he was not prepared to spit out other people's preordained responses. His faith was not that narrowly defined, nor so simply explained.

After the quiz, which Jones had obviously failed in the eyes of his accusers, the group recommended he resign from the Chapel Hill Church unless the situation could be clarified and confidence be restored in his ministry through the Synod.[72]

Jones responded by saying that if they thought him a heretic, they should bring charges against him to Presbytery. Patterson answered by reminding Jones that it was the individual minister's responsibility to notify Presbytery if he had experienced a change of views since his ordination. Jones in turn replied that there had been no change in his views that would require such action. Patterson once again urged Jones to

---

[71] Patterson interview.
[72] Complaint, Exhibit No. 4.

make a break with the church, basing his arguments on the following points.

1. That Jones had done a good job in Chapel Hill, but if a new church were started Jones would not have the field entirely to himself and would not be so successful in the same way;

2. That Jones had been in Chapel Hill eleven years and that was long enough to stay;

3. That the Chapel Hill Church needed buildings and as long as Jones was there they could not secure money from the people in the state who had "big" money. It "would be easy" to raise $200,000 for the church with new leadership.[73]

The meeting was adjourned without relief or victory for either side. The group had not been mollified or appeased, and Jones was as determined as ever to stay on as the minister of the Presbyterian Church of Chapel Hill.

Several of those who had met with Jones in Greensboro were members of the Presbytery's Council, and they now pressured it to entertain seriously, for the first time, the possibility of a second Presbyterian Church in Chapel Hill. Plans were begun to make a recommendation to the June 13 meeting of Orange Presbytery concerning the Chapel Hill situation.

---

[73] Complaint, Exhibit No. 3.

Interlude

Since coming to Chapel Hill in 1941, Jones had been a leader in the struggle for social change in the town. That made him the center of much public and media attention, but it meant that his family was placed squarely in the limelight, too. As the pressure intensified for Jones, so did it for his wife Dorcas and their three children. In the summer of 1952, Jones was at the peak of his ministry thus far, with a large and supportive membership at his church, with frequent requests to speak at churches and colleges all over the South, and with the respect and love of the majority of Chapel Hill's most prominent citizens. The demands on his time and energy were increasingly severe, and even the mild-mannered Preacher Jones felt the need to take some time off. He had done so every summer since arriving in Chapel Hill, packing his family into the car and heading for the mountains for a six-week vacation.

For the first few years they stayed with their friends Hal and Hester Hart, near Brevard—the couple Jones had taken his family to after the bus incident of 1948. The Harts had a farm called Little Pines, which they ran during the summer as a tourist resort. The Joneses stayed in their own cabin on the property, a tenant house with no electricity or running water, and would delight in becoming a part of daily farm life there. Preacher rode with Hal Hart to the local markets, and once helped him buy a cow; Bettie Miles would bring in the cows at milking time, or saddle the horses for guests wanting to ride; the adults would play shuffleboard while the children went down to the pond to swim.

The family would also help out around the house, taking up any slack should the need arise. Once Jones found Hal collapsed in a barn, his appendix ruptured. He rushed him to the hospital, and returned to the farm to lend a hand running it while Hal was recovering. Hester spent the next few days with Hal in the hospital, so Dorcas took over some of her household duties, and Bettie Miles and Virginia were even conscripted into waiting on the guests during meal times, a job they enjoyed immensely. It was during this hectic time that Dorcas received her first, and only, tip—$15 handed over by a grateful guest as he was leaving.

Mostly the summers there were a time to work hard and play hard, a time to enjoy life to the fullest, to get back to being in and around nature, to appreciate the simpler, less complicated things in life. In the evenings, as guests piled into the living room and filled the sofa, chairs and even the floor, Charles would sing for them, accompanied on the piano by his friend Lee Brooks from Chapel Hill, whose family also spent their summers at Little Pines, or by his old friend Alvin Moore who often came by to see the family while they were in the area.

As the race issue heated up in Chapel Hill, and as he became somewhat uncertain as to his own future there, Jones decided to pay for his own little retreat in the mountains. In 1949, he and Charles McCoy, a former student at UNC, together got the money for a down payment on a piece of property in Etowah, just outside of Brevard. The parcel of land had been two small farms, about 27 acres in total, with two buildings on it. One was the main farmhouse, which was at first rented out to pay for the mortgage on the property, and later sold. The other was a tenant's house, with no electricity or running water. It was this three-room cabin that the Joneses made their summer home for the next 11 years.

The summer vacations would always begin with the long drive into the mountains, the children and luggage in the car, and a trailer attached to the back of it. Mattresses, linens, dishes—everything had to be brought in for each trip. And then, because there was also no road up to the cabin, it all had to be carried the quarter mile through the woods. Fifty-pound blocks of ice for the ice box were fetched by car from Brevard and then carried as quickly as possible, reaching their destination ten or fifteen pounds lighter. The first few summers especially, much of the time was spent fixing up the place to make living there a little easier. The first job was always for Preacher to put on a brave face and go through the cabin armed with a hoe, shooing out the snakes that had made it their home over the winter, and then clearing out the rolls of snake skin that had been shed. Such was his dislike of serpents that very often Dorcas and the children would watch him come sprinting out of the front door, across the porch and into the safety of the yard well before the snakes deigned to make their exit. Cutting the long grass around the house could also prove hazardous. One time he was making good progress riding on his mower when he ran over a beehive. When he saw the furious swarm he leapt off the mower, fell face down on the ground, and then was up again running, but without his glasses which had come flying off in the melee. Fortunately, he managed to escape with only a few, minor stings, and later retrieved his glasses from the newly mown field. But despite the occasional mishaps, it was his love for nature that made him return to this spot every year, the chance to be with his family and to escape for a little while the hectic life that awaited him in Chapel Hill. This six week period every year was his time of renewal, a chance to refresh his mind and body through physical labor, through a more elemental struggle to work in harmony with the forces of nature, and to spend time with people who were accustomed to doing just that. He never stopped thinking about the problems and issues that were his motivating force, and he still loved to talk with anyone about anything, but while in Etowah his primary concern was fetching water from the spring behind the house, or deciding which part of the property needed tending to or clearing up first. He also worked hard on the house, putting into practice the skills he had learned in his wood-working classes at high school—some of the few classes he had genuinely enjoyed. He built a screened-in porch at the back of the cabin, so the family could eat out there at meal times. He also screened in the long front porch, in the process creating a bedroom for Bettie Miles. It was she, in fact, who made numerous trips through the woods with her father, each at one end of a heavy oak board or roll of screening, back and forth until both porches were completed.

Jones also reveled in the chance to talk with people like his neighbors, the Logans. They were a black family who owned the land adjacent to the Jones property. Preacher especially enjoyed the older Mr. Logan, who one day agreed to teach the young preacher how to plough behind a mule. He explained, and then showed him, what geeing and hawing were, and soon allowed Preacher to take over. After a while, Jones, concentrating hard but enjoying himself immensely, yelled over to old Mr. Logan to ask how he was doing. The old man looked at him a moment and said, "Well, you be geeing when you should be hawing, and hawing when you should be geeing—but it don't matter 'cos that mule's got lots of sense."

While staying at Little Pines, and in the early years at Etowah, it was the production of food that kept the Joneses busiest, the children included. There were a number of large farms in the area, whose fields were rented by large cannery corporations based in Florida. Migrant workers were brought in to pick the crops of vegetables every year. And although there were quite a few late-ripening plants, and some first-time ones that were missed, the corporations found it was not profitable to send the pickers through the fields a second time. There was usually a week or so between the time the fields were picked and then ploughed under, and during this time the local people were allowed to go out and pick whatever they could find for themselves. The whole Jones family would join a few local villagers, spending several days a year in the various fields picking peas, green beans, and lima beans. Over the course of the summer, they would collect bushels of vegetables, as well as fresh tomatoes and corn gotten from nearby farmers, and the fresh peaches bought at local markets. The family would then take the bushels of one type of fruit or vegetable to the cannery and spend the day working to preserve their pickings for the winter, making two or three trips a week to get through their entire stock. The cannery was set up in the Brevard elementary school's cafeteria, and was always extremely busy in the summer months. Women and children sat outside snapping beans and shucking corn, working in the shade of the large trees. Inside, there were large sinks for washing the produce, and long tables upon which the cans were set out and filled with the various fruits and vegetables. Lids were then pressed onto the tops of the cans, usually by the children, and then the adults would take over, sealing the tins with a hand-turned tool much like a can opener, only having the opposite effect. Once sealed, each can was labeled as to content and then hand-stamped with a number assigned to that family, then loaded into a wire basket large enough to hold several hundred cans. The basket was then lowered into one of two giant pressure cookers, and the cans left to process for the prescribed time. Once adequately cooked, they were lifted out and left to cool for a few minutes, before being sorted according to family number for taking home. For most people, these sessions at the cannery lasted all day, with children doing as much work as they could, peeling, snapping, shucking, sorting. It was the custom for any family, having canned its own supplies, to offer assistance to other families—though often their work done, the children would be free to play for a while. This made the long days at the cannery into social occasions, chances to meet and talk with new people, and this was reason enough to make visits there one of the highlights of Preacher's summer vacation. And of course once the work was done, there were upward of two thousand cans of beans, peas, corn, tomatoes and several different fruits ready to be loaded into the trailer and driven back at the end of the vacation to Chapel Hill, where most of them would be opened up to help feed the countless students who found their way to the Manse near dinner time through the subsequent winter and spring. In fact, those students had full run of the Manse while the Joneses were away, as Charles and Dorcas never considered locking the doors and depriving those in need of a place to eat, sleep or shoot a game of pool. Preacher himself would occasionally have to return for a night or two, called back for a funeral or some other emergency. But after doing what he could there, he would always head back to his summer retreat where he could again sink gently into the slow and peaceful mountain existence that so recharged his soul.

Chapter Six

Faith Under Fire

"As men so often do, we seek justice out of a deep back-
ground of injustice. But we who seek are also the South; we
ask because our history has made the question unavoidable;
but still we ask in that friendly but insistent tone which is
the South at its best." - CMJ.

On Sunday May 18, 1952, Jones was in the pulpit of his Chapel Hill church. His sermon that morning reflected the essence of his family's summer vacations, the simple living amid nature's complex, unfathomable beauty. And it captured also the central tenet of his religious faith and teaching, an undefined and learning approach to Christianity that stood in contrast to the dogmatic stricture of some of those who were beginning to marshal their forces in opposition to him.

> "When we believe that through Jesus, God has spoken to reveal the infinite meaning and possibilities of life; that in Jesus God offers not codes or rules to be slavishly followed but a disclosing of God's ways with men and His purposes for men;- then

one has a grasp of the life-giving tradition of the Christian Church."[74]

However, less than a month after hearing this sermon, those members of the Chapel Hill Church who did desire a more traditional Presbyterian ministry received good news. A meeting of the Orange Presbytery had been held at the First Presbyterian Church in Burlington on June 13, and the last item on the Council's agenda was the matter of a new Presbyterian Church for Chapel Hill.[75]

The report began with a consideration of the March 2 petition, which stated that, "The present plant is inadequate for a total Sunday School program, and the crowded conditions necessitate two different services each Sunday morning. The Chapel Hill community has grown to a total of some 15,000 year round residents; and there is an exceptionally large number of Presbyterian students in the University, approximately 1,100 in 1951-1952."[76]

The Council's reply to the petition seemed to treat the request seriously, and on its stated merits, additionally noting the importance of the existing Presbyterian Church in Chapel Hill. "We have met on two occasions with the petitioning group and have conferred with a number of ministers and laymen across the Presbytery, and even the Synod of North Carolina, because we believe the Chapel Hill Church touches and influences every church across our Synod and many churches across our Southland."[77] Council member E. Frank Andrews subsequently moved that "on this date Orange Presbytery appoint a Commission to

---

[74] Jones, C.M. Sermon at Chapel Hill Presbyterian Church. May 18, 1952.

[75] Minutes of the Presbytery of Orange, CLXXXIII, No.2, p.5.

[76] Ibid., p.7.

[77] Ibid.

organize the church, ordain and install officers and give such guidance as shall be necessary." The motion was carried without opposition.

A second Presbyterian Church in Chapel Hill seemed then to be a solution to many of the problems that had beset the existing one. A month before the meeting in Burlington, in fact, Jones and Elder Frank Edmister had written to Charles Perry, the lay chairman of Orange Presbytery's Council. The letter stated that the Deacons and Elders of the church had met to discuss the formation of a new church, and then requested a letter be written to document their resolutions. "Our group would not oppose the establishment of a new church. We respect the right of everyone to worship as best fits his need, and should want to assist and cooperate, if the project is undertaken."[78] But the letter went on to emphasize the need for further expansion at the existing church in any event. "Even if another church is organized here, it would still be necessary to enlarge the facilities of the present Church for student work, religious education and services of worship."[79]

Thus, when Andrews' recommendation to set up a new church was passed by the Council, the central issue appeared simply to be the need for a new church to cope with the growth of Chapel Hill, and overcrowding at the existing church. There was little mention of the ideological differences between Jones and the petitioners, nor between Jones and the Council. However, a second motion made clear that there was more involved. It called for the funds currently going to Jones' student work be diverted to pay the pastor's salary at the new church. Had this

---

[78] Jones, C.M. Edmister, F.H. Letter to Charles Perry. May 21, 1952.
[79] Ibid.

recommendation passed, it would have amounted to a vote of no confidence in the Chapel Hill Church and would have crippled Jones' ministry to the University students. Even with a new Presbyterian church in Chapel Hill, the existing one had made plain its need for an enlargement of facilities, so with that knowledge, any diversion of funds by the Presbytery would have been a clear and damaging censure. Predictably, the motion was hotly contested by many at the meeting. It was one thing to propose a new church in Chapel Hill that would complement the ministry of the existing one, but to punish that existing congregation, to deprive a large group of worshippers in the process was simply not acceptable. After much debate, and when it was clear the motion would fail, a substitute motion was offered, one that bypassed the issue of money altogether. The substitute motion read as follows: "That a Commission of ten persons, five ministers and five elders, be appointed as a Judicial Commission to organize the new church at Chapel Hill; and, at the request of the Session and the Congregation of the Chapel Hill Church, have authority to work with the Session of the Chapel Hill Church to be formed; in order that a thoroughly Christian and unified Presbyterian program may be made effective in the city of Chapel Hill and on the campus of the University. Furthermore, the Commission is empowered to investigate thoroughly the total situation in the Chapel Hill Church and to report back to the Presbytery."[80] The Council immediately elected the ten-person Judicial Commission, the five ministers being: Z.T. Piephoff, of Bessemer Church, Greensboro; J.M.

---

[80] Minutes of the Presbytery of Orange, CLXXXIII, No.2, pp.8-9.

Garrison, of the Church of Covenant, Greensboro; J.S. Whitley, of Leaksville Church; G.D. Jackson, of Ashboro; and G.A. Taylor, of Northside, Burlington. The five Elders elected were: C.W. Perry, F.L. Knight, E. Frank Andrews, M.E. Yount, and D.J. Walker.[81] Five of the Commission members—Piephoff, Whitley, Perry, Andrews and Yount—were also members of the Council of Presbytery who had recommended the transfer of Synod funds away from the Chapel Hill Church. As a result of this, the Commission would be accused on more than one occasion of having an inherent bias against Jones and his church. It was a criticism the Commission was never able to effectively counter, or overcome.

The formation of the Judicial Commission raised an interesting question as to the motives of the Council—from where did the idea of an investigation of the "total situation" of the Chapel Hill Church come? The petitioners themselves had no ostensible disagreements with Jones' on social issues, their request was for a more traditional Presbyterian ministry offered as an alternative to, not a replacement of, Jones' church. Moreover, they did not request the transfer of funds from the existing church to the new one, nor did they call for or recommend any kind of investigation into the activities of the Chapel Hill Church. Clearly, the motivation came from within the Council itself, with the petition merely a vehicle to justify the establishment of the Judicial Commission, whose very name clearly belies the group's purported primary role as organizer of the new church.

---

[81] Ibid., p.9.

This accusation of bias was expressed most strongly in a statement later released by thirty-nine members of the Chapel Hill Presbyterian Church. The statement referred to a meeting even before the establishment of the Judicial Commission, between representatives of the Orange Presbytery and church officers. "The meeting with our officers was very revealing. A meeting which started out ostensibly to get our opinion on the establishment of a new church turned into an open attack on Mr. Jones. In the course of this attack it was stated that our church needed support for its student program but that this support would not be forthcoming as long as Mr. Jones was pastor. Mr. T. Henry Patterson stated that he had been deluged with letters from 'across the synod' demanding Mr. Jones' dismissal. We asked how many letters constituted a deluge. Mr. Patterson finally defined it as 18 letters. When forced to produce this deluge at a later date, Mr. Patterson could locate but two of them, one-ninth of a deluge."[82] But whatever the motivations and biases, the investigation of Preacher Jones and the Chapel Hill Presbyterian Church had begun.

Three weeks later, on July 8, the Summer Adjourned Meeting was held at New Hope Presbyterian Church near Chapel Hill and there Charlie Jones made a request to be allowed to work outside the bounds of the Orange Presbytery for a year. He had received a grant from Save the Children Foundation to work in a ten-county area of the East Tennessee mountains. His job would be to aid in improving the educational conditions in the many one-room schoolroom communities by

---

[82] Lyons, S. et al. Statement regarding Judicial Commission's final report. Undated.

attempting to motivate the local school board to assume greater responsibility for quality education. Though he would be away for a year, when accepting the grant it was agreed he would return to Chapel Hill once a month to preach.

When the request went to the floor of the Presbytery, a number of concerns were raised about the advisability of a one-year leave of absence for a minister whose church was under investigation. Those objections were in the end over-ruled and the request was granted. It would appear from this approval that apart from the Council of Orange and the Judicial Commission, the Presbytery was not expecting all that much to happen with regard to the investigation into the Chapel Hill Presbyterian Church. Jones, on the other hand, seemed to view the matter with some seriousness. Before his request was made, he typed out a statement given to his elders for consideration. A temporary pastor could be engaged to carry on the daily, general work of the Church, he suggested, and a good preacher brought in to "keep the congregation and students in attendance." He went on:

> "I believe such an arrangement as this might cushion the shock of my leaving as far as the congregation is concerned. It would put Presbytery in the place where it could relieve itself of an investigation (if that investigation were solely to force me out). If they wish to continue the investigation then that is still possible for them.

> "It would enable me to assure both congregation and Presbytery that we are not running away under fire nor being forced out against my will. It is not so important to do this for Presbytery but it is important for the Church."[83]

---

[83] Jones, C.M. Statement regarding request for leave of absence. Undated.

With the passage of Jones' request, there followed a Called Meeting, one specially convened, at the First Presbyterian Church of Burlington on July 20. It was convened for the purpose of allowing Irving E. Birdseye of Hillsborough to become associate minister of the Chapel Hill Church. He had been minister of the Hillsborough Church since 1947 and also served as permanent clerk of the Presbytery, and the matter was something of a formality, with Jones' request passed earlier in the month.

However, Presbytery refused to approve the appointment, instead voting to defer any decision on the matter "until the Commission…[makes] its report." Two days later, the News of Orange County, a weekly paper, carried a report of the Called Meeting, and in doing so shed some light on the decision made by the Presbytery. It said that among the leaders voting against the appointment of Birdseye was the Rev. Marion Huske who "sounded the call for a more conservative approach [in Chapel Hill], charging that an 'iron curtain' separated the Chapel Hill Church from the rest of Synod."[84] Birdseye had become the first, but by no means the last, casualty of the Chapel Hill controversy.

The Judicial Committee was called to meet for the first time by chairman Z.T. Piephoff on July 1, at the First Presbyterian Church of Burlington, and that meeting was primarily organizational.

---

[84] Presbytery Refuses to Approve Call of Birdseye While Chapel Hill Probe On. The News of Orange County. July 31, 1952. p.1.

Representatives of the Chapel Hill Church met with the Commission and gave it general data about the church to prepare the Commission for the first working session scheduled for July 21-22. The Commission also met with petitioning group and quickly voted to inform them "that the Judicial Commission stands ready to organize them into a Church whenever they want it."[85] This early declaration had an immediate effect—it subtly shifted the burden of action for a new church onto the petitioning group, thus allowing the Commission to change what had been its secondary assignment into its main priority: the investigation of the Chapel Hill Church and Charles Jones.

The Commission held its first meeting on July 21 at the Chapel Hill Presbyterian Church. The Session was expecting a somewhat relaxed and friendly discussion, concentrating on the possible formation of a new church and how both churches could best work together to serve the needs of the community. It was not to be. Z.T. Piephoff opened the meeting and told the officers that their request to have a member of the Session present on the Commission, "to hear all evidence to be taken" could not be approved.[86] This was the Commission's response to a letter sent by the Chapel Hill Church ten days earlier, requesting the right to hear evidence and cross-examine witnesses that it claimed was an "elementary right and common courtesy."[87]

---

[85] Minutes of the Presbytery of Orange, CLXXXIV, No.1. p32.

[86] Complaint to the Synod of North Carolina by the Chapel Hill Presbyterian Church, Exhibit No. 20.

[87] Lyons, S. et al. Statement regarding Judicial Commission's final report. Undated.

But worse was to come. The Commission then handed the Session members a lengthy questionnaire, prepared and presented much like a personality test but with a theological emphasis. There were 38 questions in all, and each officer was asked to write down his answers.[88] The officers were told "to put down in reply to some of the 'easy' questions the first thoughts that occurred to them."[89] The officers were shocked and upset by this surprise test and the apparently belittling tactics the Commission was using. Moreover, they were confronted without warning with questions like, "What does Jesus Christ mean to you?," and "What to you is the most important part of your faith as a Christian?," and "What is your view of future life?"[90] Some of the officers refused to answer all of these questions, feeling it was "improper to expect an immediate and thoughtful answer."[91] Finally, the officers agreed to answer the questions after being guaranteed that "time would be set aside for discussion of [the] questions" after they had been answered.[92] This did not happen, the meeting being adjourned thirty minutes after the questionnaires had been handed in, and much of that time being spent discussing in a not altogether friendly manner the tactics used by the Commission.

The officers left the meeting feeling deceived and mistreated, and utterly convinced the Commission was out to railroad them and Preacher Jones. The Commission, they felt, was not interested in the progress the Chapel Hill Presbyterian Church had made, but was looking to trip up its pastor and officers by laying surprise theological traps.

---

[88] Complaint, Exhibit No. 21.
[89] Ibid., No.20.
[90] Ibid.
[91] Ibid.
[92] Ibid.

On the other hand, the Commission felt sure that Jones and his officers were responsible for the way the Church had wandered from the Presbyterian path, leaving its faithful flock behind for the sake of an un-Presbyterian pursuit of racial equality.

The second day of the investigation in Chapel Hill was opened up to Church members, notices having been posted on the Church bulletin board inviting people to come and talk to the Commission. In all, forty-seven people spoke to the Commission and interviews were transcribed from thirty.

In interviews some years after the controversy, the secretary of the Commission, Aiken Taylor, remembered that "every interview in the church was given in the spirit of a person who was coming to say: This is a wonderful thing of which I am a part and I feel quite sure that as soon as you understand it clearly, you will find it just as wonderful as I think it is."[93] The people who came before the Commission held the same belief that members of the Session had, the belief that this investigation was a mere misunderstanding, and that once it was all explained, the Chapel Hill Presbyterian Church could carry on its work, continue being a progressive force in race relations and other social causes. The witnesses testified to the Commission that they "thought Charles Jones was the man [of] the hour in [Chapel Hill]."[94]

It was clear from the reaction of the Session to the questionnaire, and from the turn-out of Church members testifying on behalf of Jones, that anyone connected with the Chapel Hill Church saw the investigation as

[93] Taken from Thesis by Rev. Edward Johnston, Aiken Taylor interview done March 18, 1971.
[94] Ibid.

nothing short of a witch-hunt. As feelings ran high from the beginning, people throughout the town of Chapel Hill were forced to immediately choose sides: for or against Jones. And caught in the middle of this rapid polarization was the group who had initially petitioned the Presbytery for a second church in Chapel Hill. Obviously disapproving of what they saw as Jones' straying from the Presbyterian doctrine, they likewise were not necessarily out to see him removed from his job.

The Commission held a brief meeting on September 18 and decided the next step was to interview the officers individually, before discussing with them the results of their questionnaires.[95] The interviews were scheduled for October 8-9 in Chapel Hill, and all but four officers were interviewed. At the start of each one, Chairman Piephoff read an introductory statement which emphasized the nature of the Commission's work and made plain that they were "not interested in rumors," just the facts.[96] They also told the officers that the Commission had been "impressed with the scope and size of the church's program and the way its members felt about its minister."[97] They were also told that the Commission had been told that there were many ways in which the Chapel Hill Church was "not Presbyterian in the strictest sense."[98]

The questions posed by the Commission were based on the questionnaire that had been issued in July, with each member of the Commission privileged to ask further questions. The response of the

---

[95] Ibid.
[96] Minutes of the Presbytery of Orange, CLXXXIV, No.1, p.34.
[97] Ibid.
[98] Ibid.

officers was complete honesty. Fundamentally, they knew that Preacher Jones and the Chapel Hill Presbyterian Church enjoyed great support in the community, and that all the social action they had engaged in was rooted in the Christian concepts espoused by Jesus. What they did not seem to understand, at least at first, was the Commission's emphasis on the Presbyterianism of Jones' ministry.

The Commission interviewed Jones a week after the officers, inviting him down to Greensboro. Again, it was a question and answer session with the Commission trying to pin down Jones' theological beliefs. Jones in turn appeared vague and undecided to the Commission members.

The interview began with Piephoff asking Jones if anyone had been allowed to join the Church without being baptized first. Jones replied that as far as he knew, that had not happened. Piephoff and Dr. Yount then asked questions relating to the election and ordination of officers of Jones' church, and it seemed clear from that moment on that in some ways, Jones had "let slip" some of the more structured Presbyterian practices.[99]

Commission members tried asking specific questions of Jones to get a sense of his beliefs, to see if they conformed to the Presbyterian view. But more often than not, Jones refused to be pinned down—not being intentionally evasive, just unwilling to give a narrow form or definition to his beliefs. Sometimes he would turn the question around. Rev. John Whitley asked him, "Concerning the person of Christ, do you believe

---

[99] Judicial Commission hearing, interview with Charles M. Jones. Presbyterian Church of the Covenant, Greensboro. October 17, 1952.

that he pre-existed before coming to earth?" Jones response was unhelpful: "The thing that bothers me about that is this. In what form do you think he pre-existed?"[100] When pressed further, he replied, "Let me put it this way. I don't want to evade it. I would not say I don't believe that Jesus existed as a person before his birth. I don't know. It would be my interpretation."[101]

The conversation between Whitley and Jones on this point is somewhat reflective of the interview, a Commission member trying to confine Jones' interpretation of the Bible or hold him to a specific view on some other theological point. And each time, Jones unwilling to claim that he could really know the truth of the question at hand. On the same point, Whitley asked: "It follows then that you do not believe that Jesus was God incarnate?"

Jones: "No, that wouldn't follow at all."

Whitley: "Whether it follows your particular reasoning there, or whether it follows the question? You do not believe that Jesus was God incarnate."

Jones: "Yes, I surely do that."

"Incarnate?"

"Yes."

"And he just began being God there and then?"

"Well, let's say that God came in human flesh then."

"For the first time?"

"Yes, for the first time."

---

[100] Ibid.
[101] Ibid.

"Did not exist, pre-exist then."

"In human flesh?"

"No, in spirit."

"Well, I don't know John. It is the kind of thing you can't know. I do know that God was in the flesh here. But whether there was a pre-existent personal form, I don't know."[102]

Other questions dealt with his views on the virgin birth and the bodily resurrection of Christ, the former he acknowledged he did not believe in, and the latter he professed to believing in the resurrection of a "spiritual body… [that] at least had some quality different from the present body."[103]

Rev. Garrison told Jones the Commission recognized his ability to reach people from the pulpit, and questioned him about the "central emphasis" toward which he preached. Jones replied, "…if I would put it briefly, it would be to bring the light and truth of Christ in the New Testament to the full life and need of the student of the community."[104]

That was not enough, though—there was still the issue of Jones' allegiance to the Presbyterian doctrine. Garrison asked him, "Do you do any teaching of these young people, these students, that might be called, well, say, Presbyterianism? You know what I mean by that."

In response, Jones told the Commission about a Dr. Hugh Thompson Carr who had been asked to write for a Presbyterian publication. He had wanted to write about Christian values, but had been told, No, write about Presbyterian values. Dr. Carr was right, said Jones, to make the

---

[102] Ibid.

[103] Ibid.

[104] Ibid.

point that they were the same thing and refuse to write the article on any other grounds. Jones went on, "…it seems to me the basic so-called Presbyterian doctrines of sovereignty and grace and truth are not peculiar to Presbyterians. So if you preached a good balanced diet, if you will, a good balanced Christian sermon, you would preach what Presbyterians hold."

Garrison pushed on: "Do all Christians hold these doctrines or not? Aren't you teaching Presbyterianism?"

"Yes, but you do not claim it as the sole."

"Yes, I know. Why don't you give Presbyterians credit for it?"

"It looks to me as though it is obvious preaching from a Presbyterian Church. It would be misleading to put it the other way. Presbyterians preach it. Don't Methodists? Don't Baptists? When you come to fundamentals? I think Dr. Carr was right. He preferred to write on what Christians believe."[105]

The questioning continued, touching on Jones' work with younger people at the church, his attempts to bring more people into the Church, and his attitude towards those of other denominations, including Jews. But time and again the Commissioners brought the issue back to that of the Presbyterian doctrine. Rev. Aiken Taylor, of Burlington, told Jones, "I am still on the point that the fundamental doctrines of the Christian faith are preached from your pulpit and yet we don't find those fundamental doctrines in the experiences of your people." Jones tried again to explain his point of view. "…With the exception of occasional sermons,

---

[105] Ibid.

like on forgiveness of sins or sinners and grace and faith, I do not do what you call doctrinal sermons. That the sermon more or less springs first of all from the human need, and then the teaching of the Bible is brought into that need so that it isn't a system of doctrine."[106]

Jones was also grilled by the Commissioners on whether someone could have a satisfying religious experience outside of the Christian faith. Jones made the point that he would not be in a position to tell someone their experience was unsatisfying, if they told him it was. He told the Commission that in his view, that person would be able to get more satisfaction if they let Christ into his or her life, but he would still not be in a position to contradict that person's claim to a satisfying religious experience. Both sides used Gandhi as an example, the Commission wondering if Jones thought Gandhi's claim to a "fully adequate experience" over-rode the Holy Scriptures, Aiken Taylor asking, "Is there no objective validity to a religious experience in Christ then, apart from that validity as it happens to me?"[107] Again, Jones tried to make his questioners understand the personal nature of his creed. "I can look at [Gandhi's] whole system and say, it seems to me, that here Christ will even reach you. But if Mr. Gandhi comes back and says to me, 'I don't need that, see? I don't feel the need of it at all. I am perfectly satisfied.' I have still got to show his testimony that he was satisfied. I can come back to Mr. Gandhi and say, 'But in my experience this has been true.' But it seems to me that that's as far as in all humility you can go. He could do the same thing with you and say, 'Well, now, after all

---

[106] Ibid.
[107] Ibid.

you've got to have what I have. You can't possibly have a satisfying religious life."[108]

Jones was asked about the Scriptures, his belief in their fallibility. His reply was, "Not every verse, nor every chapter is equally valid. But all Scripture inspired of God is the infallible rule."[109]

He was also asked whether he thought his beliefs had changed since he had moved to Chapel Hill. The question harked back to the first confrontation between Jones and T. Henry Patterson, when Patterson had urged Jones to leave the church, reminding him that if he had changed his theological views, it was his responsibility to step down. At the time, Jones had told him there had been no real change. Jones faced the question again, this time asked by E. Frank Andrews, who said he had heard that Jones had claimed that the community had influenced his thinking to a degree. "Did I understand from that that since you have been in Chapel Hill Church that your thinking was different from what it was when you were in Brevard.?" Jones responded, "Well, I had hoped I'd grown some. I gave you the wrong impression there if I gave you the impression they had changed me. It's kind of a mutual thing that goes on. I think it happens in any church. Any minister that doesn't have through his congregation something happen to him, there is something wrong with him. He's outside of it and I would rather put it that that congregation has had an effect on me surely. I hope I have had an effect on them also. A kind of mutual growth going on. Fundamentally, I don't think I have changed in fundamentals since I have left Brevard."[110]

---

[108] Ibid.
[109] Ibid.

The question of the virgin birth was raised again, this time by Dr. Yount. Jones told him that while he did not believe in it, neither did he write it off as an impossibility. "I see it as not fundamental. That the authority of Jesus does not rest in the virgin birth and that he could have been born of ordinary parents which, incidentally in Isaiah in the new version, by the way, translates the passage, 'born of a virgin,' as 'born of a young maiden.' Just a translation."[111]

The meeting continued, with Commissioners insisting on direct answers to some of their questions, answers Jones was clearly not able to provide. The Commissioners took turns covering every aspect of Jones' ministry. The wanted to know about what they saw as practical deficiencies in Jones' church, such as record keeping and the proper ordination of elders. They asked about the number of students who came to him on a regular basis, whether there were some of them whose faith was more orthodox than Jones' own beliefs, and how he handled that, how they handled it. The meeting came to an end finally, with Jones being thanked by Aiken Taylor and Rev. G.D. Jackson and assured that testimony on Jones' behalf had "profoundly impressed" the Commission. The transcript of the meeting ends with Jones' words, "I appreciate the spirit in which we have worked."[112]

The conclusion of this meeting marked also the conclusion of the Commission's formal gathering of information. Third parties were still able to submit material to the Commission, however. Each member of the Commission was given copies of all the interviews, the sessional

---

[110] Ibid.
[111] Ibid.
[112] Ibid.

records and the controversial questionnaires from the officers. In preparation for the final report, each member was asked additionally to consider all he had heard orally in the interviews and "to read over and over again that which had been written in our files."[113]

The Commission met on November 20 at the Bessemer Presbyterian Church near Greensboro to write its final report. The end result was a 12-page document that began by detailing its investigational and information gathering efforts. The report stated at the end of this introductory section:

> "The Commission feels it has acted fairly and impartially in the collecting of evidence, admitting only that which is, in its opinion, first hand information. It has not admitted hearsay and it feels that its findings are fully and adequately supported by its own first-hand knowledge and/or true and sufficient evidence."[114]

The report proper begins with a detailed analysis of the Chapel Hill Church, an apparent endorsement of the ministry of Charlie Jones.

> "The Chapel Hill Presbyterian Church is an active, cosmopolitan congregation of people from many walks of life but especially from the University community. This congregation is possessed of a strong social concern, is united, above all other ties, by a common affection and regard for its pastor and is motivated by a controlling principle that can best be described as the ideal of the

---

[113] Minutes of the Presbytery of Orange, CLXXXIV, No.1, p.35.
[114] Ibid., p.37.

brotherhood of man as it was set forth in the teachings of Jesus. The great majority of its members support and actively defend the pastor and the total program of the church, finding here, in their opinion, their spiritual needs fully met and honestly striving to dedicate themselves to an ecumenical ideal that envisages a union of human differences of every kind under the social ministry of the Church."[115]

This initial paragraph seemed to dispel fears of a biased Commission predisposed towards finding nothing but bad in the Church's ministry. The report continues in the same vein. "The outstanding characteristic, according to officers and members, is the spiritual atmosphere generated by and centered in the pulpit ministry of this Church. It is a spiritual atmosphere in which widely separated theological viewpoints feel equally at home."[116] Unquestionably, this was an accurate reflection of Jones and his ministry, and it was also a positive beginning. But soon the Commission's concerns were written into the report.

"This church declares that it is not interested in denominationalism in general, nor Presbyterianism as such, but rather in the practical application of Christianity in terms of an active demonstration of Christian brotherhood."[117] And despite being a church where "hundreds of ... students flock to the regular services and testify that they have had their religious doubts settled here, their religious needs met", the Commission claimed that "outstanding Presbyterian students on the campus have turned from this Church to others in their search for a church home

[115] Ibid., p.38.
[116] Ibid.
[117] Ibid.

while at the University."[118] Section One ends with a brief paragraph that again shows the vast gap between the priorities of the Commission, and that of so many at the Chapel Hill Presbyterian Church. "It is, finally, a church led by officers with a keen and active interest in the practice of religion who are, at the same time, unusually uninformed respecting the soteriological tenets of the historic Presbyterian faith."[119]

The next section deals directly with the Church School and religious education at the Chapel Hill Church. The report stated that the Church School program was "severely restricted" as a result of inadequate facilities, and added: "Again, sharp differences of opinion exist within the Church respecting the effectiveness of the Church School program". Some felt, said the report, that it was very helpful, while others thought it too secular, and that "the classes are essentially play periods and that a strong Biblical basis for the lesson material is missing."[120] Despite the poor facilities, though, the report listed nine different study groups, as provided by the Church's Religious Education Committee to the Commission.

The Commission then moved on to discuss the Youth program, which, "as distinct from the Student Work, is not developed and is inadequate."[121] While acknowledging that "students flock to the services of the Church", which, it added, "in view of the size of the University and the success of other local churches in attracting students, may or may not be especially significant."[122]

---

[118] Ibid.
[119] Ibid., p.39
[120] Ibid.
[121] Ibid.

The Commission stated, "Several interested persons take issue with the declared effectiveness of the Church's impact upon the University life, affirming that, in their opinion, the secular atmosphere prevailing in organizations on the campus such as the YMCA may be due, in some measure, to the Church's influence."[123]

The final point of the section concluded: "In view of the Presbyterian enrollment on the campus, which is in the neighborhood of 900, the Commission feels that the student program in this Church needs to be strengthened.... We believe the problem to be inseparable from the general testimony and position of the Church itself."[124]

The Commission then dealt with the work of the women of the Church, finding a "well-organized, active group of circles... undertaking numerous projects and contributing liberally."[125] Again, though, the Commission noted that there were differences of opinion as to how 'Presbyterian' some of the study courses should be, and differences in the views of members of the women's circles "regarding the conduct of the Communion services in the Church."[126] Given the intellectual climate of the University community and the large number of church members, some theological differences in any church group or subgroup was perhaps inevitable, yet the Commission seemed to take such divergence of opinion as a sign of failure on the part of Preacher Jones and the officers of the Chapel Hill Presbyterian Church. And it was this latter group the Commission addressed next, turning the spotlight on

---

[122] Ibid.
[123] Ibid.
[124] Ibid.
[125] Ibid., p.40
[126] Ibid.

what it saw as a number of problematic areas visible from the sessional records.

"It is distinctly evident that the Church has drifted into a habit of carelessness respecting certain jurisdictional matters." And later: "Respecting annual reports, and the records of the Church, a certain carelessness is again evident", and "the annual reports also display a certain carelessness... discrepancies frequently appear in these reports."[127]

Moving on to the members of the Session, the report noted the "noticeable unanimity," which although commendable also caused problems such as the following:

1. Unbaptized persons received into the membership of the Church on Profession of Faith without baptism. "This, in the opinion of the Commission, constitutes a serious violation of our denominational policy."[128]

2. New members were not received before the congregation, but instead met privately with Jones, with their affiliation to the Church then announced in the Bulletin. "Although this practice does not represent an essentially serious departure from ordinary procedure, it is undesirable in a Church small enough not to have its services unduly interrupted by the reception of large numbers of people."[129]

3. The Session did not ask the questions outlined in the Book of Church Order of persons received into the Church. "This represents a direct violation of essential Presbyterian procedure."[130]

---

[127] Ibid., p.41.
[128] Ibid., p.43.
[129] Ibid.

4. The Session received an ordained Presbyterian minister into the Church, indicating that the "Session is unaware of certain jurisdictional provisions in our Book of Church Order."[131]

5. Several of the Church's elders and deacons had not been ordained nor properly installed, some of these serving for a number of years. "Again, the Commission takes a serious view of this 'omission.' Historically, the position of the Presbyterian Church has been that ordination for elders and deacons is fully as important as for ministers."[132]

As a result of these, the report went on, the officers were "not instructed in the Standards of our Church" and thus were uninformed about the theological position of the Church. Moreover, there existed "a general feeling that it is relatively (for some, absolutely) unimportant that this Church be Presbyterian in the strictest sense."[133] The Commission did acknowledge, however, that these administrative lapses and dearth of Presbyterianism at the Chapel Hill Church dated back to the days of Parson Moss. "Carelessness respecting the administration of the sacraments is not a new thing in this Church."[134] But it was the fact that "there has been little change in this Church respecting its attitude toward Presbyterianism in twenty-five years"[135] that seemed most to antagonize the Commission. But this admission raises the question of why act against the pastor now? If such problems were so old, why had the Presbytery not seen fit to address them before? While it is possible that Jones and his Session were somehow the straws that broke

---

[130] Ibid.
[131] Ibid.
[132] Ibid.
[133] Ibid.
[134] Ibid.
[135] Ibid.

the camel's back, one other possible conclusion could be that the Church's lack of Presbyterianism was merely a cloak the Presbytery chose to hide behind. Whatever the truth of the Commission's motives, its description of Jones' place in the hearts of his parishioners seemed accurate, and its analysis of Jones' ministry was detailed, taking up three of the twelve pages of the report.

"The Pastor of this Church is deeply loved by the vast majority of the active officers and members. There are those who frankly consider him an embodiment of Jesus," the Commission wrote. "He has been a fearless champion of the ideal of the brotherhood of man.... He has not been stayed, in his efforts to present to his people a picture of practical religion at work, by criticism or threats.... Many indicate that, in their opinion, he is the 'finest Christian in the Community.'"[136] His sermons, the report noted, were the "soul of the Church's spiritual life" and had been described to the Commission as "seminars in religious experience," and as "challenges to individual thinking." The report adds, "In the opinion of some, Mr. Jones, as a preacher, is without peer in American Protestantism today. His sermons are earnest, simple discussions of practical problems, largely ethical in content."[137] Inserted into this litany of praise for Jones' preaching, and despite the Commission's recognition that "the pulpit ministry occupies the central place of interest and importance" for those who viewed the Chapel Hill Church as their religious home, there was an admission that: "The Commission has not made an effort to hear Mr. Jones preach."[138] This might not

---

[136] Ibid.
[137] Ibid.

have appeared so serious an investigative omission had the Commission left Jones' sermonizing uncriticized. However, the report said that some people had found "that the Pastor does not preach a gospel in which the concept of 'salvation' is sufficiently central. In short, criticisms of Mr. Jones' pulpit ministry are, generally speaking, theologically oriented."[139]

And herein, apparently, lay the problem with Jones' ministry overall. "It should be said that the Commission found it difficult to ascertain the exact nature of Mr. Jones' theological convictions."[140] While the exact nature of it may have eluded them, the Commission did feel able to characterize this theology as "a philosophy that considers religious feeling more important, and in some sense the controlling principle, when compared with religious truth.

> "It has had the practical effect of making doctrines appear to be the product of human efforts; of making religion something for man to work out for himself; of making God Someone to be sought out and found. In the final analysis, the emphasis falls upon man instead of upon God, and doctrines become what man thinks they ought to be instead of what they are, no matter what man thinks."[141]

The report said that while this may appear a wonderfully inclusive way of practicing a religion, "it puts the cart before the horse."[142] The Commission wrote: "Those who follow it, in effect, believe they can love

---

[138] Ibid.

[139] Ibid., p.47.

[140] Ibid.

God before they really know Him; trust him before they have heard what He intends to do; treat him familiarly before they have found out whether it wouldn't be better to be afraid; seek Him before they know <u>why</u> He may be found; call upon Him without giving a thought to what brings Him near—in short, tell Him what they are prepared to believe about Him, instead of listening to hear what He may say."[143] The Presbyterian doctrines, the Commission stated, were given, not found, and must precede any religious experience. While Presbyterians were allowed to interpret and analyze, the report said, they were not free to alter, censor, ridicule or deny it, nor "cast it aside in favor of other possible varieties of religious interpretation."[144]

The report concluded by stating that "the Commission does not feel that the Pastor, the officers of this Church, or the members (to the extent they reflect their spiritual leaders) have always been true to the Record of God's Revelation as it is interpreted in our denominational standards."[145]

After finishing the report, the Commission passed two motions. The first was that Jones should be asked to resign from the Chapel Hill Church, effective no later than December 1, 1952. A letter to this effect was drafted and then sent by registered mail on November 21. The letter stated that "for the welfare of the church, its own life as well as its relations to Presbytery and Synod", Jones should make a clean break with the church, and as soon as possible.[146] The second motion was that Jones' officers, for "the present and future good of the Church", should

---

[141] Ibid.
[142] Ibid.
[143] Ibid., p.48.
[144] Ibid.
[145] Ibid.

also indicate their intentions to resign.[147] This message was to be conveyed to them verbally when the Commission made its full report on November 30.

The final business of the Commission that day was to discuss the extent of its authority in the matter, specifically whether it had the authority to enforce its findings, or whether it could only report back to Presbytery. The members decided that the authority to implement decisions was implied by the mandate to investigate, and that they would carry out their decisions as far as mutual consent permitted. If challenged, they would refer the matter to the Presbytery.[148] To this end, a timetable was outlined:

1. Advise Jones at once of the Commission's decision by Registered Mail.

2. Meet with the Officers of the Chapel Hill Presbyterian Church November 30.

3. Meet with the members of the congregation on December 7.

The short notice for Jones' resignation and for the meetings with officers and the congregation implied that the Commission fully expected compliance from all those involved. Such was not to be the case. In a letter sent by return mail to Aiken Taylor, as clerk of the Commission, Jones said: "Your letter asking for my resignation from the pastorate of the Chapel Hill Church has been given careful consideration. Since I disagree with the finding of the Commission on which this

---

[146] Ibid., p.36.
[147] Ibid., p.35.
[148] Ibid.

request was based I cannot conscientiously do as requested."[149] He then stated that he hoped the Commission would present its findings, recommendations, and all supporting evidence to the Presbytery for its consideration and decision.

On November 30, the Commission and the Session met in Chapel Hill. The Session members already knew of the Commission's request for Jones' resignation, and as such they were prepared for an unfavorable report. The meeting was formal and polite, the atmosphere cool. The Commission members "came into the room and shook hands with individual officers and then seated themselves on one side of the room and the officers sat on the other side."[150] The Commission's report was then read to the officers, and they in turn were asked to resign, being told that the request was "not open to discussion or debate."[151] Dr. Van Hecke, the Session's spokesman asked whether officers would be given a chance to reform, whether there was any way they could comply with the report and right the wrongs cited in order to avoid the mass resignation. The Commission said that this was not possible.

As the meeting broke up, Aiken Taylor engaged in conversation with the Rev. Robert McMullen, assistant pastor at the Chapel Hill Presbyterian Church, and Dr. John Graham, saying at one point, "Why can't you fellows see that our suggestion is the best way, and comply with it? Don't you want the Synod's money?" Dr. McMullen replied immediately, "This church is not for sale."[152] After the meeting had adjourned, the members of the Session sat stunned. They were also

---

[149] Ibid., p.36.
[150] Complaint, Exhibit No. 2.
[151] Ibid.

upset that Jones might have been punished as a result of their failings. So on December 3, the officers made a counterproposal to the Commission which offered again to correct those errors of the church that had not been placed directly at Jones' feet. A later statement by Church members summed up the sentiment that lay behind the offer: "It is clear from the Commission's report that the major errors were those of the officers. The Pastor was blackened chiefly by association with his officers."[153]

The Session's proposal included the retirement of those officers whose six year terms would have been completed by March, 1953, and a restructuring of the length of terms for elected Elders. These new and existing elders would then be properly ordained and complete a course of study in the standards of the Presbyterian Church, a course that would be satisfactory to a panel of senior Presbyterians agreed upon by the Commission.

This proposal was dealt with by the Commission when it returned to Chapel Hill four days later, on December 7, for a meeting with the entire congregation. The details of the report and the Commission's intention to see Jones and his officers removed from the Chapel Hill Church had generated a great deal of interest, within the Church and beyond. An editorial in the Greensboro Daily News the day before showed how the controversy had begun to nudge its way out of Chapel Hill, out of that town's Presbyterian Church, and into the light of day. It would continue to gather momentum, gaining the attention of inter-

---

[152] Complaint, Exhibit. No. 19.

[153] Lyons, S. et al. Statement regarding Judicial Commission's final report. Undated.

ested parties nationwide (including one national magazine) until its conclusion.

The editorial was entitled Controversy at Chapel Hill, and editors had printed within it statements from the University paper, the Daily Tar Heel, and the Chapel Hill Weekly. The Daily Tar Heel's statement read, in part: "... doesn't the Commission consider the total imprint of the Presbyterian minister and the church's program on the minds of the students, faculty and townspeople, more important than technical impression which may be disputed by theologians? The Commission is throwing away a vital growing religious community. For it to shake the foundation of this church which has meant so much to students particularly is a disservice to the community."[154] This contrasted with the more conservative views of Louis Graves, editor of the Chapel Hill Weekly, who wrote: "It seems clear that the officers of the church... are not really thorough believers in what are commonly accepted as Presbyterian doctrines. They may be men of excellent character, deserving and receiving the esteem of their fellow citizens; they may be splendid Christian gentlemen in the sense of being animated by the true Christian spirit as understood by most people; but, if Presbyterianism means what it is taken everywhere to mean, they are not Presbyterians. The Presbyterian Church here is a Presbyterian Church, not an Ethical Culture Society. It looks as if the officers and other members of it who are not Presbyterians had better leave it and hire them a hall of their own."[155] The Greensboro Daily News took a neutral line, which was

---

[154] Editorial: Controversy at Chapel Hill. Greensboro Daily News. December 6, 1952

itself a shift in position. It was this paper that had referred to the bus riders in 1947 as "this fresh crop of martyrs" and spoke out against "this sort of seemingly unnecessary embroilment… for purposes of personal exploitation."[156] However, this time the paper merely stated neutrally: "The Daily News knows the splendid reputation both of members of the Judicial Commission and of the pastor and officers of the church. It is to be hoped that their controversy can be settled with both sides considering the greater rather than the lesser good of the individuals involved, the community and the church."[157]

One opinion, offered in the form of a letter in the same issue of the Greensboro paper, came from the Reverend R. Murphy Williams, a distinguished, retired Greensboro clergyman. He wrote to the editor:

> "The report submitted by the body of ten fine Christian men appointed by Orange Presbytery to investigate the condition of the Chapel Hill Church, as reported in the Press, was quite a shock to me; and, I believe to thousands of Presbyterians in North Carolina.

> "I have not studied the report, but it seems to me that the action of the Commission was drastic and the suggestion that all the officers resign is enough to humiliate the personnel of the Chapel Hill Church, as it would have been to any other church in the Synod.

---

[155] Ibid.

[156] Editorial: North Carolina Can Take It. Greensboro Daily News. April 16, 1947.

[157] Editorial: Controversy at Chapel Hill. Greensboro Daily News. December 6, 1952.

"For forty years there have been criticisms hurled against the ministers of that church, notwithstanding the fact that many of them have been as sweet-spirited Christians as I have ever known, outstanding in character and ability.

"I have not always shared all their views by any means, but that does not mean they were not sincere and devout Christian men, who preached the everlasting gospel of the blessed God.

"Chapel Hill is a most unique and cosmopolitan community, made up of citizens who have come from the ends of the earth, with a training and background that might cause them to express their Christian convictions in terms that might differ from mine. The ministers and officers in the Chapel Hill Church realized this and have conscientiously endeavored to make the church an open door of the gospel of Jesus Christ.

"They have had a tremendous responsibility, as I well realize from my forty years ministry at the door of one of our largest and greatest institutions of learning.

"I feel sure that no church in North Carolina would appreciate being subjected to the scrutiny given to the Chapel Hill Church by this committee of sincere Christian men....

"Who would dare say but that the Chapel Hill church through its ministry has honored and glorified Jesus Christ as the Savior of men and brought honor and blessing to our beloved church?

"To remove this minister and these honored officers of this church in this unprecedented manner in my humble judgment would be a blot on Orange Presbytery and the Synod of North Carolina."[158]

When the Commission came to Chapel Hill that afternoon to report its findings, more than four hundred people packed the Presbyterian Church, eager to hear what it had to say.

The Commission had prepared a six-page report for the Church members, wherein it said it was inclined to accept the Session's offer, with one minor alteration. This showed for the first time, on the part of the Commission, a somewhat more conciliatory approach towards the Session, an approach that would not be extended to Preacher Jones.

The presentation made to Church members that day was remarkable for its lack of specificity. Here was a document urging the congregation to throw out its much-loved pastor so that the Church might have a new beginning—one that very few members had ever sought. The Commission made it plain that its position on Jones was non-negotiable, while allowing one of two options with regard to the Session. First, Church members could endorse the officers' counter-proposal as accepted by the Commission, or, second, they could ask the entire Session to resign as originally proposed by the Commission. Whichever was decided, urged the Commission, it needed to be done by the end of February, 1953, at the latest.

The presentation to the congregation was designed to explain how the Commission reached its conclusions, and to help members decide which course of action they should take. However, the members were constantly asked not to look for specific wrong-doings, but feel the "shape of things that are."[159] No charges were being pressed against

---

[158] Williams, R. Murphy. Letter to the Editor, Greensboro Daily News. December 8, 1952.

Jones or the Session members, the Commission said, rather it was the general "pattern" of behavior that warranted such extreme action. Rather than "framing charges against specific personalities,"[160] the easiest thing was for Jones and the entire Session to resign. The Commission repeated this non-specific view of its investigation several times, and officers of the Church later claimed that the Commission did so because of a lack of faith in its own evidence.[161] The officers based that claim on the words used by the Commission in referring to its own official report that it had made available to the church's members. "In the reading of this report we urge that you do not attach too much importance to individual items here and there but try to feel the 'shape of things that are' from this report."[162]

Church Elders had their own view of how the report should be viewed, and produced a one-page Guide to Consideration of Commission's Report for church members attending the meeting. The officers said they recognized the value of the Commission's criticisms and undertook to make use of them to improve the Church. The guide reiterated the Elders' willingness to "administer, consistently with the Book of Church Order, the examination, Baptism and presentation of new members; the instruction and ordination of new officers."[163]

However, the officers did want to make clear that they took issue with the Commission's report on the following points:

---

[159] Commission of Orange Presbytery. Report to congregation of Chapel Hill Presbyterian Church. December 7, 1952.

[160] Ibid.

[161] Lyons, S. et al. Statement regarding Judicial Commission's report to congregation. Undated.

[162] Commission of Orange Presbytery. Report to congregation of Chapel Hill Presbyterian Church. December 7, 1952.

1. That we accept the sacraments with mental reservations. On the contrary, we believe the sacraments are means of grace and aids to the Christian life.

2. That the emphasis of this Church is primarily ethical and secular, without religious motivation. Instead, we have always insisted that the starting point for ethics is in our Lord and Savior Jesus Christ, who reveals to us how both God and man are to be loved.

3. That we place Christianity in a position of opposition to Presbyterianism. But they are not mutually exclusive and this Church encompasses both.

4. At various places in the Report, and in particular in the last two pages, the Commission has substituted its own interpretation of Presbyterian doctrine for the Confession of Faith. We are the more conscious of this since our recent course of study of the Confession of Faith, which we plan to continue.[164]

Accompanying the guide was a printed resolution that was, in effect, a statement of confidence in Jones. It called him a "Christ-centered man, a devoted worker in the promotion of the Kingdom of God in Chapel Hill." It was acknowledged that his views might not have been in exact agreement with the members of the Commission, but added: "We feel from long experience with him that there is ample room for these views within the traditional framework of historic Presbyterianism."[165] The document ended:

---

[163] Complaint, Exhibit No. 2.
[164] Ibid.

"We are firmly convinced that the welfare of this church in its work for the Glory of God would best be furthered by continuing its present leadership. We therefore recommend that the following resolution be adopted by the congregation:

"'The congregation of the Chapel Hill Presbyterian Church expresses its confidence in Mr. Jones and requests the Commission to withdraw its recommendation concerning him.'"[166]

Just before the end of the meeting, twelve new members were received into membership, a distinctly unusual occurrence for a church in the midst of such a controversy.[167] The meeting adjourned after deciding to set the following Sunday, December 14, as the time to vote on the Commission's findings and the officers' own recommendations.

At roughly the same time as the congregational meeting was being held at the Presbyterian Church, the Reverend Richard Jackson was delivering a sermon at his United Congregational Christian Church of Chapel Hill. Entitled Authority in Religion, he later mailed a copy to Jones, writing at the top, "Thought you might like to see this. Hope everything works out for you so that you can continue your work in Chapel Hill."[168]

For anyone interested in the Presbyterian controversy brewing in Chapel Hill, this sermon could have been interpreted as a poke in the eye for the Commission, and conceivably the Presbytery, for their

---

[165] Ibid.

[166] Ibid.

[167] Greensboro Daily News. December 8, 1952. p.1.

adherence to doctrine over the less dogmatic, but unquestionably Christian, deeds at the Presbyterian Church. And Jackson's mailing a copy to Jones was a valuable message of support from a fellow minister. Though Jackson made no specific references to the controversy, to Jones, or to the Commission, in the sermon, he proposed that he and his congregation "think together this morning about the kind of authority Jesus exhibited—which made such a lasting impression on the people of his day."[169] He compared Jesus' authority with that of the Scribes.

> "The authority of the Scribes was external in contrast to the authority of Jesus which was intrinsic. The authority of the scribes was attached to their office. As you know, they were the recorders of the official religion. They presumed it was their business to defend the faith. Because of their familiarity with the records, they were able to quote unquestionable, conclusive evidence in matters of faith and morality.

> "Jesus, on the other hand, did not live in such a prison house of quotation marks. While the Scribes drew stale water from old cisterns, the words of Jesus… were like streams of fresh living water—because he appealed to the hearts and consciences of men. The truth of which he spoke was grounded in the Universe itself."[170]

---

[168] Jackson, Richard L. Copy of sermon, and letter to Charles Jones. December, 1952.
[169] Ibid.

He talked about the notion of freedom as it related to theology and the human mind, the importance of it, and the decline in formal, rigid church authority. "However, much as we deplore it, external religious authority still persists in some quarters."[171]

He said there was a place for doctrine, but those espousing it had better be sure they were right. "But whatever the doctrine, we need to remember that religion is always deeper and more basic than our creeds. It created them in the first place and will persist long after the present forms have passed. 'Religion,' says Dr. Harry Emerson Fosdick, 'cannot be essentially described in terms of his temporary clothes—its churches and creeds. Religion, at its fountainhead is an individual, psychological experience.'"[172]

This illustrated the central issue around which the controversy would revolve. The question of race would later surface and further polarize the two sides, but for now the controlling factor in the struggle for Jones' ministry was the theology of the Chapel Hill Presbyterian Church. For Jones and those to whom he ministered, Jesus' teachings were fundamental and primary in the religious experience. For the Commission, and much of Presbytery, that was not good enough. The authority and place of the Presbyterian Church had, they believed, been questioned by Jones' ministry and relegated to second place. Preaching

---

[170] Ibid.
[171] Ibid.
[172] Ibid.

the gospel of Jesus was all very well, they were saying, but to remove the cloak of Presbyterianism and let the gospel stand on its own was simply unacceptable.

Chapter Seven

Grace Tested

"Jesus accepted no tradition unthinkingly. The past had authority only as it won his inner conviction and improved the practice of life. Tradition was neither to be swallowed nor to be rejected; it was an instrument and not an end. It was a heritage of past achievements which had made human advance possible." - CMJ.

Two months after his request to work for the Save the Children Federation in Tennessee had been approved, Jones and his family were on their way to Kingsport, a city a little larger than Chapel Hill, situated in the north-east corner of the state. They arrived in the late summer, settling into a three-bedroom apartment at 1225 Watertree Street.

Jones' mission with Save the Children was to travel out to the rural counties and meet with the superintendents of education, his primary aim being to improve conditions at the tiny, one-room schools in their districts. It was a job he enjoyed immensely. He would leave early in the mornings, climbing into his Jeep and heading out of town and up onto the winding roads of the mountain country, heading for small towns and communities a million miles away from the theological and political war that was being waged in Chapel Hill. Though he made frequent trips back to North Carolina, preaching once a month at the Presbyterian Church, and though the conflict there was always in the back of his mind, it was once again the beauty and peace of the mountains that meant such problems *could* remain a little more distant, a little more in perspective, and a little less consuming. He would ride the mountain roads in his Jeep, his daughter Ginnia by his side, both of them singing made-up opera songs as they wended their way through the hills and valleys. They would always keep one eye on the gas gauge, both knowing that Preacher had a penchant for running his Jeep, or any other vehicle he was driving, as far as he could without refilling, seeing how far an empty tank would take them—sometimes they would coast on fumes into a service station, though just occasionally he would not make it that far. Many times, he would take his other daughter, 18-year-old Bettie Miles, with him, and they would ride out to the schools and county seats that were his temporary parish. They would stop at the small country stores where members of the community could often be found, gossiping and passing on tidbits of local news. Jones would relish the opportunity to talk with the store-keepers, local tradesmen and other customers.

There was also a practical reason for his making himself known in the smaller towns. He had been warned before coming to Kingsport that one of the area's chief informal industries was the production of moonshine, illegal liquor. He had been told that every now and again, the government would send out 'Revenuers' to try and catch the mountain people making and selling their drink. And sometimes these revenuers would go into the mountains but not come out, disappearing for ever in the wilds of the Tennessee mountains that was home to some independent-minded, determined, and potentially dangerous men. One time, in fact, Jones and Bettie Miles were riding in their Jeep and noticed they were being followed. Jones kept driving and the car behind stayed with them, every mile. The only thing to do was to keep going, and eventually Jones and his daughter found themselves alone on the road once again. By stopping in at the local stores, he could explain to people why he was there and what he was doing exactly, hoping that people would get the message he was here to help their children, not take away their liquor.

The schoolrooms that Jones saw were mostly primitive, accessible by dirt roads and devoid of many basic services like heating or running water, though the Tennessee Valley Authority had begun to provide them with cheap electricity. His main areas of interest were in seeing that better health care became available to the children. This meant finding, for example, a dentist who would travel the county with his chair and visit the various schools to provide dental care—for some children, the first they had known. Jones also worked to provide better nutrition, specifically helping the schools install proper stoves so that the children could have hot lunches. As well as working with local school officials, he also had a great deal of contact with the children, something he enjoyed immensely. He would get to know them as best he could in the short time he spent at each school—he met one young lad by the name of Peeflo, an odd name he had not heard before, even with all the time he had spent in the mountains of North Carolina, Virginia and Tennessee. Jones was sitting with the children when the teacher called on Peeflo to sing. Jones turned to one of the boys sitting next to him, asked where the name came from, and was told, "Oh, the first time he came in here, he peed on the flo."

Jones also took the time to help some of the children personally when they needed special care or attention. At one of the schools a young boy had gotten a reputation for not paying attention and for being a troublemaker. It was discovered, though, that he was in fact deaf, and had not followed instructions because he simply had not heard them. Needing to see a specialist, Preacher offered to drive the boy to one in Bristol, a slightly bigger city about fifteen miles away. They set off in Jones' Jeep, driving along in silence as the boy did not do much talking on account of his lack of hearing. After a while, though, they came to the bridge over the Holston River. As they began to cross it, the boy looked out and caught sight of this huge body of water, cried out, "God A'mighty, what a creek!"

After just a few weeks in Kingsport, parishioners at the Presbyterian Church in Sturgoinsville, who were without a minister, learned that Jones was in town and asked him to preach. He was glad to do so, and began preaching there every Sunday, missing services only when he was in Chapel Hill or away doing his work for Save the Children. The church in Sturgoinsville was small, its congregation about forty strong. But as with all his other churches, the members took an instant liking to him, and the congregation grew throughout his time there. They were so enthusiastic that they even asked him to organize a few extra activities at the church, including Bible classes, and again, he was delighted to do so. Another element of Jones' personality that resurfaced here was his pleasure in meeting and talking with men older than he. In the past, he had forged friendships with Mr. Stickney in Gordonsville, Mr. Verner in Brevard, and old Mr. Logan in Etowah. It was as if he liked to draw out and share in their wisdom, hear about their experiences and views on the world, listen to their philosophies on life. His own ministry was centered on relating Jesus and his teachings to the everyday world, and it was as if the insight and intelligence of these men were somehow extra beacons he could use to shed light on the world's comings and goings. This time, in Sturgoinsville the man was Sam Miller, a local farmer who would talk with Jones for many hours about religion, theology and life in general. Such discussions provided Jones with a perspective he did not always have access to in the highly educated environs of Chapel Hill, giving him a way to connect his religious views with a different world, one that he knew and loved, but also one that sometimes eluded him.

However, while in Tennessee Jones was still an integral part of what was happening to his church in Chapel Hill. Throughout his year away, and in addition to his monthly visits home, Jones was in contact with a number of his friends and church officers, and in December of 1952 he received a first-hand account of the Commission's meeting with the congregation from Lee Brooks.

"Yesterday afternoon's meeting was really quite an event. Dr. McMullen announced as we sang the hymn, 'The Church's One Foundation,' any one who had come expecting a cat-and-dog fight might want this opportunity to leave, because there would be no discussion and no voting until the next Sunday.

"It was the first chance I had to see the Rev. Joe Garrison who was delegated to read the six-page report. Rev. 'Achin' Taylor had done the reading of the first report to the officers a week ago. Rev. Joe evidently had something of the tension that sometimes afflicts a professor when he is giving out examination papers and has asked the class to please wait until the first instructions are given. Often a few students will be curious and peek at the last page or two. Well, Brother Joe stood looking over the assembly as the six-page report was being distributed, and then with some asperity said, "I see already some of you looking to see what is on the last pages." Everyone detected a somewhat belligerent air which was hardly dispelled by his attempt at prayer. He read without more than a dozen words of interpolation.

"Well, let us carry it on through to the uttermost limit. If a heresy trial is what they want, let 'em have it. Denominations hate that sort of thing because they are <u>always</u> the losers. As for you, there will always be the glory of God to be preached as you can do it, for many a church and pulpit will be blessed to have you."[173]

The day that Brooks wrote the letter to Jones, the <u>Greensboro Daily News</u> gave its own report of the meeting—and put it on the front page. The paper gave a detailed account of the meeting, stressing the disagreements between the Commission and the officers. It also hinted that the congregation received the Commission's report with utter disbelief, and in turn the Commission was itself shocked by the strength of the reaction to its findings. But, the findings of the Commission had been no great secret, nor had the fact that the congregation of the Chapel Hill Church was supportive of Jones and his officers. So while surprise may not have been the initial reaction, the meeting served to establish clearly who was on which side.

However, reaction to the growing crisis in Chapel Hill did come from Orange Presbytery, who requested a meeting with the Commission to hear its report. Recognizing the storm that was brewing, the Commission members met among themselves, and decided "it would be the better part of wisdom to call a halt to all its activities—accepting a status quo in the investigation—and wait until after this called meeting of Presbytery, before proceeding further."[174] Reflecting the increasing urgency of the situation, the meeting was originally scheduled for December 18, but for procedural reasons was delayed first until January 6, and then, to suit all parties, finally called for January 20, 1953.

---

[173] Brooks, Lee M. Letter to Charles and Dorcas Jones. December 8, 1952.

[174] Minutes, p. 60.

Before that, however, on December 14, the Chapel Hill Presbyterian Church was host to the congregational meeting "to consider the Report of the Judicial Commission of Orange Presbytery and to take such action as may be thought best regarding matters growing out of it."[175] The meeting was moderated by Dr. Robert McMullen, who was serving as the interim minister in Jones' absence.

The first item of business was a resolution supporting Jones. It was offered by Dr. Wallace Caldwell, and ended with these words: "The congregation of the Chapel Hill Church expresses its confidence in Mr. Jones and requests the Commission to withdraw its recommendation concerning him."[176] The congregation then held a secret ballot, and the resolution was approved by a resounding 156 to 14 vote, as strong a vote of confidence as any minister could hope for. Next, Dr. Raymond Gould presented to the congregation the officers' counter-proposal which provided for a limited term system. Afterwards, Dr. Henry Brandis offered two resolutions which carried:

"Resolved, that the congregation has confidence in the present officers of the church and approves their decision not to resign and their proposals to the Commission.

"Resolved, that while it appreciates the spirit of the Commission's offer to serve as its representative, the congregation believes that it should be represented in all matters before the synod by its own pastor and officers."[177]

---

[175] Complaint, Exhibit No. 2.
[176] Ibid.
[177] Ibid.

This resolution reflected a constant concern of those in Chapel Hill—Preacher Jones, the officers, and now the congregation—that they were being handicapped every step of the way by not being allowed to see, and then address, for themselves the evidence being compiled to sink their pastor.

Finally, Dr. M.T. Van Hecke presented for adoption the paper entitled A Guide for the Study of the Commission's Report which highlighted the differences the officers had with the report. The paper was adopted and the meeting adjourned. Battle lines were now more clearly drawn— the congregation had rallied, almost unanimously, behind Jones.

On December 15, the Greensboro Daily News printed another front page story, giving an account of this congregational meeting. In it, the paper quoted interim pastor Dr. McMullen as saying, with humor and sincerity: "There is a general feeling that [the Commission is] not the Assembly of Divines—but then we're not either."[178]

The same day, the Presbyterian Outlook emphasized the importance of the case, asserting: "Not only our entire church but the general public as well is watching with keen interest to see how Orange Presbytery will solve the problem."[179] The editorial cautioned against overly hasty action, stating that "an unwise and hasty solution will do serious harm to the reputation of the Presbyterian Church and to the progress of the Kingdom in Chapel Hill and beyond—for many years to come."[180] The article was written by editor Aubrey Brown, who was himself waging a battle for a change in the Book of Church Order, so that in situations

---

[178] Davis, Burke. Presbytery is Given Challenge. Greensboro Daily News. December 15, 1952.

[179] Brown, Aubrey. Editorial. Presbyterian Outlook. December 15, 1952.

[180] Ibid.

such as these Presbyterian ministers would have the right to face their accusers. Thus far in the controversy, at least in this editorial, Brown would only comment that a "forced resignation of pastor and officers would not be the wisest solution of the problem."[181] However, as the controversy gathered momentum, the Presbyterian Outlook would come to be seen as a champion of the pro-Jones forces, and a thorn in the side of the Commission. But Brown's contention that those condemned by the Commission should have been able to meet and answer all charges in person was a key claim being made by Jones himself.

On the other side of the fence sat the Presbyterian Journal, a conservative and independent paper. On New Year's Eve, it printed an editorial in support of the Commission. "For some years it has been common knowledge that the Presbyterian Church at Chapel Hill has departed from the accepted standards, not only of Presbyterianism, but also of evangelical Christianity."[182] The article outlined the Commission's report and strongly supported its findings. It concluded by saying, "the issue at stake is one which goes to the very heart of our Church and her faith."[183] The opposing views printed by the pro-Jones Outlook and the pro-Commission Journal were the beginnings of an intense media battle between the two organizations. Over the next few months, the Outlook would run twenty editorials and articles about Chapel Hill, while the Journal would run ten. Again, individuals and religious groups purporting to be representing the same organization had faced

---

[181] Ibid.
[182] Dendy, Henry B. Editorial. Presbyterian Journal. December 31, 1952.
[183] Ibid.

off against each other, choosing opposing sides to which they devoted themselves faithfully.

The secular news media also began to take sides, much of the press in North Carolina seeming to side with Jones. One reason for this was simply that many of the writers were graduates of the University in Chapel Hill and had come to know and respect Preacher Jones during their time there. This respect and admiration was carried over and reflected in the way they viewed the controversy as newspaper people. That Jones' impact on the lives of people extended beyond their youth would become extremely apparent. As news of the case began to spread, letters began pouring in to Jones, to members of the Judicial Commission, and to members of Orange Presbytery. One was sent to Howard Newman, clerk of Orange Presbytery, by Philip Riddleberger who lived at the time in Sacramento, California. He wrote:

> "As a youth and a young man I lived in Virginia and obtained my professional education in North Carolina. I came to know Mr. Jones as the minister of the Chapel Hill Church through regular Sunday church services, which I attended by making the trip from Durham. These services, together with services of worship at the church of the Fellowship of All Peoples, with Dr. Howard Thurmond in San Francisco, remain for me the most valued and influential in my life, mainly so, it seems now, because these churches under the guidance of these men fulfilled, more completely than I had known, the spirit of one who spoke, 'For where two or three are gathered together in my name, there am I in the midst of them.'

> "In several relations I came to know and increasingly respect and admire Mr. Jones. It is difficult to fully evaluate the lasting influence of one person upon another mutually seeking satisfactory human values. My own practice of certain human values must be the ultimate test. Yet I can trace certain seeds of

human growth to the influence of these men of Christ-spirit. I am indebted to Mr. Charles Jones in this way."[184]

By the turn of the year, Charlie Jones was a well-known name across the state. People had been following the news stories, interested not just in any theological differences between Jones and the Commission, but also curious as to why the Presbytery might want to get rid of a preacher who was so loved by students, faculty and townspeople, and one whom even the Commission viewed as a Christ-centered man, exceptional social and spiritual leader, and a wonderful teacher, and example, of Jesus' gospel. The ever-present undercurrent of race also bubbled near the surface, with frequent references in news articles to the various incidents in Chapel Hill that Jones had been a part of, including the Battle Park picnic in 1944 and the bus protests in 1946.

Such was the situation faced by members of Orange Presbytery when they met with the Commission on January 20, 1953, to discuss its report and try and make some sort of decision or resolution that would calm or even end the looming crisis. As far as the congregation of the Chapel Hill Presbyterian Church was concerned, the resounding vote in support of Jones dealt decisively with the issue of his removal, and the officers counter-proposal to the Commission seemed to be an adequate 'new beginning' as sought by the Commission. For its part, the Commission had indeed been willing to accept the officers' proposal, but it had not softened its view on Jones removal—a new start was only a new start if Jones was not a part of it.

[184] Riddleberger, Philip. Letter to Howard Newman. December 27, 1952.

The Presbytery meeting was officially called to "hear the report of the Council regarding the formation of a new Presbyterian Church in Chapel Hill."[185] Even at this stage, when the controversy was as public as it was, the Presbytery still kept up the charade that this was all about a new church. The reading of the Commission's report, by secretary Aiken Taylor, took over five hours. In fact, it was the manner of this reading by Taylor that later formed the basis for one of the complaints against the Commission when the case was appealed to the Presbyterian Synod of North Carolina. Henry Brandis and John Graham, two elders who represented the Chapel Hill Church at Presbytery, claimed that Taylor showed marked bias in the way he read the Report, that he "employed a tone of voice and inflections which manifested a definite personal animosity to the Reverend Charles M. Jones; [that he] departed from the text of the Report to make a personal assertion that Mr. Jones was deliberately evasive in his conferences with the Judicial Commission; and [that Taylor] attempted to change the wording of the Report in an attempt to modify some of its theological assertions."[186] It even became necessary at one point in the reading for the Chairman of the Commission to instruct Taylor "to confine himself to the written text of the Report."[187]

When the report was concluded, it was mid-afternoon. In a move clearly designed to consolidate and confirm its authority, the Commission asked for clarification of its instructions. Commission member Rev. Joe Garrison moved that the Commission be "clothed

---

[185] Minutes, p.32.

[186] Complaint, Exhibit No. 2.

[187] Ibid.

with full authority to continue its work and conclude the matter."[188] The motion caused considerable debate and several substitute motions were offered in attempts to rein in the Commission a little—all these failed and the original motion was carried. The result, then, was that the Commission had full authority to act, to correct the situation in Chapel Hill however it saw fit.

The high tension of the controversy had its effect on members, notably Aiken Taylor who, at that same meeting, resigned from the Commission. A second member, George Jackson, was to move out of the Presbytery's jurisdiction, so he too stepped down. They were replaced by two ministers, H.R. McFayden, of the Bethel Church near Oak Ridge, and J.P.H. McNatt, of the Brentwood Church of High Point.

Just five days after the Presbytery meeting, and almost unnoticed, the Judicial Commission realized it's primary, or at least its stated, goal: the establishment of a new Presbyterian Church in Chapel Hill. On Sunday, January 25, at 3 pm, the Judicial Commission held an organizational service in the University's Institute of Pharmacy building. The sermon was preached by Dr. Connolly Gamble of Union Theological Seminary at Richmond, entitled 'The Foundation of the Church'. After the sermon, the Commission organized the church by receiving certificates of membership from twenty-four people, eleven as affiliate members, and two children by baptism.[189]

So after nine months of investigation, meetings and controversy, the original mission of the Commission had been carried out. However,

---

[188] Minutes, p. 61.
[189] Ibid., p.81.

with its authority confirmed by the Presbytery and with the establishment of the new church completed, the reformation of the existing Presbyterian Church now gained the full attention of the Commission. But just as the Commission scrutinized Jones and his ministry, so did its own not-so-hidden agenda come under the keen and watchful eye of the public.

The Durham Morning Herald had covered the Presbytery meeting in depth, calling it an "emotion filled debate", one that gave the Commission "the power to fire" Preacher Jones. The Herald also reported that the Commission had agreed "not to push the resignations of the officers if the pastor was dismissed," but stood firm in its resolution that the Chapel Hill Church could not make a start without a new minister.

Jones' chief spokesman at the meeting had been Frank Graham, the former President of the University of North Carolina and international mediator for the Federal Government. An elder at the Chapel Hill Presbyterian Church, he spoke movingly in defense of Jones, stressing the need for fairness based on Christian principles. "Our problem can be settled in a Christian spirit with values to both the church and to the Presbytery. If the Spirit of Christ is moving in our hearts, and we come here not to destroy someone, or to humiliate someone, then we can settle our problems in a Christian spirit. If this is not true, then I am wasting my time being here."[190]

Unfortunately for Jones and Graham, his words fell on deaf ears, with the Commission more concerned with working to conclude its

---

[190] Durham Morning Herald. January 21, 1953. p.1.

business than enter into it with the Christian spirit. Between the January 20 and subsequent April 23 meetings of Presbytery, the Commission met nine times. One of these was on January 29, when the Commission voted to "request the resignation of Jones as Pastor of the Chapel Hill Church immediately."[191] Eleven days later, Jones came down from the Tennessee mountains to meet with the Commission at the Covenant Church in Greensboro, where he was informed of their decision. The official account of the meeting is brief, with the minutes of Presbytery stating:

> On February 9, 1953, at the Covenant Church in Greensboro, N.C., was a conference with the Rev. Charles M. Jones at which time he was asked for a second time for his voluntary resignation. At the conclusion of the conference he was given until the 14th of February at noon, to give the Commission his answer."[192]

However, Jones gave a full account of that meeting himself as part of the appeal to the North Carolina Synod. He stated:

> "I met at the request of the Commission. The meeting was opened with prayer and the Chairman read a résumé of the official actions of the Commission to that date and the resolution of Orange Presbytery giving them full authority to conclude the investigation and act.

---

[191] Minutes of Presbytery of Orange, CLXXXIV, No. 1, p.84.
[192] Ibid.

"The Chairman also read a paragraph from a letter of mine in answer to their letter of November 21, 1952, requesting my voluntary resignation—'In accordance with my ordination vows I submit to the government of Presbytery and hope that the Commission will present its findings, recommendations and all supporting evidence to the Presbytery for their consideration and decision.'

"The Chairman then informed me that after much deliberation they had called me to request my voluntary resignation immediately. Referring to the sentence just quoted he suggested there was no other course I could take.

"I pointed out that no supporting evidence had been offered the Presbytery for their decisions and asked if they would be willing to tell me on what basis they called for the resignation. The grounds given by the Chairman were—'for the welfare of the Church.' I pointed out that the officers were unanimous in their opinion that the welfare of the Church would not be served by my resignation and the congregation was also well nigh unanimous in that opinion. I asked if they would be willing to state specifically how the welfare of the Church called for such action.

"One member of the Commission stated he believed I deserved an answer to my request and he said he voted for the action not because of the welfare of the Chapel Hill Church alone, but for the welfare of the Church in a larger sense, i.e. the Synod and the Assembly. I asked what evidence they had that there was such widespread and general dissatisfaction. Since we had not been shown any concrete evidence of this I could not resign on that count. No other member of the Commission volunteered any comments in specific ways in which the welfare of the Church would be benefited by my leaving.

"I then requested the Commission for time to consult with the officers of the Church before I answered their request, stating that I did not feel able at the time to answer either yes or no without that consultation. The Chairman then informed me he had neglected to tell me that they considered this meeting confidential. Since this was the first meeting we had held without a stenographer to record what had been said I expressed concern at having a confidential meeting without some accurate record being kept of not only the proceedings but the questions and answers.

"I replied to the Chairman's notice that this meeting was confidential that I was sorry I had not been told for I would not have remained in the meeting where I would be bound to hold in secrecy matters that were of concern to us all in the church. I insisted on my right to report to the officers of the Church on the meeting. It was agreed that since they had not so stated that the meeting was a confidential one that they could not expect me to regard it as such.

"Then there was considerable time spent in discussion. Some members of the Commission expressed their opinion that the Presbyterian government was an insincere and false statement inasmuch as they were now acting as Presbytery and I would not abide by their decision.

"I explained to them that only in a technical sense were they the Presbytery and that actually no evidence had been presented to Presbytery and inasmuch as their first report contained errors and distortions that we had no opportunity to answer I did not feel they had complied with my request.

"I also explained that in reality they (acting as Presbytery) were not making a decision. They were asking me to make the decision for them, i.e. to remove myself. This I would hope I could do if I were convinced it were the honest thing to do and for the welfare of the Church. I felt they had no right to expect me to remove myself for the welfare of the Church when I did not believe that to be the case. If they believed this was necessary, then they must make the decision in accord with their convictions and not insist I act against my convictions. Some members of the Commission were unable to see this distinction and felt I was not acting with integrity.

"Then the Commission offered to let me give them my resignation, which they would hold and give me time to accept other positions that had been offered me. As they put it, 'You can leave with a clean record.' Again I tried to explain why I could not agree to do this but with little success.

"I repeated my request for permission to consult with the officers of the Church and I requested that they consult with the officers of the Church before any action was taken for we believed we ought to sit down together and try to find a way to work out the differences.

"I was sent from the room while they discussed my requests and in about thirty minutes was recalled and informed of three actions they had taken. First, they would give me until Saturday noon to consult with my officers and give them a reply. Second, they planned no consultation with the officers of the Church until after they had settled my relationship. Third, they were informing the officers of the Church that as of that date and time all actions of the officers were subject to review and approval of the Commission.

"During our discussion, I stated that I would give no statement to the newspaper without informing them. I could not promise to keep the meeting confidential."[193]

The following day, February 10, the <u>Durham Morning Herald</u> ran a front page headline, "Commission of Orange Presbytery Asks Jones to Resign Or Be Fired."[194] There was no comment from Jones, and Commission Chairman Z.T. Piephoff told the paper: "We have made it clear that we will make a report at the proper time."[195]

Jones had kept his promise not to talk to the press before giving the Commission his answer, and as he also said he would do, he consulted with his friends at the Church before making any decision. That decision was sent to the Commission in a letter dated February 14.

"Your request for my voluntary resignation from the pastorate of the Chapel Hill Presbyterian Church, on the grounds that it will be for the welfare of the Church, has been carefully considered. I must decline the request.

"The officers of the Church, by a unanimous vote, and the members of the Church, by a vote of one hundred fifty-six to fourteen, have expressed their conviction that the pastoral relationship should be continued for the welfare of the Church. This is based upon the experience of the past twelve years, during which the people, officers and pastor have

---

[193] Complaint to the Synod of North Carolina by the Chapel Hill Presbyterian Church, Exhibit No. 6.
[194] Durham Morning Herald. February 10, 1953.
[195] Ibid.

worked together in a spirit of confidence and affection, for the advancement of a Church program designed to meet the unique needs of this congregation, campus and community.

"You have stated in your report and in conference with us that the Chapel Hill Church does not have the confidence of Presbyterians in the Synod. At no time has the Commission presented to us substantial evidence of any such lack of confidence. On the contrary, I have received from members, officials and ministers of Presbyterian churches in various parts of the State and region, and from many former students and professors in the University in other parts of the country, unsolicited messages of confidence and encouragement for the work of this Church. Some of them were copies of letters sent to you.

"You have informed us that Presbyterians who are financially able to contribute to the work of this strategically located church will not do so if the present pastorate continues. However, our people and I feel that no minister or Church should inhibit the free expression of the Spirit of Christ because of the possible withdrawal or granting of financial support.

"As a Presbyterian minister, I am under the authority of the Presbytery. In refusing to resign I am not defying your authority. I can not with honesty voluntarily sever my connection with this Church and say that it would be for the welfare of the Church or indeed for the welfare of southern Presbyterians at large.

"If, however, in the judgment of the Commission, it is for the welfare of this Church and Presbyterianism that this pastoral relationship be dissolved, and if you take such action, I will obey your order."[196]

The same day as Jones' reply to the Commission, the congregation of his church held a one and a half hour informal meeting at which they discussed ways of "combating the certain firing of their minister."[197] The acting pastor Robert McMullen, who had thus far during the controversy played a very low key role, suggested two possible avenues to follow. The first was for members of the congregation to issue a complaint against the Commission's procedure to the Synod of North Carolina. The second option was to follow the complaint, if sustained at the Synod, to the General Assembly of the church in the hopes of reversing the Commission's decision. While the members of the congregation were rallying around Jones, some of his ministerial colleagues tried a last ditch effort to persuade the Commission to back down. They addressed a letter to the Commission which read as follows:

> "We, the undersigned ministers in Chapel Hill, have been asked many times in the last few months: 'What is happening to the Presbyterian Church in Chapel Hill?'

> "The way in which this question is answered will affect every other congregation in this community and many throughout the State. This means that the influence and welfare of all our churches rest, to some extent, in your hands and depends upon the way this whole matter is resolved. For this reason we earnestly seek for an answer to the above question.

---

[196] Complaint, Exhibit No. 7.
[197] Greensboro Daily News. February 15, 1953.

"No doubt the Commission of Orange Presbytery has its reasons for conducting its investigation in secrecy, but because it has issued no official statement of the charges and testimony, it is impossible for the people to know the nature of Mr. Jones's fault in the eyes of the Commission.

"There have been various interpretations given: theological, racial, economic, political, administrative, etc. All of us would welcome some light in this matter. Since the church exists to proclaim the truth in love, we feel that a demonstration of the 'truth in love' in this particular case would ease the burden of anxiety in the minds and hearts of many sincere Christians, and clear the position of the minister, the local congregation, the Presbytery and the members of the Commission.

"From our contacts with the University students, faculty and townspeople, of all faiths, we discover anxiety, dismay and discouragement among those who had looked to the Chapel Hill Presbyterian Church for its pioneer thinking on social issues and its spiritual leadership in the community. Because the influence of this Church is widespread, this same attitude of distress will reach out wherever it is known. We fear there is a growing suspicion that the Church and its ministers are being penalized for the very things which have distinguished it in the minds of many Christians. A direct statement from your Commission would go far in alleviating this suspicion."[198]

---

[198] Complaint, Exhibit No. 13.

The letter was signed by seven ministers: Richard Jackson, C.T. Boyd, J.C. Herrin, W.M. Howard, David Roston, Maurice Kidder and David Yates. Their earnest plea, though, was to no avail, and the Commission pressed ahead as determined as ever. On February 17, the Commission met and officially dissolved Jones' pastoral relations with the Chapel Hill Church effective March 1, 1953. The decision was based on, or justified by, Paragraph 76 of the Book of Church Order, which allows for such extreme measures if "the interest of religion imperatively demands it."[199] Jones was informed of the decision in a letter dated February 24.[200]

Interestingly, the vote to dismiss was not unanimous. Rev. Joe Garrison was the lone dissenter, writing that instead of taking such drastic action in removing Jones, the Commission should have followed a course "in keeping with the great heritage of the Presbyterian Church and . . .the Christian spirit of tolerance and forgiveness."[201] He favored "the return of the 'sense of responsibility and the fact of accountability to the pastor and officers of the Chapel Hill Church' by requesting them to set forth in specific terms the proposed changes deemed necessary and adequate by them."[202] He was, in effect, ready to go along with the church's counter proposal, to support the compromise approach that would have rectified most of the procedural and doctrinal deficiencies identified by the Commission. But he was the only Commission member to feel thus.

---

[199] Complaint, Exhibit No. 9 and Minutes, p. 85.

[200] Complaint, Exhibit No. 8.

[201] Presbyterian Outlook. March 9, 1953.

[202] Ibid.

On March 1, 1953, the congregation issued its response to the firing of their pastor at an informal meeting attended by about one hundred and fifty people. A six-man steering committee was appointed to draw up a formal complaint against the Presbytery to the Synod. In the meantime, Jones was not to preach or perform any official duties at the church, pending the final outcome of the situation.[203]

The day after this meeting, Preacher Jones stood before the Institute of Religion at the United Church in Raleigh. He presented a paper to the Institute entitled 'Some Problems of Religious Freedom.' Despite his obvious and high-profile experience in this matter, the very first words of his talk were, "I am not here this evening to use this forum as a sounding board for the presentation of the Chapel Hill side of our current controversy. That would be taking advantage of the forum, of you, and of the Commission of the Orange Presbytery with whom we are working."[204] For him even to claim that his Church and the Commission were working together was an example of his generosity of spirit—by the time he spoke those words, all of Jones' requests for a fair and open hearing of all the evidence in the case had been denied, all attempts at compromise had been rejected, and he had been removed from his pastorate.

Although Jones avoided broaching one touchy subject, he did not shy away from the one that had gone unmentioned throughout much of the Chapel Hill controversy. He began by talking about the basic freedoms people have to choose their church and worship with their friends. But,

---

[203] News and Observer. March 2, 1953.

[204] Jones, Charles M. Some Problems of Religious Freedom. Paper presented to the Institute of Religion, United Church, Raleigh, NC. March 2, 1953.

he added: "We must bear in mind that even that freedom of religion is not actually a fact for all of us. Many of you in this audience this evening know that you are not free to go to any church you may choose in the city of Raleigh on next Sunday. Because of your dark skin some would turn you away. Others would segregate you. Others might be too polite to shunt you to the front, rear, of the balcony, but someone would surely mutter, loudly enough for you to hear it, 'They have their own churches; why don't they go to them?'"[205] Jones went on to give his definition of freedom.

"Christian freedom involves not only adventure of the mind and spirit but also calls for an adventure in fellowship. It involves the right to 'love one's neighbor as oneself', to be free to share life's joys, sorrows, pleasures, trials, problems, satisfactions, and afflictions with <u>all</u> of God's children. That is Christian freedom."[206]

He also touched very briefly on a subject that would, in just a few years, become a central tenet of the civil rights movement—civil disobedience. "Civil laws often conflict with the Christian conscience and it is a very difficult thing for a man to make a choice when the State says 'No' and the Christian conscience says 'Yes'. This conflict is most acute as regards military service and enforced segregation. The whole evening could be spent on what the Christian is to do when the State says 'No' and Christ says 'Yes.'"[207]

But despite outward pressures on Christianity, Jones said, "most of our problems of religious freedom arise in the Church itself. The

---

[205] Ibid.
[206] Ibid.
[207] Ibid.

Church has often been the denier of freedom. This is tragic because actually the function of the Church is to help people do better with other people what they could not do so well alone."[208]

Despite making no direct reference to the Chapel Hill controversy, Jones was framing his argument according to the way he saw the situation unfolding at his Church. "There are two camps in Christendom and the dividing line is drawn by the varying emphasis put on two aspects of Christianity. The first [is] the 'institutional' emphasis; the second [is] the 'vital-spiritual-prophetic' emphasis." Jones wryly acknowledged a difficulty with his representation of the institutional model, not being the one he would ascribe to. "If I do not fairly present the institutional approach I hope some of you will correct me. The difference between these views is not chiefly in the message preached. Nor is it that one produces good people and one bad. All the saints are not in one camp, and all the devils are not in the other." Both sides, he said, agree that Jesus was their guide as to what God wanted of them. "The conflict is with respect to what the institutionalists think is essential, most important and divine."[209] And these are, he said, the heads of the religions, the creeds and the infallibility of the Church structure. "With such a major emphasis the Church becomes authoritarian and legalistic. It may become tyrannical, depending on the quality and character of its ecclesiastical leadership."[210]

Preacher talked about authoritarianism in its most basic form, as he had come across it in recent months in Tennessee while on his way to

---

[208] Ibid.
[209] Ibid.
[210] Ibid.

preach. "Turning on my radio as I drive to church I frequently hear something like this: 'Friends, I believe this old Book. It is the word of God. I believe every word of it and I believe it means what it says. The pulpits are full of non-Bible-believing preachers…' and so they rant. Crude, ignorant, yes; but most often, sincere.

"This literalistic, authoritarian approach to the scriptures is not limited to the so-called ignorant. There is a sophisticated form of it…. Many a person is not free to handle the Bible with intelligence and integrity because he has run afoul of a sophisticated theory of literalism and infallibility of inspiration that is deep in Protestantism. It is just as authoritarian in its sophisticated form as it is in its crude form."[211] Jones talked about the emphasis on creeds which become "a final summary of truth" and the rites and rituals, like baptism, "that may often become the most essential and the most emphasized part of the church."[212]

He talked about the "emphasis on buildings, money, and numbers," the precision of facts and figures required of preachers when they make their reports: "…the numbers added to the church, the numbers lost, the numbers dead, the numbers retired, the amount of money contributed to benevolences, the amount of money contributed to building expenses, new buildings put up, amount paid to the preacher, and current expense. All of our reports are numbers, statistics.

"I know that it is much harder to measure spiritual and ethical progress than it is to measure monetary and numerical progress….

---

[211] Ibid.
[212] Ibid.

Would not the following questions be embarrassing for any of our churches to answer? Are there any slums in your city? Are the city ordinances on sanitation enforced there?...Were civil liberties violated in your town this year? What progress have you made in bringing the judgment of God on discrimination in your town?"[213]

Then Jones turned to the approach he called 'spiritual-prophetic' and in doing so explained his own type of ministry.

"It is an approach to Christianity which is fundamentally ethical. It believes that our relationship with God, on God's part, depends on His grace and forgiveness but, on our part, demands right relationships with our fellow man. This conception of Christianity believes in the Church as a following of men in faith, worship, and service. It believes in saving people, both individuals and society. The word 'secular' is not in its vocabulary because there is nothing secular. It demands all of man's mind, heart, soul and strength."[214]

But Jones said tradition did have its place in the Church—Jesus himself, despite sometimes shunning ancient Judaic tradition, relied on it in times of crisis. "When he goes into the temple and finds graft and corruption, He becomes angry and cries, 'My house shall be a house of prayer; you have made it a den of thieves.' That is a combination of two quotations from the Scriptures: one from Isaiah, the other from Jeremiah. Now I have no idea that Jesus thought, 'Now here is a good chance to quote Scripture'—not that! But that which was deep within Him welled up in time of crisis and need."[215]

---

[213] Ibid.
[214] Ibid.
[215] Ibid.

Jones said he believed that the two sides of institutionalism and spiritualism were not only compatible, but necessary. "Because our institutionalist friends may insist that all of the past is essential and divine, we must never let it turn us away from what should be carried from the past into the present. The past is to be honored and used, but not worshipped."[216]

He ended: "Actually these 'institutionalists' need the 'vital-spiritual-ones', and the 'vital-spiritual-ones' need the 'institutionalists'. They need each other not merely to develop toleration, but for the completion one of the other. Humility and love will bring more than toleration into this conflict—it will bring a creative spirit of God to work."[217]

By the time Jones dealt with this issue in Raleigh, the perceived struggle between the ethicists and the dogmatists had spread across the state, and was even reaching national proportions. A story released by the Associated Press appeared in the Charlotte Observer on February 21. "The Orange Presbytery's judicial commission was charged today with using extreme prejudice in its probe of the Chapel Hill Presbyterian Church officers and pastor," the news article began. And on the day before the Commission wrote to Jones informing him of the termination of his pastorate, the Chapel Hill case made the pages of Time magazine. In an article adorned with a picture of a smiling Jones, Time gave a background account of the case, referred to his work with blacks, and reported that the Judicial Commission and Jones were in a deadlock. In discussing the Commission's report, the magazine also quoted

[216] Ibid.
[217] Ibid.

Professor of Journalism Phillips Russell, the man who had brought Jones to Chapel Hill in the first place. Russell had told the writer, "The report gives the impression (and this is said with due reverence) that if Jesus Christ were found occupying the pulpit here, He might be ousted on the ground that, although a Christian, He could not be called a Presbyterian."[218]

That feeling was apparently widely held. The Time article unleashed an avalanche of letters, written to Jones and to the Presbytery. The vast majority of these expressed their support for Preacher, and their dismay at the intransigence of the Presbytery. And the letters came from far and wide.

Architect William Gray Parcell, from Pasadena, California, wrote: "Don't change your line. I just wrote Time as follows: 'Escaping the tough brambles of Jonathan Edwards and the lush swamps of Billy Graham, the Rev. Charles Jones of Chapel Hill hurdles St. Paul and lands in the lap of Jesus, where a lot of us would do better."[219]

Jones also received a letter from the minister of a church in Westport, a sawmill town of 600 people in Oregon. Reverend Kerr told Jones, "I am writing to you to say a loud 'Bravo' to you... as you are probably aware, there is a growing and vital body of liberal, and wholly sincere, real Christian forces in this country that, like yourself, cannot be stopped."[220]

From Evanston, Illinois, a postcard with a message of support sent by a Methodist minister. "Dear Brother Jones: I want to add my voice to

---

[218] Pastor v. Presbytery. Time Magazine. February 23, 1953.

[219] Purcell, William Gray. Letter to Charles Jones. March 4, 1953.

[220] Kerr, Rev. Keith. Letter to Charles Jones. March 2, 1953.

the multitudes who are deploring what is happening to you and your fine works in Chapel Hill. I can scarcely credit my eyes as I read the reported recommendations of the Commission. Your work was and continues to be a real beacon for College work. It will be a tragedy if anything interferes with its effective continuation. Let me know if I can be of any assistance—any way."[221]

James Taylor, a Professor in the Psychology Department at North Carolina College at Durham, wrote expressing his dismay that fellow-Christians could have taken such action against Jones. "I do not have to point out to you, that History and the future are on your side. You are not the first, nor will you be the last person to be persecuted, abused, and condemned for daring to do the right as you have understood it. It has been such souls, however, that have changed the course of History, and have become revered and esteemed by millions long after the names of their detractors have been lost in oblivion. Knowing this I am sure that you will continue to be guided by the precepts of Him who you have tried to follow."[222]

Very few of the letters of support directly referred to race as being one of the central issues, concentrating more on the injustice of un-Christian-like judgment on the part of the Commission, or berating the Presbytery for insisting on an adherence to Presbyterian doctrines at the expense of social justice. But as well as letters of support, Jones did receive some from people obviously angry at his work with blacks. One such letter came at the end of February, one page long and typed in a

---

[221] Bosley, Dr. Harold. Letter to Charles Jones. March 6, 1953.
[222] Taylor, James T. Letter to Charles Jones. February 26, 1953.

random mix of capital and lower case letters. The lines were pressed close together, making the reading of the letter extremely difficult. It came from Denmark, South Carolina, and was sent by a sixty-eight year old man, P.D. Buie, who said he had been born in Red Springs, Robeson County, North Carolina. He told Jones, "…if you are of the South the Ku Klux Klan must be a sleep. Mr. Rev. are you ashamed of your home town or is it the reverse ashamed of you. Your kind is why we of the South have to keep our powder dry and Klan at full people strength. Why don't you take the African trash your people left down here back to Africa…. Where all the Southern red-blooded men have gone I don't know, my pals, from down here a white man's country, and when we got through of your seat you resign and leave Chapel Hill faster than you come there…. I won't get an answer to this because your people don't like the truth, neither have the brain to answer." He signed the letter as "My good deed for the day."[223]

This long and incoherent letter contrasted with the pithy note sent by the Rev. John Stevenson, of the Midwest Community Church in Wyoming. "Dear Sir: the Alger Hiss type of ethics seems to have invaded your pulpit. Remember your solemn ordination vows."[224]

In fact, Jones did reply to as many of these letters as he could, thanking people for their support or, to those speaking against him, restating his hopes for a conclusion to the affair that might prove satisfactory to everyone. A fairly typical response was sent to Tom Sanders of the Forum Committee of the Student Cabinet at the Union Theological

---

[223] Buie, P.D. Letter to Charles Jones. February, 1953.

[224] Stevenson, John R. Letter to Charles Jones. February 21, 1953.

Seminary in New York. He thanked Sanders for his encouragement, telling him that the Church had appealed the Commission's decision. He added: "We are trying to find common ground on which our Church, myself and the Presbyterian authorities can work together with confidence, affection and creativity. It has been difficult, for the Investigation Commission has majored mostly in trying to find fault (of which we cannot claim to be free) and has not tried to understand the problems of our Church, its work, or its spirit. We shall continue to use reason coupled with the Christian spirit until we have exhausted all means of an understanding."[225]

The firing of Jones prompted more than just letters though, from his many supporters within the Chapel Hill Church. There was even talk of members abandoning the Presbyterian Church and forming yet another one, with Jones as its pastor. With the specter of this possibility looming, McMullen wrote to Jones in Tennessee to express his concern. He said that although he understood Jones would not intentionally provoke "a mass exodus," he might "be willing to serve as pastor of a group making such an exodus if they were led by someone else."[226] As ever, McMullen was in a difficult position, constantly trying to observe the often conflicting loyalties that were his duty to the Presbytery, his responsibilities to the Chapel Hill Presbyterian Church, and his personal friendship with Jones.

The resentment felt by many members of the Chapel Hill Church was mirrored by that felt by members of Orange Presbytery, and in particular

---

[225] Jones, Charles M. Letter to Tom Sanders. March, 1953.
[226] McMullen, Rev. Robert. Letter to Charles Jones. March 12, 1953.

by members of the Judicial Commission, as a result of the drubbing they were receiving in the media. The local press had for some time sided with Jones, and the Time article had not helped the Presbytery's image any. Now, even the religious press seemed also to be lining up alongside Jones.

On March 4, The Christian Century published an article entitled, 'Deplore Secrecy in the Jones Case.' The article read as follows:

> "Secrecy in church affairs, as well as in the conduct of the public business, is certain to arouse suspicion and to invite trouble. That should be pretty well understood by this time, but it seems to be a lesson which has to be learned again and again. The latest instance to appear in the news concerns a Presbyterian commission in North Carolina. It has told Charles M. Jones, for twelve years the beloved minister of the Chapel Hill Presbyterian Church, that he must resign or be fired. Seven Protestant clergymen of this university community have asked the commission to state the charges and the evidence on the basis of which it has laid down its ultimatum. They declare that the secrecy with which the commission has carried on its assignment to investigate this minister and his church, which is standing loyally behind him, has created a 'growing suspicion' in the community. The ministers do not say so, but the suspicion concerns the investigators more than the investigated. Charles M. Jones is widely known as 'the finest Christian in the community.' One direction taken by his Christian conviction has made him defend the rights of minorities in his community, and to welcome Negroes to the services of his church. But this is not named as a reason for the demand that he resign or be fired. Another report is that the minister has 'deviated from strict Presbyterian doctrine,' although in what respects is not specified. But all of this is only whispered, and Dr. Jones' colleagues are entirely right in

demanding that it be brought out into the open. Injustice flourishes and the whole church is brought into disrepute by ecclesiastical secrecy."[227]

That same week, the Chapel Hill controversy took up all of the first two pages of The Presbyterian Outlook, and several more pages further within the issue. (Coincidentally, following the two main pieces dealing with the controversy, there appeared a large article by Dr. Charles Logan, entitled 'How to Start a New Church'). One of the articles dealing with the Chapel Hill case was an editorial, which again addressed the cloak of secrecy that the Presbytery had used to smother any kind of appeal by Jones. "We find it difficult to believe that any minister or elder on the commission would feel that he had been treated justly if the positions were reversed and if such action were taken without the substantiation of definite charges and the privilege of hearing and confirming or refuting them."[228]

The editorial quoted, and agreed with, the Greensboro Daily News: "'The longer the commission refuses to make these grievances perfectly clear, the more the impression grows that: (1) they are not sound enough to stand public scrutiny; or (2) the real motivations behind the ouster action involve practices which the Presbyterian Church itself does not sanction.'" The editorial stated that the congregation of the church faced an almighty task to preserve its "dynamic church" in light of the controversy, and ended by saying, "They deserve our prayers. They will need them."[229]

---

[227] Deplore Secrecy in the Jones Case. The Christian Century. March 4, 1953.
[228] Editorial. The Presbyterian Outlook. March 9, 1953.
[229] Ibid.

The longest article in the issue was entitled 'Chapel Hill Procedure Called 'Travesty of Justice''. The article was mainly a printing of the 1,200-word statement released by members and elders of the church in support of Jones. The statement included the somewhat mocking reference to the "deluge" of letters T. Henry Patterson, the executive secretary of Presbytery of Orange, claimed to have received, and when pressed was able to come up with two. Patterson read the <u>Outlook</u> article and was outraged. He wrote the magazine's editor, Aubrey Brown, to express the fact that he "was hurt beyond measure" by the repetition of the story which, he claimed, was "completely untrue."[230] Patterson's letter reflects the frustration with the media he and his colleagues felt at the time. "I have usually found [<u>The Presbyterian Outlook</u>] a fair paper presenting both sides of any important matter, but I have certainly been completely overwhelmed by the 'one-sided' presentation of this case…. We have expected criticism and exaggeration in the public press but we certainly have not expected a Church paper, representing our great Denomination, to join forces in such untrue, unfair and unjust criticisms of the work of a duly appointed Commission of five Ministers and five Elders, who have been sincerely seeking to perform the difficult task, placed upon them, in a truly Christian and Presbyterian manner with the best interests of the Church and the Kingdom of God at heart."[231]

Patterson's letter was also one of the few times the question of Jones' work with minorities in Chapel Hill was addressed by anyone at the

---

[230] Patterson, T. Henry. Letter to Aubrey Brown. March 13, 1953.
[231] Ibid.

Presbytery. Patterson said he knew Brown thought "that the race issue was central in this entire matter." But, he added, "You will note the Race question is not even mentioned in the Report except as Charlie Jones is lauded and praised for his courageous Christian stands for great social reforms. The race issue is not the case and Presbytery has steadfastly refused to permit [it] to be even mentioned on the floor or brought into the case in any way."[232]

Harold Dudley, executive secretary of the Synod of North Carolina, was also concerned about the unfavorable press coverage, and on March 9 he wrote a letter to Frank Price, who was elected Moderator of the General Assembly the following June. He said:

> "The distorted newspaper accounts of the Chapel Hill Church affair are provoking so much adverse criticism of our whole church, that it seems to me an answer ought to be made by somebody in defense of the Presbyterian system. I have just come from Chapel Hill, where I went to ascertain what I had suspected, namely, that the releases all originated from one source, a special correspondent of the newspapers who is a deacon in the church and one of those who was 'called on the mat' regarding his standing as an officer in the church. The newspapers, including the editors, have swallowed 'hook, line and sinker,' everything that this man has released."[233]

---

[232] Ibid.

[233] Dudley, Harold. Letter to Frank Price. March 9, 1953.

Dudley also wrote the editor of the <u>Raleigh News and Observer</u>, Jonathan Daniels, expressing his concern over that paper's biased coverage. He also sent Daniels a copy of the Presbyterian <u>Book of Church Order</u>, which was the legal authority upon which the actions of the Commission had been based. Daniels responded a few days later, but not in the way Dudley had hoped. "I agree with you that there has been much unfortunate publicity with regard to the Jones case, and I am at a loss to understand why the Presbytery did not early and clearly make known specific charges against Dr. Jones."[234]

It seems that this was the central point under the brightening media spotlight. By pressing upon Daniels the rules and regulations of the Presbyterian Church he was hoping the editor would understand better the reasons for the Commission's decisions. But what Dudley, and many other members of the Presbytery failed to understand was that to the press and public, who were not cognizant of every small nuance of the case, the central issue was fairness. It looked more and more like Jones had been railroaded, and the more the Presbytery tried to defend itself behind its shield of rules and doctrines, the more people thought it had something to hide. People knew that no court in the land would try and convict a man, and one so patently Christian, without so much as a glimpse at the evidence, or a chance to cross-examine his accusers. So those same people failed to understand how Orange Presbytery could do just that, and expect to get away with it.

---

[234] Daniels, Jonathan. Letter to Harold Dudley. March 16, 1953.

And so the battle in the media continued, with the <u>Presbyterian</u> <u>Journal</u> as the lone gun defending the Judicial Commission and the Presbytery. On March 18 it published an article on page three, in support of the Commission and its findings:

> "The Judicial Commission of Orange Presbytery has our sympathy because they assigned to them a difficult and unpleasant task. It has been a matter of common knowledge for many years that the pastor of the Chapel Hill Presbyterian Church had digressed far from evangelical teaching and preaching. In a university town, known for its groups of extreme liberals, both among the faculty and also in the student body, such preaching was popular and the pastor had become both a symbol and a leader. The Judicial Commission of Orange Presbytery had assigned to it the unhappy and trying task of studying the situation and rendering a verdict.

> "Nowhere more than on our college and university campuses do we need ministers with a vital Christian faith and message and an ability, by the power of the Holy Spirit, to impart that faith to the young men and women who come under the influence of their ministry. Personality is desirable; scholarship will help; but, above and beyond all else there is the absolute necessity that the Gospel of the Lord Jesus Christ shall be preached and His Name—not the preacher's—exalted.

> "We as a church have passed through a sobering experience in this particular case. We owe it to all who are involved to pray for them. We also owe it to the students who in the future

come under the influence of our own particular denomination to see that such a development shall not occur again."[235]
Five days later, the <u>Presbyterian Outlook</u> offered an opposing view.

"According to published accounts, part of the indictment brought against the Chapel Hill (N.C.) church by its presbytery is a 'controlling philosophy of religion' which is said to include, as its first principle, 'that being Christian is more important than being a Presbyterian.'

"To some, it may seem inconceivable that such a charge would be made against a congregation by any Presbytery. Perhaps the published report did not quote the document correctly. Other more cynical readers may doubt that such a congregation exists. But so far as it goes, this is a true indictment.

"The present writer has visited in that church from time to time, and has always come away with a heart of thankfulness for having seen Christianity in action. What a church is, is not merely to be heard; it is to be seen and felt. And this, not on one day alone of seven, one hour out of 168, but through every day and week. This church did not make the impression it is not Presbyterian; but it did convey the conviction that for both minister and officers and people, being Christian is more important than being Presbyterian.

---

[235] Presbyterian Journal. March 18, 1953.

"But if this be a true indictment, it is an honorable one. If the Chapel Hill Church has anything to repent of, let it at least not repent of this, that in their fellowship being Christian takes first place. Furthermore, it does not stand alone. There are other congregations known to the writer, and no doubt others unknown to him, in the Southern Presbyterian church, where Christianity takes first place. If this be heresy, it is a spreading one."[236]

The differences between the two articles highlighted the differences between the opposing sides of the debate—neither saw it, or would address it, as the other did. For supporters of the Commission like the Journal, Jones had elevated himself and his own agenda while diminishing the importance of Presbyterianism, and consequently, the Presbytery. Jones' own supporters viewed the action of the Commission as nothing more than an unjustified maneuver to reign him in, put the brakes on his social development work (particularly his work with blacks) and reassert the Presbytery as the central authority of the church. Most importantly, though, Jones, his officers, and all those behind them, wanted their day in court. They never openly questioned the sincere and honest intentions of those trying to oust Jones, and this made the secrecy all the more frustrating. The Presbyterian Outlook published two more letters, long ones, from those affiliated with the church who wrote demanding that the whole affair be brought into the open. The Reverend Watt Cooper had been a student pastor at the

---

[236] Foreman, Kenneth J. Christian First. Presbyterian Outlook. March 23, 1953.

Chapel Hill Church from 1933-36. He said, "This affair has gone too far now to be passed over by the majority of Presbyterians in North Carolina. Too many questions have been raised and too many of them have gone unanswered. If there is something wrong at Chapel Hill let's get it out into the open. That's the Presbyterian way."[237]

Two weeks later, the magazine published a letter by former member of the Chapel Hill Church Coy Phillips, entitled 'Elder Discusses Effect on Professors.' Phillips, who had later become an Elder in Greensboro, said that the effect of the firing of Jones would be counter-productive and lead to timidity in the pulpit. Moreover, he said, the best religious-minded educators and university professors will turn away from church. "Will the courageous not seek to serve in other fields and never enter the ministry in the first place?.... There is spiritual hunger in the land. The church needs great ministers in the pulpit, and when we have them the people will be there."[238]

On March 22, the Judicial Commission met at Chapel Hill with the officers and ordered both the Session and the Board of Deacons dissolved effective April 1, 1953. This action was taken "for the welfare of the Church."[239] Needless to say, this was bitterly received by the members, who met on March 30 to "vigorously protest"[240] the decision. The Session conceded that a number of officers had not been ordained, but maintained that they had nonetheless carried out their responsibilities with the complete confidence of the pastor and the congregation. "Moreover, they have sought since last Fall an opportunity for them or

---

[237] Cooper, Rev. Watt M. Letter to Presbyterian Outlook. April 6, 1953.

[238] Phillips, Coy T. Letter to Presbyterian Outlook. April 20, 1953.

[239] Minutes, p. 85.

[240] Complaint, Exhibit No. 24.

their successors to receive instruction, examination, ordination, and installation, so that they might become fully qualified to serve as elders and deacons, only to be denied that opportunity by action of the Commission."[241] The protest ended with a stinging rebuke, charging that the Commission "disregards the needs of the congregation and the efforts of the officers and acting pastor to work out a constructive solution of the Church's problems. As on the occasion of the removal of our Pastor, the Commission's action in removing our officers is destructive, dictatorial, and vindictive."[242]

Orange Presbytery scheduled a meeting for April 23 to acknowledge the Chapel Hill Church's official complaint, and to elect respondents to defend the Presbytery's position before the Synod.[243] The Judicial Commission also met, twice in fact, to discuss the complaint. At the first of these, on April 9, the Commission passed a resolution that enhanced the aura of secrecy that surrounded their investigation and decision-making: the resolution stated that if the case were appealed to the Synod, the Commission would be "on record as opposing the omission of the reading of any part of the Commission's record."[244] This meant, essentially, that while the representatives were denied access to the Commission's evidence, the Synod would be obliged to read everything the Commission had compiled. At the second meeting ten days later, the Commission approved a paper entitled, 'Guide to An Understanding of the Acts of the Judicial Commission; Re: The Chapel Hill Presbyterian Church.' The paper was the Commission's defense of

---

[241] Ibid.
[242] Ibid.
[243] Minutes, p. 86.
[244] Minutes, p. 85.

itself. It deplored the role of publicity, stating that "trial by public opinion to which all concerned have been subjected not only has rendered a disservice to all, but has resulted in unnecessary confusion with the Presbytery in general."[245] Jones was accused of breaching the Commission's confidence, and the attitude of the officers was also criticized. The 'Guide' concluded by listing the following nine problem areas as identified by the Commission:

1. The failure to ordain and properly install officers who, subsequent to their sometimes irregular election, performed the official and sacred functions of elders and deacons and served on important Presbytery and Synod committees.

2. The failure to conform strictly to the <u>Book of Church Order</u> in the conduct of services of ordination when these were held.

3. The failure to require the profession of faith specified by the <u>Book of Church Order</u> of non-professing Christians received into the Church.

4. The failure to baptize unbaptized adults received on 'profession of faith'.

5. The failure to encourage parents to bring their children for infant baptism.

6. The appalling ignorance of the saving tenets and doctrine of the Presbyterian Church on the part of both officers and members.

---

[245] Ibid.

7. The toleration of religious convictions among the officers—both elders and deacons—which are wholly incompatible with the basic doctrinal position of the Presbyterian Church; and the presence of active officers who affirmed that they could not subscribe to the Standards of the Presbyterian Church, nor to the Apostles' Creed.

8. The failure to meet the spiritual needs of the students at the university in a manner agreeable to the best interests of the Presbyterian Church.

9. The notable lack of harmony among Presbyterians in Chapel Hill which has existed to the dishonor of religion over a period of many years.[246]

Interestingly, despite the Commission's apparent disgust at the 'trial by media', this document managed to find itself onto the pages of the May 6 issue of the <u>Presbyterian Journal</u>. But harder to understand were some of the conclusions reached by the Commission. To claim a "notable lack of harmony among Presbyterians" flew in the face of the massive vote of confidence Jones and his officers had received from those Presbyterians. And the remarkable work Jones had done to attract and engage the students at the University seemed also to contradict the words of the Commission—though in addressing this point the Commission had said Jones had failed to reach them "in a manner agreeable to the best interests of the Presbyterian Church," which seems in itself a telling indictment of the priorities of the Commission,

---

[246] Ibid.

and, assuming the Commission spoke for those who had formed it, an indication that Orange Presbytery was also more interested in its own salvation as an institution than in the salvation of the students.

Chapter Eight

Heresy or Travesty?

"Religion is more than a matter of beliefs and practices. Religion has at its heart the intention to make the world a better place." - CMJ.

The secrecy surrounding the Judicial Commission's work was one of the chief frustrations for Jones and the Chapel Hill Presbyterian Church. In March of 1953, after notifying the Commission of the Church's intent to complain to the Synod, Henry Brandis, Dean of the University of North Carolina's law school and a communing member of Jones' church, wrote to Z.T. Piephoff requesting that the evidence collected by the Commission be made available to those resisting its attempt to oust Jones and the officers.[247] Specifically, Brandis demanded to know "where, and during what hours, the full transcript of the Commission's proceedings, including all evidence received, will

---

[247] Complaint, Exhibit No. 26.

be available for perusal and study by one or more of the complainants."[248] He requested permission to make copies of any evidence made available, and also requested "a statement from you as Chairman of the Committee indicating what, if any, oral testimony, letters, documents, or evidence of any kind, was considered by the Commission which has not been made a part of such transcript."[249] The response came a week later, and was suitably vague: "Let me hasten to assure you that as soon as it is possible for the Commission to meet and consider these requests it will do so and inform you of its decision."[250]

The meeting of Orange Presbytery on April 23 to acknowledge the official complaint from the Chapel Hill Presbyterian Church was documented in a letter from Harold Dudley, the Synod Executive, to Albert McClure, the Synod Moderator, and written two days after the meeting. He described it as a heated encounter, centering on the demand for full access for those at the Chapel Hill Church to all the evidence. The Presbytery decided to deal with the problem by dividing the evidence into two categories, public and confidential, sending both packets to the Synod for its hearing. Dudley also stated that, according to the Presbytery's Stated Clerk, Howard Newman, the Chapel Hill Church was not to have access to the confidential evidence, which was to be made available only to the Synod's Judicial Commission, if such a body was created.[251]

This struggle over secret evidence between the Commission and the Chapel Hill Church was further revealed in the correspondence

---

[248] Ibid.

[249] Ibid.

[250] Ibid.

[251] Dudley, Harold. Letter to Albert McClure. April 27, 1953.

between Newman and Milton Van Hecke, representing the Chapel Hill Church. Van Hecke wrote Newman after the meeting on April 23 to request "immediate access to the record of the case compiled by Presbytery's Judicial Commission, in order that the complainants may have adequate opportunity to examine, copy and study the record, transcripts and evidence relied upon by the Commission to complete the preparation of their case on complaint."[252]

Van Hecke's letter was written after he had been given the floor to make his case for making public the evidence. Recognizing the unlikelihood of this happening, he suggested that just six members of the Chapel Hill Church be allowed to see all the evidence, and they would in turn keep what they had seen confidential. Piephoff countered by saying the Commission had turned over evidence to the Presbytery on condition of confidentiality, and were it to be made public, the Commission would have to take it back, rework it, and then present it anew, causing a long delay in any proceedings. Dr. T. Henry Patterson added that he felt it dangerous to reveal the contents of the confidential documents, as they contained material "that would turn brother against brother and stir up bad feelings that it would take years to heal."[253] However, Aiken Taylor supported the motion, saying all evidence had come to the Commission voluntarily, and not confidentially, and had been declared confidential by the Commission, which meant that in effect "a man could not even see his own words."[254]

---

[252] Van Hecke, M.T. Letter to Howard Newman. April 23, 1953, and Complaint, Exhibit No. 27.

[253] Complaint, Exhibit No. 27.

[254] Ibid.

Two elders from Greensboro then took up the case for the Chapel Hill Church. McKibben Lane compared the Commission's investigation tactics to McCarthyism, and Arthur Cooke, a lawyer, cited the fundamental right of confrontation as guaranteed in the Bill of Rights, "a requirement that the witnesses face the accused and that opportunity for cross-examination be given."[255] In response, he was told that a minister in the Presbytery had surrendered these rights to his brethren, and did not have the same protection in the church courts as in the civil and criminal courts.[256]

The meeting ended with a motion that all the evidence, and thus the responsibility for the decision as to confidentiality, be passed onto the Synod. The motion passed easily.

On May 14, 1953, the Synod convened a special meeting to hear and act upon the complaint by the Chapel Hill Church, at White Memorial Presbyterian Church in Raleigh. In all, forty-six ministers and elders from eight of North Carolina's nine Presbyteries were present. No one from Orange was present, as in an appeal to a higher court, the Presbytery in conflict does not have a direct voice, being allowed to speak only through its respondents. The Synod accepted communications from both the Chapel Hill Church and Orange Presbytery. The Chapel Hill Church requested that the Synod establish a Judicial Commission of its own to adjudicate the case. In doing so, the Church specified three grievances. The first claimed irregularities on the part of the Presbytery's Commission in the proceedings; the second alleged

---

[255] Ibid.

[256] Ibid.

[257] Minutes of the Synod of North Carolina, One Hundred and Fortieth Annual Session.

234 / F a i t h , G r a c e a n d H e r e s y

prejudice in the case; and the third grievance was that the judgment offered and action demanded by the Commission was unjust. In turn, the Presbytery respondents denied the charges, but joined in the request for a Synod Commission. Since both parties were in agreement on this point, the Synod voted to appoint such a body comprising one minister and one elder from each presbytery except Orange. Following selection of the Commission, the Synod moved to adjourn the session to allow their Commission to make a report. The Synod also ordered that all documents in the case be turned over to the new Commission.[257]

The Synod Commission met that same day, and elected the Rev. Price Gwynn, of Red Springs, to be its Chairman. The first working session was scheduled for May 22, again in Raleigh at the White Memorial Presbyterian Church.

Despite the sometimes complicated church procedure, the religious and news media continued to keep tabs on the controversy. The Presbyterian Outlook, in its May 25 issue, reported that the Synod had given the case to a special commission and that the complaint against Orange Presbytery had been signed by more than 130 members of the Chapel Hill Church. It further explained to its readers that the Synod had the right to "affirm or annul the action of Orange Presbytery's Commission in whole or in part or it can send it back to the Presbytery with instructions as to procedure."[258]

The Greensboro Daily News gave the meeting front page coverage. It too reported that the Synod had established a commission, but added

---

[258] Presbyterian Outlook. May 25, 1953. p. 3.

"that an appeal will be made to the [General] Assembly, the Church's highest court, whatever the decision of the Synod's Commission."[259]

The first meeting of the Synod Commission was held on Friday, May 22, 1953, at 9:30am. There were eight ministers and seven elders present. Also present were Dr. Van Hecke, Dr. Frank Porter Graham, and Dr. John Graham, representing the complainants, and the Reverends T. Henry Patterson, Z.T. Piephoff, and Aiken Taylor, who represented the respondents. The meeting began with an informal discussion of the duties of the Synod Commission and its procedures. There was also a reading of the complaint from the Chapel Hill Church, and a review of the records of the case. It was explained to both sides that no new evidence would be allowed—the role of the Commission was to review only the evidence that had been previously admitted.[260]

Dr. Frank Porter Graham was the first to speak. Despite his lack of height, his personality and intellect demanded attention and respect. He told the Synod Commission that he did not want to be a "hit-and-run" speaker, and that he was open to cross-examination on any point. Graham told the Commission, "In my opinion we have a dynamic Presbyterian Church of great value to our University, our State and this region. That church should be encouraged to go forward. . . I have never felt the Spirit of Christ more real in any church. It expresses and acknowledges its failures, it prays for forgiveness for its mistakes. Some irregularities were involved, several things which should have been

---

[259] Greensboro Daily News. May 15, 1953. p. 1.
[260] Synod Commission Minutes, p. 2.

done were omitted, but I don't think that those shortcomings require our minister to be taken from us."[261]

Graham said that the Church had welcomed the organization of a new Presbyterian Church, wanting to see all Presbyterians have their religious needs met in Chapel Hill. He told the Commission that Jones was always available to help those who needed him, in an emergency or otherwise, and he said that support for Jones came in great part from students, but that people across the country have been positively influenced by him. And he urged the Commission not to pay heed to the rumors and gossip that had surrounded the controversy.

"There have been rumors abroad of all kinds of beliefs or lack of beliefs in the Chapel Hill Church. Some say that here are atheists—and we even hear that Chapel Hill and the Church is a hotbed of communists. Others say that there are Unitarians on the roll of the Church. All of these are just rumors and cannot be based on facts."[262]

And Graham mentioned the race issue, something that the Presbytery's Judicial Commission continued to ignore, and deny when asked if it was a factor in their judgment. "Charlie Jones took the hard way—he and his wife have suffered. During the war, the Navy had a big training program on our campus, and some of those Navy students were Negro. The laws of our state required that they be housed apart from the whites, but when Sunday came, there was no separate church. They came to our church—a few of them—and they were seated just as you or I would have been. They were not taken to the balcony or stuck

---

[261] Synod Commission Minutes—Testimony Notes, p. 1.
[262] Ibid., p.2

in some corner. Anyone who comes to the Chapel Hill Church can sit anywhere there is a vacant seat. Forty members of the Church withdrew immediately following this episode—but twice that many joined. The officers stood behind Charlie in his stand about this."[263] Finally, Graham told the Commission, "I know of no minister who could be put ahead of Charlie Jones—there may be others his equal, but I know of not one who is above him."[264]

Van Hecke spoke next, and began by laying out the Chapel Hill Church's biggest grievance. "The representatives of the Complainant are unable to comment on the Presbytery record. We have not been allowed to see large portions of it."[265] He went on to raise six issues that he saw as being important to the case. They included Jones' ministry, whether Orange Presbytery's Judicial Commission acted properly according to the <u>Book of Church Order</u>, the issue of fair play and whether it was, in a larger sense, in the interests of the Presbyterian Church to remove Jones and his officers, the bias of the Commission and Orange Presbytery, the needs and wishes of the congregation, and whether it was too late for "redemptive measures".[266]

On this point Van Hecke said, "We have tried to discuss the situation and possible solutions with the Orange Presbytery Commission, but they refused to listen to us. We could not sit in a group and discuss the problem, trying to work it out together. The Commission has refused to listen to our suggestions. We hope the Synod's Commission will listen and will let this problem be discussed in a spirit of give and take. There

---

[263] Ibid., p.3.
[264] Ibid.
[265] Ibid., p.4.
[266] Ibid., p.5.

is a constructive way for settling the problems in Chapel Hill, and all we are asking is an opportunity for finding and following this way. Taking our minister from us, and refusing us a voice in the matter does not seem to us the way."[267]

After a few questions from the Synod Commission, T. Henry Patterson took the floor to speak for the Respondents. He began by saying that the Chapel Hill Church had made unjustified personal attacks on him, saying, "we begged Charlie [Jones] not to let the situation in Chapel Hill become filled with lies and hate."[268] He also denied the claim that the Presbytery had used funding as a way to threaten or coerce the members or officers of the Chapel Hill Church.

Z.T. Piephoff spoke next, saying that there had been no irregularities of procedure during the investigation. And he addressed the Complainants chief concern, the issue of secrecy. "We had a perfect right to hear all who wished to appear before the Commission—and we had a right to protect their names by silence, if this was the action we deemed wise. It is true that the material which is classified as confidential was not all so classified by the persons who appeared before us—but the names of those persons are confidential. Our reason for keeping this information within the Commission was that we did not feel the names should be divulged."[269] Moreover, he said, a trial had not been conducted and no charges levied against anyone, which meant that according to the Book of Church Order, the Commission was in no way

---

[267] Ibid.
[268] Ibid., p.8.
[269] Ibid., p.9.

obliged to turn over evidence and testimony to the Chapel Hill Church or Jones.

He went on to say that the testimony contained no rumors or hearsay and was completely reliable. "The Commission does not feel it has broken any trust or acted unethically in anyway."[270] Elder Jack Hooks, sitting on the Synod Commission, asked Piephoff for the exact reason for Jones' dismissal, and was told, "The interests of religion imperatively demand it."[271] Synod Commissioner Reverend Harry Moffett followed that up by asking, "Did you make an exhaustive effort to find interpretation of the phrase 'interests of religion'?" Piephoff answered, "Yes. There seems to be no such interpretation." To that, Moffett said, "I wonder why the General Assembly did not state more clearly what was meant by this."[272] It was a question that had occurred to many people, simply because the subjectivity inherent in interpreting that phrase, combined with the secrecy under which the Judicial Commission had operated, made it difficult for the Chapel Hill Church and Preacher Jones to defend themselves—they did not know the evidence against them, nor did they know against what standard they were being judged. Moreover, Moffett concluded the discussion with an endorsement of the Chapel Hill Church, which was tantamount to a rebuke for the Commission. He said, "As a former University pastor, let me speak about the work with students as I see it. It seems to me the Chapel Hill Church did an excellent job with graduate students, a group which is often inadequately served. This is one of

---

[270] Ibid.

[271] Ibid., p. 13.

[272] Ibid., p. 14.

the problems of student workers everywhere... but this church was reaching the students I believe."[273]

Aiken Taylor was the last of the Respondents to speak. He also addressed issues like the lack of ordination of elders, denied that the Judicial Commission relied on rumors and hearsay for their conclusions, and said the interviews with the officers of the Chapel Hill Church did not violate Presbyterian procedures. He added, "The investigation was begun in a hostile spirit, but this spirit soon melted and I would say that these interviews were in the best possible spirit."[274]

But, said Taylor, this spirit did not spread through every facet of the investigation. He said the Commission did indeed try to work with the Chapel Hill Church, but without success. He felt his own integrity had been called into question.

> "In Exhibit 19 the Complainant states that I tried to bribe the Church, and then in Exhibit 18 they state that I resigned because I did not approve of the Commission's action on the question of money from the Synod. This makes me look like I am a two-faced person, saying one thing to the Church and another to the Commission on which I had served and worked.

> "Fathers and brethren, it is important that they make me look like a person whose word cannot be trusted, for you see, I served as clerk of the Commission, and if my own personal

---

[273] Ibid.
[274] Ibid., p. 16.

word cannot be relied upon, then you see, they think that the work I did as Clerk of the Commission can also not be relied upon."[275]

T. Henry Patterson concluded the Presbytery's defense with a final statement.

"Orange Presbytery holds the pastor of this church responsible for the fact that the elders and deacons have not been properly examined, ordained and installed. Charlie Jones is a member of the Examining Committee of Orange Presbytery, and has examined ministers coming into the Presbytery. It is foolish to say that he forgot to examine the officers in his own church.

"The Commission dealt with Mr. Jones as they felt they had every right to do—and indeed they had this right."[276]

After each of the Complainants and Respondents had spoken, the Synod Commissioners questioned the men on the points they felt were of importance. But the questions themselves gave the impression, in some cases, that there were pre-existing biases even in this new Commission. Loaded questions such as, "Were the officers aware of the flagrant neglect of high school students?," when no such "flagrant neglect" had been established, forced defensive responses from the Complainants. On the other hand, Rev. Moffett would occasionally step in and appear to be speaking up for the Chapel Hill Church. When asked about whether all of the Presbyterian students at the University had been reached, Dr. John Graham told the Synod Commission that it

---

[275] Ibid., p. 15.
[276] Ibid., p. 17.

was hard to say exactly what percentage had been. Moffett spoke up, adding: "You can never tell how many students who worship in a University church are Presbyterians. In the University church where I served we sent student visitation teams to each new Presbyterian student. I was never accused of heresy, but I did not reach all of the students, Presbyterian students that is, in the University."[277]

Dr. John Graham concluded the testimony by telling the Synod Commission that the real issue in the case was "Does the Presbytery have the right to circumvent the Book of Church Order?"[278] To support his claim, he quoted D.J. Walker, a member of the Presbytery's Commission, as saying, "In general our form of church government guarantees the same rights in these matters as does our American form of government, and I did not feel that these rights had been accorded, especially the right to confrontation, the right to cross-examine, and the right to be heard fully."[279]

Graham then recommended that the case be referred back to the Presbytery "with the request that they allow due process to operate."[280]

The meeting was then adjourned, with plans to reconvene the following Wednesday morning, May 27, for a report to be written.

The Synod Commission met again at the White Memorial Presbyterian Church in Raleigh, and spent the morning in informal discussion, and then after lunch each member of the Commission was given the chance to voice their opinion as to what should be done. That afternoon the members voted on the four-part motion that follows:

[277] Ibid., p. 19.
[278] Ibid.
[279] Ibid.
[280] Ibid.

"In accordance with paragraph 294 of the <u>Book of Church Order</u> [see Appendix One], the Judicial Commission of the Synod of North Carolina answers the complaint of the Chapel Hill Presbyterian Church against the Presbytery of Orange by sending the matter back to the Presbytery of Orange with the following instructions for a new hearing:

That the new hearing be held immediate and in accordance with paragraph 189 of the <u>Book of Church Order.</u> [See Appendix Two].

That the dissolution of the pastoral relationship of Reverend Charles M. Jones and the Chapel Hill Presbyterian Church be continued until the issue of the hearing is settled.

That the present direct oversight of the Chapel Hill Presbyterian Church by the Presbytery of Orange continue until this hearing is concluded, or as long as the Presbytery may deem necessary short of that time.

That the Reverend Charles M. Jones and the Chapel Hill Presbyterian Church be given the opportunity by the Presbytery of Orange of due process and trial as soon as possible, if so desired by either party, in accordance with paragraph 189 of the <u>Book of Church Order</u>."[281]

---

[281] Synod Minutes, p.21.

The Commission voted on each section of the motion separately. Section one was approved 13-1; section two was approved 10-4; and sections three and four were approved unanimously. The motion as a whole was then voted on and approved unanimously.[282] However, two groups within the Synod Commission made a point of clarifying their positions, on the record. Two elders on the Commission, R.L. Corbett and James L. Brandon, stated: "In voting for the motion (as a whole) we did so with no idea of sustaining the complaint of the Chapel Hill Presbyterian Church but with the hope this action might bring about a workable solution in this matter."[283]

On the other side were the four men who had wanted to see Jones back in the pulpit until the matter was resolved. The Reverends Harry Moffett and Thomas Hamilton, along with Elders W.G. McGavock and Philip Howerton, stated for the record: "Our votes were in the affirmative to this motion as a whole for the sake of arriving at as much unanimity of action as possible. At the same time, our opposition to No. 2 of the motions remains unchanged."[284]

The next meeting of the Synod was held at the First Presbyterian Church in Raleigh, on June 2. The meeting was brief, with the Synod members hearing the report of its Commission. Since Orange Presbytery was excluded from the vote, the Commission's report and recommendations, presented by Commission Chairman Dr. H. Price Gwynn, was approved unanimously. In effect, the Synod's vote upset the Presbytery's stance in relation to due process, siding with the Chapel

[282] Synod Commission Minutes, May 27, 1953, p. 2.
[283] Ibid.
[284] Ibid.

Hill Church. The <u>Greensboro Daily News</u> the next day saw the Synod decision as leading to an ecclesiastical trial or a compromise.[285]

A friend of Jones wrote him on the day of the Adjourned Meeting of Synod giving his interpretation of the events.

> "Everyone here is overjoyed. Beyond it's particular application, Synod's decision has wholesome significance in a frightened world of witch hunts and McCarthyism.

> "Piephoff told McMullen in Raleigh yesterday Presbytery (not Commission) to carry out Synod's instructions. Piephoff, Patterson and Taylor stunned.

> "Understand minority on Synod Commission wanted to reinstate you pending settlement or trial, but were defeated. Strong implication in Synod Commission's statement that your doctrinal deficiencies are intolerable. So a settlement will not be easy. No hope you could come back wholly free.

> "Fear examination or trial by Presbytery likely to be far from impartial, unless Synod establishes liberal leadership."[286]

So the Presbytery was stunned. But as predicted, there was an immediate appeal lodged with the General Assembly by the Presbytery's leaders. The appeal was based on two points:

---

[285] Greensboro Daily News. June 3, 1953.
[286] Unknown to Charles Jones. June 2, 1953.

1. That the Synod of North Carolina acting through its Judicial Commission, erred in sending this matter back to the Presbytery of Orange with instructions that 'a new hearing be held' in accordance with paragraph 189 of the <u>Book of Church Order</u>.

2. That the Synod of North Carolina acting through its Judicial Commission, erred in the use it made of paragraph 189, point #4, by suggesting an 'optional' trial, whereas, this paragraph makes a trial mandatory.[287]

The response from the Synod was for the Moderator, A.B. McClure, to appoint five members of the Synod Commission as respondents. They were: Harry Moffett, S.H. Fulton, Price H. Gwynn, Phil Howerton and R.D. McMillan. These men were to appear before the General Assembly at its meeting in Montreat on June 4.

The General Assembly of the Presbyterian Church is the final court of appeal in all ecclesiastical cases involving lower courts of the church. It is composed of commissioners of all the presbyteries on a representational apportionment of one layman and one clergy commissioner for each 4,000 members. In 1953 there were 744,922 Southern Presbyterians with 2,954 ministers and 3,733 churches. The meeting was held at the Assembly conference grounds in Montreat, North Carolina, with several hundred commissioners from all over the denomination present.[288]

---

[287] Patterson, T. Henry, Piephoff, Z.T. Letter to Harold Dudley. June 4, 1953.

[288] Minutes of the Ninety-third General Assembly of the Presbyterian Church in the United States. June 4-9, 1953, p. 340.

On June 5, the <u>Greensboro Daily News</u> speculated as to how the General Assembly would handle the case, and reported the appeal as coming after the Synod had "rapped the procedure of the Presbytery."[289] The paper said that the General Assembly would probably appoint its own judicial commission to hear the case. In fact, that is what happened. The Assembly indeed referred the case to its standing Judicial Committee, minus its members from the Synod of North Carolina, constituting it as a commission for the purpose of the Synod review.

The General Assembly's Commission was chaired by Dr. E.T. Thompson, professor of Church History at Union Theological Seminary in Richmond, and a former teacher of Jones. Thompson was something of a controversial churchman himself, both widely respected and disliked because of his outspoken liberal views on church affairs. In fact, in the early 1940s, at his own insistence, he had been tried for heresy and acquitted by his own Presbytery, to refute baseless charges that had been lodged against him by some leaders of the conservative wing of the denomination. While his chairing the Commission was undoubtedly a relief, if not a positive blessing for Jones and the Chapel Hill Church, all parties recognized his ability as a parliamentarian and his essential fairness in any ecclesiastical proceedings.

The Assembly Commission reviewed the record of the case and then heard representatives from both the Synod and the Presbytery. When all the parties had been heard, the Commission spent some considerable

---

[289] Greensboro Daily News. June 5, 1953, p. 1.

time coming to a decision. Concerning the first complaint of error by the Presbytery, the Commission voted 16-15 to sustain the complaint, which affirmed that the Synod had been in error when deciding to refer the case back to the Presbytery.[290]

The vote was not a straightforward one—thirteen members of the General Assembly's Commission felt so strongly they lodged a complaint of their own against their own Commission's action. Among the signers was the Commission's chairman, Dr. E.T. Thompson. This new complaint was signed by all of the lawyers on the Commission and read as follows:

1. Sustaining the Presbytery's complaint, in this case, seems to condone what has largely been interpreted, within and without the church, as 'Star Chamber' proceedings;

2. Sustaining the Synod's ruling would not have had the effect of changing a Presbytery's authority, under proper circumstances, to proceed under paragraph 76 of the Book of Church Order to dissolve a pastoral relation;

3. Sustaining the Synod's ruling would have indicated that, where investigation produces information leading to a reasonable presumption of guilt, the responsibility of the investigating body should then be discharged under provision of Paragraph 189 of the Book of Church Order.[291]

---

[290] General Assembly Minutes, p. 65.
[291] Ibid., p. 66.

The Commission then voted 25-6 not to sustain the Presbytery's second specification of error, wherein the complainants claimed the Synod had erred when it stated "that the Rev. Charles M. Jones and the Chapel Hill Church be given the opportunity by the Presbytery of Orange of due process and trial as soon as possible, if so desired by either party, in accordance with paragraph 189 of the <u>Book of Church Order</u>."[292]

The action of the Commission was approved by the General Assembly, and the minutes record the meaning of the decision:

1. It left intact the authority of the Presbytery to dissolve the pastoral relationship where the interest of religion imperatively demanded it, without the necessity of a formal trial.

2. It continued "in full force and effect" the dissolution of the pastoral relationship that existed between Jones and the Chapel Hill Presbyterian Church.

3. It continued "in full force and effect" the special oversight of Orange Presbytery over the Chapel Hill Presbyterian Church.

4. It afforded Preacher Jones and the Chapel Hill Church the right of a formal trial "should it be so desired."[293]

This action led the <u>Greensboro Daily News</u> to carry a front page story entitled "Firing of Jones Upheld by Church's Assembly" and stating that thirteen of the thirty-one members of the Assembly's Commission filed a dissent to the action. The story went on to say that "although the Commission said the dismissal will continue in effect, it will be neces-

---

[292] Ibid., p. 65
[293] Ibid.

sary for the Presbytery to hold a formal trial in the case if either Jones or the Chapel Hill Church request it."[294]

The Presbyterian Outlook was also following events closely, and told its readers of the hard work and late hours the Commission had endured. It said that the "practical effect of the Assembly's action differs in only one respect from the action of the Synod's Commission since Synod did not restore the pastoral official relationships. It eliminates the necessity of a preliminary hearing which might have led to a trial."[295]

The Presbyterian Journal in its June 13 issue gave much the same report.

Thompson himself wrote to Jones after the hearing, expressing his dismay at the outcome.

> "I regret that the Assembly's Commission on which I served could not act more constructively than it did. I am afraid that not only you and the Chapel Hill Church, but also the cause of Christ has suffered considerable harm, far beyond the borders of the state."[296]

The effect of the General Assembly's ruling was to uphold the historic right of each Presbytery to determine who will serve in its churches. But there was an apparent inconsistency in its findings. While reaffirming that a Presbytery could remove a pastor "without the necessity of a formal trial", this particular case was seemingly deemed an exception, with Jones being granted precisely that right. And the likelihood of a trial increased when, on June 15, Jones wrote from Kingsport, Tennessee, to the Reverend William Currie, the Presbytery Moderator. The letter was directed towards Orange Presbytery as a whole.

---

[294] Greensboro Daily News. June 9, 1953, p. 1.

[295] Presbyterian Outlook. June 29, 1953, p. 6.

[296] Thompson, E.T. Letter to Charles Jones. June 20, 1953.

"Brethren,

"It is desirable for both our sakes that my ecclesiastical status be clarified.

"The Commission of Orange Presbytery in conference with me prior to my removal asked me to 'voluntarily' resign from the Chapel Hill pastorate stating they would permit me to release the resignation and give me time to find other work so that I might leave 'with my record clear'. It is a matter of record that I refused this course of action. When the Commission removed me from the pastorate it was expressly stated to the press that there were censures or charges against me and that I was in good and regular standing in the Presbytery but the 'interests of religion imperatively demanded' my removal.

"At no time has the Commission offered definite reasons why such action was demanded for the interests of religion. In various reports and statements the Commission has mentioned 'serious irregularities' and 'confidential information' in such a way as to give rise to all kinds of speculation and rumor.

"I therefore request Orange Presbytery to join me in asking the Synod of North Carolina to set up a Commission to hear all charges and receive all evidence against me and to make judgment on the same."[297]

---

[297] Jones, Charles M. Letter to William Currie. June 15, 1953.

So while Jones was considering taking the matter to trial, he clearly was not keen for Orange Presbytery to sit as his judge and jury, the outcome of such a trial likely to be something of a formality. Of course, for Jones' request to be realized, it had to be agreed upon by Orange Presbytery which was now faced with a chance to end the controversy in its favor. Moreover, to concur with Jones' request was to admit to its own prejudice.

Howard Newman replied to Jones in the name of the Presbytery in a letter dated June 29, and expressed his own doubts as to such a transfer. He also stated that the Presbytery moderator, Currie, had also expressed doubt over a transfer, and that he had sought an advisory opinion from the Assembly Stated Clerk, Dr. E.C. Scott, who told him:

> "Synod has no connection whatever with the matter in its present status. Mr. Jones has the opinion that Synod will need to be brought into the matter but this will not be true unless there is a conviction after a trial and he decides to appeal to Synod."[298]

Despite the seeming harshness of the tone, there were still some hopes for a non-confrontational resolution to the crisis. Frank Price, Moderator of the General Assembly, wrote to Jones the same day as did Thompson.

> "I am sorry that I have not had the opportunity to meet and talk with you since my return last year from China. From Bob McMullen and many other friends I have heard about the fine work that you have done at Chapel Hill through the years.

> "I understand that you have asked Orange Presbytery for a trial, preferably by the Synod of North Carolina. Yesterday afternoon I had a long talk about the matter with Dr. Ernest T. Thompson who knows you and was Chairman of the Judicial

---

[298] Newman, Howard. Letter to Charles Jones. Junes 29, 1953.

Commission at the recent General Assembly. You are familiar with the judgment of that Commission by a very small majority, and with the minority opinion in which Dr. Thompson concurred.

"Dr. Thompson goes next week to the Joint Meeting of US and USA Synods of Tennessee to be held at Maryville College, Knoxville. He will be the speaker at the Bible Hour each morning, June 23-26.

"I have asked Dr. Thompson to see you and talk with you if it can possibly be arranged. Could you go to Maryville to see him sometime during next week or could you write or phone him where he could meet you if you prefer some other place? Dr. Thompson will also write you.

"It is our earnest hope and prayer that the solution of this difficult question in which you are vitally concerned shall further the unity, peace and spiritual life of our whole church. We are moving forward steadily toward Presbyterian reunion, on vital theology, interracial brotherhood and other high goals. Of course there is opposition but I am sure we can win over many of our critics and opponents by faith and love and prayer. We can do it without sacrificing any of our basic Presbyterian beliefs and methods.

"May God give you His wisdom and grace in this time of testing. Our prayers are with you. Please let me know when you receive this letter and whether you and Dr. Thompson can arrange an unhurried interview."[299]

---

[299] Price, Frank. Letter to Charles Jones. June 20, 1953.

Jones responded to Price immediately, saying that he would not be able to meet with Thompson, to whom he had written a long letter, a copy of which he enclosed for Price. The tone of Jones' letter was one of sadness, as he acknowledged the futility of a trial before the Presbytery. He wrote:

> "I have conferred with friends in Chapel Hill, mainly the officers of the Church, and we agreed that it would be impossible to get a fair and impartial hearing before Presbytery. I do not think this would be because of the defective character of the brethren but because there has been so much discussion and emotions have been so aroused that it would be asking too much of human nature (even regenerated human nature) to be fair under such circumstances. I can see nothing constructive coming out of a trial in Presbytery.

> "My request was that Orange Presbytery join me in asking Synod to hear the case. If this is refused it is our present judgment that the most constructive thing I could do would be to remove myself from the scene as the source of trouble by making a frank, simple but friendly statement and requesting Presbytery to relieve me of my vows as a Presbyterian minister.

> "I am extremely sorry the whole problem has become so complicated and filled with such misunderstandings and misinterpretations. I appreciate the efforts of many friends to bring about a good solution."[300]

---

[300] Jones, Charles M. Letter to Frank Price. June 23, 1953.

That same day Jones wrote a letter to Dr. Thompson, the man who had once been his teacher, and was now one of his many supporters. In it he apologized for not having the time to meet with him as Rev. Price had hoped.

"I am to leave here the last of this week to be away for several days in North Carolina and in the early part of July I shall be away for over a week in New York. I cannot, in fairness to my responsibilities here, leave at this time.

"I have tried throughout the whole of this event to remain sensitive to constructive solutions. Several times I have suggested to the officers of the Church that I was not personally indispensable to the Presbyterian Church at large or the Chapel Hill Church in particular and perhaps a simple, frank, non-inflammatory statement by me, followed by my request for a friendly and peaceable breaking of the relationship between me and the denomination would be wise. Every time this has been unanimously opposed.

"Following the General Assembly's decision, I met with the officers again and made the same proposal. I am not belligerent by nature and a legal approach to the problem for the sake of 'vindication', or as Dr. McMullen puts it 'to smoke them out', does not appeal to me. Furthermore, even if a trial should declare me in good standing but with certain deficiencies it would only further embitter the Chapel Hill folk for the removal order would still stand. I found no one agreed with me. When the meeting ended we had agreed that I should ask Orange Presbytery to join with me in requesting that a Commission be set up by the Synod to hear charges and evidence and judge the same. If Presbytery refuses this, it would then be proper for me to make as fair and generous a statement as I can make and request that I be divested of my office as a Presbyterian minister.

"I am enclosing a copy of a letter I have written to Orange Presbytery making the request for a Synod's Commission to judge the case. A reply from Bill Currie indicates he does not believe this will be done. He questions the legality of it and assumes that I will want a trial by Presbytery. He very generously offers to help work out a time schedule convenient to me.

"It is our agreement in Chapel Hill that it will be impossible to get an impartial and fair hearing in Orange Presbytery, and I am therefore making ready a statement that I can use if it should be necessary.

"I am sure Dr. McMullen has spoken to you and Dr. Price about the move in Chapel Hill to start a Community Church. This was proposed by a few of the officers at the time of my removal by Presbytery's Commission. The Report of the Commission indicated wholesale opposition not only to the procedures and practices of the Church but the very spirit of it. These few saw no chances for reconciliation but most of us felt the errors in the Report could be corrected and misunderstandings cleared up to the point where reconciliation would be possible. After much discussion there was complete agreement that any move to start another Church should wait until every effort had been made, including appeal to the General Assembly, to resolve our differences with the Presbytery.

"I was asked at that time by two officers if I would be willing to return to work with a Community Church in Chapel Hill. I discouraged then any movement to work up support for such a new church on the grounds that we had to make every appeal in good faith on through to the General Assembly.

"Since the General Assembly's decision, the movement to start a Community Church has revived and I have been asked if I would return. I have been asked by Dr. McMullen to make a public statement that I would not return to Chapel Hill to serve a Community Church—so you see the dilemma I have been facing.

"I have had to give the kind of answer to both that is very unsatisfactory to me. To those who have asked me to agree to serve a newly formed Community Church so that they might state that fact in approaching charter members, I have said no. I have explained to them that churches are not wholesome when formed around personalities and if a new church is needed in Chapel Hill it should be because of faiths, convictions and needs irrespective of the ministerial leadership involved. I have told them that I did not want to lead a 'mass movement' from the Presbyterian Church of people who would feel it necessary to be loyal to me. When they ask if I will refuse to return if a Community Church is organized and a call extended to me I have said such a call would have to be considered on its merits.

"There are those who honestly believe the Report of the Commission, the removal of the officers, and the refusal of the Commission to let the Church elect officers means a determination to destroy the spirit and the program of the Chapel Hill Church for the Commission reports the conditions they dislike are of long standing. While there has been active support for our Church both in the Synod and General Assembly, in the final analysis it is with the Presbytery the people must work and live and the gulf between the Presbytery and Church seems wide. They believe that the strength of the Presbyterian church in Chapel Hill, while it may have been unfair to the

denomination to be such, was in its lack of strict denominational emphasis. There are many unchurched people in Chapel
Hill that a Community Church might reach. Such is their contention and they are trying to discover just how great this need
might be.

"I recognize the subjective element that will tend to force itself
on me when I must make a decision and I am trying to keep
myself free from it that I may be led into a constructive and
good decision.

"I again want to express my appreciation for the work of you
and others when so much of it is undeserved on my part."[301]
That same week, Jones received a letter from Dr. McMullen dealing
with that very issue. Up to this point, McMullen had been in a difficult
position, attempting to perform his job as temporary pastor at the
Chapel Hill Church under the watchful eye of Orange Presbytery. Keen
not to upset the Presbytery further, yet believing in Jones, he trod a narrow and treacherous path. Now, however, he did not shy at making his
feelings about a new Community Church felt. He had been opposed to
the idea when it was first broached, writing to Jones in March of 1953 to
express his hope Jones would have nothing to do with a new church in
Chapel Hill because doing so "will definitely contribute to the weaken-
ing, perhaps to the breaking up of this congregation and surrendering
the cause."[302] If anything, his feelings had strengthened.

---

[301] Jones, Charles M. Letter to Dr. E.T. Thompson. June 23, 1953.
[302] McMullen, R.J. Letter to Charles Jones. March 12, 1953.

"In regard to your coming here to be pastor of an independent church, I fear I am of the same opinion still. I can see many reasons for your not doing so. You will recall that those stated to you are

"1st., It will weaken the Church which you have led for so long so as to make it extremely difficult to secure a suitable pastor to carry on its liberal tradition.

"2nd., It requires many of your friends to make a decision which you should relieve them of making. It is stated that principle is more important than person. It is for this reason, I suppose, that you insist that those wishing to join from this or any other Church should do so because they wish to be in a Community Church regardless of whether you returned here or not. I submit that the only way this can really be done is for you to definitely eliminate yourself from the picture by stating that you will not serve the church. Then the issue will be quite clear cut and those withdrawing will do so on principle and not because of a loyalty to a person. Otherwise the issue will be confused and you might find yourself serving a Charlie Jones Church rather than a Jesus Christ Church, as Harry Smith put it to you.

"3rd., It would not be helpful to many of those who are strongly advocating your return here as pastor of a Community Church. Many of them tend to adore you more than they should. Some of them need a greater loyalty to Jesus than they now seem to have. It was because of such a conflict that Harry Moffett decided to leave Texas. He wished to eliminate himself and force his devotees to a fuller dedication to Jesus Christ.

"4th., It would not be helpful to the other churches in this town. Dick Jackson and his church have for some time had a committee working on a plan to develop themselves into a Community Church. Your plan would, of course, kill this. How many liberals from the Episcopal, Methodist and other churches would leave them to join your church I do not know. If a significant number did so, it would tend to turn all of the other churches in the city towards a very conservative type of church. This would not be a healthy situation for any of them. Doubtless your old friends would give you a hearty welcome into the Ministerial Association and into the Council of Churches, though some of them would wonder how the Charlie Jones they have known could have done this to their churches.

"5th., It will not do you any good. You would disappoint many of your staunchest supporters, not only in Chapel Hill but in the Synod and General Assembly. You did not ask me for my opinion but permitted me to give it to you. You might be asking the opinion of such friends as Dick Jackson, David Yates, Kelsey Regan, Harry Moffett, or any other of your staunch friends throughout the country. Further, I believe it might also harm you personally. It would be quite unusual if the publicity you have received did not cause you to become spiritually proud. Your coming here would tend to develop in you a desire for adoration which would not be helpful to your friends and would be very dangerous for you.

"Again, assuring you of my continued prayers for you as you make these important decisions, and with warmest personal regards to you and Dorcas, I remain, Yours cordially. R.J. McMullen.

"P.S. Since writing the above I have run into a couple who are most devoted to you and among our best Church workers. They said with deep feeling that they hoped you had too much sense to come back here as pastor of a Community Church. I said that your doing so would put many people on the spot. She replied that it would certainly embarrass them for they were devoted to you. He said that they might lose some of their respect for you if you came. This would make it easier to stay in the present Church as they felt they should. R.J.M."[303]

On June 29, Howard Newman wrote to Preacher Jones and stated officially that they would not accede to his request to move a trial away from Orange Presbytery and have it before the Synod. "No provision is made in the <u>Book of Church Order</u> whereby the procedure you suggested could be followed, and, as Stated Clerk, I shall have to so advise Presbytery."[304]

Jones replied immediately, thanking Newman for dealing with the matter and investigating the possibility of transferring the trial. He ended the letter by saying, "I know you must have some feeling for the difficulty of the decision I must make now. I do not know that a trial before Presbytery would be constructive in its results. I do not mean in the sense of giving me a clean slate or of convicting me, but I mean in the larger sense of being constructive for me, the Church and the Presbytery. We are all so close to the problem and see it with unclear vision."[305]

[303] McMullen, R.J. Letter to Charles Jones. June 20, 1953.
[304] Newman, Howard. Letter to Charles Jones. June 29, 1953.
[305] Jones, Charles M. Letter to Howard Newman. July 1, 1953.

Now was the time for Jones to make one of the most important decisions of his life. He was, in a sense, in limbo—dismissed from his church but with no charges levied against him, and at the same time seemingly made to feel unwelcome in Chapel Hill by some of those most devoted to him. So he faced either a trial he could not win, and which he felt would hurt the Church in a broader sense even if he was cleared, or he could step down gracefully now and perhaps lose forever the chance to preach in Chapel Hill.

Orange Presbytery met on July 16 at New Hope Presbyterian Church, with the Chapel Hill report scheduled for the afternoon session. Jones and some of his supporters were present, as was Dr. Price Gwynn, Chairman of the Synod Judicial Commission.

The first issue before Presbytery relative to the Jones case was the request for a change of venue. Though rare, such a change to the Synod could have been made if the Presbytery had concurred with the request, even though the Stated Clerk of the Assembly questioned its validity. If the Presbytery concurred, it would then be up to the Synod to decide whether or not to receive the case. During the morning session, the Moderator, Currie, appointed a committee to study Jones' request for a change of venue and report to the afternoon session. When the time came for the report, the committee chairman, J.M. Millard surprised the meeting by recommending that the Presbytery go along with Jones' request and endorse a change of venue. This recommendation caused quite a stir, and was vehemently opposed by Presbytery Executive T. Henry Patterson. When the vote was finally taken, the committee's recommendation was defeated.[306]

---

[306] Presbytery Minutes, p. 27.

The Stated Clerk then said that the Presbytery stood ready to try Jones if he requested such a move. By this time, though, Jones had decided that this was simply not something he wanted to put himself or the church through. Instead, he asked permission to make a statement to the Presbytery regarding his status. He spoke for 45 minutes, a statement he later condensed to be printed in the Presbytery minutes. His statement presented his reasons for requesting a change of venue, and, being denied this, his decision to leave the Presbyterian ministry.

"I have asked you, Orange Presbytery to submit our controversy to a Commission of your Synod of North Carolina for the hearing of all charges and evidence you may have and judgment of the merits. Your moderator appointed a committee to study the legality of my request and the wisdom of granting it or not granting it. This committee has reported to you a recommendation that my request be granted. You have turned down their recommendation.

"I asked for this 'change of venue' upon the advice of the former officers of the Presbyterian Church of Chapel Hill. All save one, not present in the meeting, concurred. We are convinced prejudices and emotions have been so aroused during the past year, that a fair hearing and just decision before Orange Presbytery is impossible. It would be of no benefit to the Chapel Hill Church, Orange Presbytery, Presbyterianism or me to have further and futile litigation in this Presbytery.

"The Book of Church Order, paragraph 263, reads in part as follows:

"'A minister of the gospel, if he has satisfactory evidence of his inability to serve the church with acceptance, may report these facts at a stated meeting of Presbytery. At the next stated meeting, if after full deliberation the Presbytery shall concur with him in judgment, it may divest him of his office without censure.'

"The Chapel Hill Church through unanimous vote of its officers and well nigh unanimous vote of the congregation has declared my ministry acceptable and helpful to them. Their devotion to the Church and its work has been both an inspiration and means of growth to me.

"But the stubborn facts remain that I do not serve the Church to the satisfaction of Orange Presbytery. I desire to report my inability to serve the Church with such acceptance and request Presbytery to divest me of office as a minister in the Presbyterian Church.

"My future is uncertain but in some capacity, lay or ministerial, I shall continue to share my imperfect and partial experience of the breadth and length and height and depth of the love of God as seen in Christ Jesus with my fellows. I shall try to grow inwardly in the grace and knowledge of Christ Jesus in my own life and the life of society.

"These purposes I believe we share."[307]

As dramatic as this pronouncement was, it would not take immediate effect—even demitting from the Presbyterian Church required strict adherence to the law of the Church. Notice of such a request had to be

---

[307] Presbytery Minutes, p. 27.

given at one stated meeting and acted on at the next stated meeting. This meant Jones was again in limbo, a three-month wait for the final disposition of his status as a Presbyterian.

Before the Presbytery adjourned the meeting, however, members voted to dissolve the Judicial Commission and normalize the status of the Chapel Hill Church by installing a new slate of officers.[308] As far as the Presbytery was concerned, then, the controversy was over. Jones was out of the Chapel Hill Church, and these new officers would be able to guide the congregation back into more Presbyterian ways. But rumblings from Chapel Hill were set to disrupt and disturb the Presbytery still—the specter of a new church, and one led by Preacher Jones, threatened to draw members away from the newly normalized Presbyterian flock. The pressure from both sides was building, and once again Jones was faced with a decision that would please many, and outrage many others. Either way, he found himself having to make a decision that was for him very personal, but a decision that would come under intense public scrutiny and put him back in the limelight.

---

[308] Ibid.

Above: Charles and Dorcas in the Church office.

Left: The Presbyterian Church, Chapel Hill.

Above: Congregants await the second Sunday service, at 11am.

Above: Preacher and the Friday night student group, meeting and eating in the basement of the Presbyterian Church.

Below: Some of the Snuffbuckets. From left to right:
Miriam Williams, unknown, John Barlow, Zan Harper, Fran Defandorf, Dave Andrews, Bill Howard, unknown, Charles McCoy, Garland Woolsey, Rev. Charles Jones.

Above and below: Two of the one-room schools Charles visited while working with Save the Children, in 1953.

Above: Rev. Charles M. Jones in the pulpit.

Above: Charlie Jones, still working, but caught in a more relaxed moment.

<u>Above:</u>Charlie with Francis Bradshaw, Dean of Students at UNC, Chapel Hill.

<u>Below:</u> Preacher in the one place he always found peace, the woods of North Carolina.

Chapter Nine

Out of the Fold

*"Those of you who know me best, and who have watched
or been involved in the ministry of this church, know that I
believe the key to the understanding of life is in the value of
human personality." - CMJ.*

Jones' resignation from the Presbytery was officially announced to
members of the Chapel Hill Presbyterian Church in a two-page letter
dated July 21, 1953.

"Dear Friend,

"You know by now of my action at the recent meeting of
Orange Presbytery. When the Presbytery did not see fit to join
me in seeking an objective hearing before the Synod of North
Carolina I asked to be released from my responsibilities as a
Presbyterian minister.

"The officers and I have all along tried to secure your advice
and keep you informed of our plans. We met after the General
Assembly gave its decision and unanimously agreed on the

above course of action to be the most constructive one. We wanted to tell you of these plans but felt if they became known to members of Orange Presbytery there would be a temptation to summarily vote down a transfer of our problem to the Synod.

"Now that our relationship is completely severed by my action, I want to express appreciation for the twelve years of association with you folk in the Church. Your voluntary assumption of responsibility in planning and carrying out the policies and program of the Church, the patience you have had with my inadequacies and mistakes, the spirit of tolerance you have shown when differences have arisen, your willingness to seek the will of God in perplexing situations, and your courage in putting Christian principles, on which we all agreed, into practice have made the last twelve years the best in my life. The old hymn, considered too sentimental by some, takes on a sense of reality as I think of these years:

"'Blessed be the tie that binds
Our hearts in Christian love,
The fellowship of kindred minds
Is like to that above.'

"There seem to be two approaches within the membership of our Church as regards the future. Some feel the quality of spiritual life and work in our Church has a place in the Presbyterian denomination. They believe they have a responsibility and opportunity to express it within the stream of the Presbyterian heritage.

"There are others within the membership of our Church who feel that when a Presbytery has sole authority to control the local church, without due consideration of the convictions of its members, freedom of inquiry and action are not allowed. They believe they have a responsibility to seek membership in a Christian Church organization that will give an expression to their convictions.

"The unity that has been ours in the past years has been a unity of spirit and intention—not a uniformity of thought and action. May the same spirit of unity continue as each makes his or her decision in the light of their deepest convictions."[309]

Jones' mistrust of ecclesiastical hierarchies was a decisive factor in the decision he was about to make. He expressed it in a letter to his friend Maurice Cobb.

"A representative of the Unitarian Church visited me here in Kingsport and made the suggestion that it might be possible to get denominational support for a Unitarian Church in Chapel Hill. I thought it over very carefully and decided against that. Not because I could not with good conscience be a Unitarian minister! But I am fully convinced now that denominationalism, even at its best, contributes to an ecclesiastical self-consciousness. Furthermore, one has to spend half his time trying to explain what a denomination stands for and how it works. This is true of Presbyterians, Methodists, Baptists and Unitarians too. A community church has problems ahead of it anywhere but I believe they can serve the community better now that the general person is no longer denominationally minded.

---

[309] Jones, Charles M. Letter to members of the Chapel Hill Presbyterian Church. July 21, 1953.

"If a community church were started in Chapel Hill and its base was not broad enough to include Unitarian, Trinitarian, Quaker etc then I should not want to serve it."[310]

The idea of Jones serving a new church in Chapel Hill was of concern to many. One day after the July 16 Presbytery meeting, former Judicial Commission member Joe Garrison wrote to Jones in Tennessee, delivering a message very similar to that of Rev. McMullen. Garrison was conciliatory, yet his chief message was simply that Jones should not come back to Chapel Hill as the minister of a new church.

"This past year has been most difficult for all of us. There are obviously two sides to most any question so that people must of necessity meet in a compromised position or else not meet. I am sure that you feel you compromised as far as you could.

"You had many people exceedingly sympathetic. The bitterest words I have ever heard spoken in a church were spoken by one of the members of the Chapel Hill Church supposedly in a Christian defense of you. The two things do not go together. I have talked to many people during the year who admittedly had no information, nevertheless, they had an opinion and wanted to express it. They were on both sides of the question.

"You have felt deeply hurt throughout this struggle. Some of the rest of us have suffered too. Many people have been hurt.

---

[310] Jones, Charles M. Letter to Maurice Cobb. July 20, 1953.

"The matter before us has been a religious matter and it can not be solved without <u>religion</u>. Here preaching and practice must meet.

"I am deeply concerned about our young people and students. They, of course, have paid the really big price. In your recent statement you suggest that your recent decision is in part in honest consideration of the welfare of the Chapel Hill Church. You have come to a place now where you can demonstrate that. As one who has tried to hold out for a 'fair trial' for you, I want to say that you are really on trial now. What you do is going to speak louder than anything that has been said by you or by others.

"I want to urge you to be very wise in your response to the efforts of many of your <u>friends</u> who will go a very long way to set up a 'reactionary' church and call you as its pastor.

"This is intended as a tribute to you, but I am very fearful of the outcome in the long years ahead.

"I, of course, know that my advice in no sense will determine your action but I, at least, have recorded my convictions and have stood up clearly so that you can see where I stand.

"I would like to assure you of my personal friendship and good wishes."[311]

---

[311] Garrison, Joseph. Letter to Charles Jones. July 17, 1953.

Jones did write a reply to Garrison, on July 22, but never mailed the letter. In it, he wrote:

> "I am aware that many individuals, groups and even the Presbyterian Church as an institution has been hurt. I am sorry for the inadequacies of mine that contributed to the hurt. Sack cloth and ashes are appropriate for most of us.
>
> "You know, of course, that there is a move to establish a community church in Chapel Hill. I have told them I felt they should consider the need for it apart from whether or not I would return. If they need a community church then they need it irrespective of who may be its first minister.
>
> "The tone of your letter, with its underlined words and a few statements of which 'I, of course, know that my advice in no sense will determine your action but I, at least, have recorded my convictions and have stood up clearly so that you can see where I stand', is a sample indicating you wrote with strong convictions. I appreciate that fact.
>
> "I trust I do not have to prove the honesty of my preaching or the sincerity of my religion by making my practice conform to your judgment. I shall endeavor to look at facts, listen to advice and make a wise decision."[312]

As word spread of Jones departure from the Presbytery, along with the possibility of his return as the minister of a new community church in Chapel Hill, many eyes focused on his next move.

---

[312] Jones, Charles M. Letter to Joseph Garrison (unsent). July 22, 1953.

The news media were still watching—Time magazine ran its second piece on Jones on July 22, announcing that he had "lost a final battle with the Orange Presbytery, which had removed him from his pulpit for showing too little regard for Presbyterian doctrine."[313] The magazine quoted him as saying, "I cannot place dogma above Christianity.... I believe [the Christian's] first loyalty is not to his denomination but to the church universal."[314]

With such announcements of his rejection of the Presbyterian Church, as well as the anticipation of his return, letters from further afield again began to pour in. As before, most were encouraging for Jones, though not all. An "Unknown Friend" wrote and told him: "You and a few crack-pot so-called Elders seem obsessed with egoism or/and ignorance and that you can run a Presbyterian Church; foolish and school-boy attitude to assume... suggestion: for your own good vamoose."[315]

Jones' friend Warren Ashby, a philosophy professor at the Woman's College of the University of North Carolina at Greensboro, wrote and told him, "since coming to North Carolina in 1946, I have learned more from you ... than from any other. I am grateful for it all; and I hope that others can receive from you as I have. This is all the more reason that I hope you will stay with us in the South, and more particularly in North Carolina. I am but one among many, doubtless, voicing a hope to you; and I know that you will live and work in the place you think you should. I simply hope that place is here: we need you desperately."[316]

---

[313] Time. July 27, 1953.

[314] Ibid.

[315] Unknown. Letter to Charles Jones. May 8, 1953.

[316] Ashby, Warren. Letter to Charles Jones. July 17, 1953.

Dr. Charles Ramsay, professor of Religion at Greensboro College, wrote about his sadness at the way things had turned out in Chapel Hill.

"When and if you leave Orange Presbytery and the ministry of the Presbyterian Church, I shall certainly feel very much less at home in the church that is left .... I cannot help regret profoundly the way things have turned out for you regarding our church. Personally I am opposed to you leaving the ministry of our church. I am so opposed to it that I at present feel I should vote—if it comes to a vote—against allowing you to do so .... You do have a spirit and a conviction—and also undoubtedly an ability to communicate the same—which our church very much needs. I wish to see this preserved in our church. I have what you might call a 'vested interest' in seeing it preserved."[317]

It seems likely that such input from friends would have, to some degree, influenced his decision about whether or not he should return to Chapel Hill. But he also seems to have used these correspondences as an opportunity to identify the issues involved, address the dilemma he faced, and set out his own feelings. He replied to Dr. Ashby in this way.

"Experiences seem to need digesting just like food does. I am in the process of digesting this one and at the same time looking at the future. So my reason for coming [back to Chapel Hill] is not entirely unselfish—I want to use you and Helen as a kind of 'digestion juice.'"[318]

To Dr. Ramsay he wrote a two-page letter, talking in more detail about his view of the controversy and its effect on him.

---

[317] Ramsay, Charles. Letter to Charles Jones. July 17, 1953.
[318] Jones, Charles M. Letter to Warren Ashby. July 1953.

"I have learned much this year. The tendency when under attack is to rush to the defense of oneself 'in toto'. For the first two months of this controversy that was my reaction. I soon realized, however, that I ought to be as honest as I could in self-examination. I have become aware of weaknesses and believe I will be better because of that knowledge.

"I have also learned how strong the tendency is in controversy to think of those who disagree as being totally evil. While not totally successful I have benefited by the necessity to attempt to keep both my feelings and utterances under control.

"I have also been forced to think through both matters of faith and practice and get down to bedrock as regards such things. This has been difficult to do with the Commission because the only session I have had with them alone was spent mostly in investigative mood and by asking questions that somehow never got us into the process of reaching to fundamentals with a view toward understanding. I don't know who made the remark expressing the opinion that if I had talked like that before [the Presbytery meeting on July 16] I'd still be pastor of the Church. Maybe so, maybe not. I don't imagine the blame for the failure to get together in a different spirit can be placed at either side's door entirely. I surely don't put entire blame on the Commission. I do believe in a kind of 'depravity' that resides in each of us as far as self-interest, security and pride are concerned and I suspect the unregenerated part of us all had a tendency to get expressed.

"I meant what I said in my statement—I feel no bitterness. I believe I had best sever my relationship as a minister to the Southern Church. I don't like to think of the Church as a battleground on which I should stand and keep in conflict with authorities. I like to think of the Church as a united fellowship seeking both the mind and spirit of Christ. I believe I can find a fellowship in which my efforts will be less under suspicion and in which my efforts would be more creative."[319]

Of the formation of a new community church in Chapel Hill, Jones told Ramsay that he had always wanted to first try and resolve the problem with the Presbytery.

"Now that this has been proven impossible the move for a Community Church has started again. My position briefly put is this: I see the danger of, in reaction to this experience, starting a Jones Church; or a church born out of frustration and resentment and revenge. Any such fellowship would be doomed to failure and do harm to the community.

"I have refused to (even since my request for dissolution of my ministry) let a new church be organized around me. I have discussed the problem with a number of friends and of course get all kinds of advice.

"Fortunately for me I have been away from Chapel Hill for a year and the ties of friendship, while still strong, have been broken enough so that the thought of leaving Chapel Hill is not an abhorrent one. Then, too, I have been offered several jobs—one as Professor of Religion and Dean of the Chapel in

---

[319] Jones, Charles M. Letter to Charles Ramsay. July 1953.

a college, the Save the Children Federation and an Advisory Committee of the National Education Association are anxious that I continue this work for another year and I have had several inquiries from Church officials in other denominations as to my willingness to work with them. This will take the heat off me in making a decision.

"How I wish I could sit down and talk through this experience and the problems of the future with you and a few other friends whose affection and confidence I have enjoyed!"[320]

Other letters came to Jones from minister friends across North Carolina, and from people who knew no more than they had read in Time magazine in places as far away as Indiana, California, and New Mexico. It was these words of encouragement and advice that he considered while planning his next trip to Chapel Hill, scheduled for July 31. He had been invited to substitute preach for the Reverend Dick Jackson at the Congregationalist Christian Church on August 2. It was before this trip that Jones made up his mind. His decision made front page news in all the local newspapers.

'Jones Made Pastor of New Church', announced the Durham Sun.[321] 'New Chapel Hill Church Names Jones as Pastor', declared the Greensboro Daily News.[322] And the Durham Morning Herald showed four pictures of Jones "accepting the call as pastor of the new non-denominational church in Chapel Hill."[323]

---

[320] Ibid.
[321] Durham Sun. August 3, 1953.
[322] Greensboro Daily News. August 3, 1953.
[323] Durham Morning Herald. August 3, 1953.

The <u>Greensboro Daily News</u> dated the story August 2, and reported it as follows:

"A scant two weeks after he quit the Presbyterian ministry, Rev. Charles M. Jones was called back to Chapel Hill today as pastor of a newly formed community church.

"The 47-year-old minister accepted the call 'with a feeling of inadequacy' at a meeting of about 80 persons—many of them former members of his church here—held this afternoon in the Institute of Pharmacy building.

"The group in rapid order adopted a brief statement of purpose, formed itself into a nondenominational community church and elected major committees to perfect its organization.

"First services of the new church will be held two weeks from now in the United Congregational Christian Church, which has extended the use of its facilities to the group for a trial period.

"In an earlier financial canvass, members of the new group pledged slightly over $7,000 toward the first year's support of the church, contingent on Jones becoming the pastor. The details of his salary and other arrangements were left up to the organizational committee elected at the meeting.

"Rev. Mr. Jones, in a 10-minute statement at the beginning of the meeting, cautioned those assembled against organizing a church 'on the basis of emotion.' This was an apparent reference to the Presbyterian controversy of the past 18 months which was climaxed by his being fired from his local pulpit last Spring and his resignation from the Presbyterian ministry on July 17.

"Although he encouraged the group to have a full and thorough discussion and to express themselves very freely before calling him—while he left the room—the preacher was called to be minister of the new church by unanimous vote after little discussion and no debate."[324]

Each of the newspapers reported that Lee Brooks, long-time friend of Jones and one of the driving forces in founding the new church, read aloud a 'statement of purpose,' which said:

"Chapel Hill needs a worshipping and working fellowship of people from varied backgrounds and faiths; a church of open membership free from denominational limitations; a spiritual home wherein there is unity in the Christian essentials, liberty in the non-essentials and charity in all things; a fellowship dedicated to the worship of God and to outgoing Christian service."[325]

The Durham Sun reported Jones words on accepting the call.

"We must weld together a family out of a lot of people who don't know each other well. We will have to use a great deal of forbearance, a great deal of thought and a great deal of prayer.

"I hope we will have some experiences—experiences not to make dogma—but experiences that we can share with people."

In order for Jones to become the minister of the new community church, though, he found there was yet more Presbyterian red tape to

---

[324] Greensboro Daily News. August 3, 1953.
[325] Durham Morning Herald. August 3, 1953.

negotiate. He wrote to Orange Presbytery asking to be honorably dismissed to the Congregational Fellowship of Ministers, so that he could take up his new post, and asking for an official letter of this dismissal.

The request was not kindly received by Presbytery. There was no desire within the organization to see Jones back in Chapel Hill as the founding pastor of a church that would inevitably take members away from the existing Presbyterian Church. The debate as to how to answer the request was heated, but finally a motion was made by Chester Alexander, who had made the original motion to set up a Commission on the Chapel Hill problem the previous year, which passed 57-22. It read:

> "Inasmuch as Reverend Charles M. Jones had already in fact demitted the Presbyterian ministry by accepting a call to an independent church, that his name be dropped from the roll of Ministers of Orange Presbytery, and if he so desired, that we grant him a letter as a communing member to the church of his choice."[326]

On September 26, Jones was notified that he had been dismissed to the United Congregational Christian Church of Chapel Hill. The letter of dismissal sent to the Congregational officials read:

> "This is to certify that Charles M. Jones is a lay member of the Presbyterian Church, U.S., and is hereby transferred to the United Congregational Christian Church of Chapel Hill."[327]

---

[326] Presbytery Minutes, p. 45.

[327] Newman, Howard. Letter to Charles Jones. September 26, 1953.

A new era, then, was set to begin. On August 28 Aiken Taylor wrote to the <u>Presbyterian Outlook</u> expressing his disappointment that "debate can be expected to continue for some indefinite time to come" and his hopes that all future discussion might avoid heated repetition of what had passed and concentrate on constructive and objective discussion of the issues raised by the controversy."[328] It is true that with his moving to a new church, tales of the controversy circulated and grew in scale. The Reverend Edward Johnston wrote about the controversy for his Master's thesis twenty years later. In his analysis of the case he spelled out the after-effects of the controversy as he found them.

> "Charles Jones' departure from the Presbyterian Church was clouded by mystery. Twenty years later some people thought he had been tried for heresy or excommunicated. Others simply wondered what happened. But few knew the impact of the Jones Controversy on the Presbyterian Church. Jones, himself, was by nature a low profile person and as such, with the exception of his summation before the summer meeting of Orange Presbytery, wrote no defense of himself or any study of the controversy from his perspective. Yet there are certain observations that need to be made in fairness to Jones and to the Presbytery.

> "Charles Jones loved Chapel Hill. It was the only place he wished to live and minister and no other option, however

---

[328] Taylor, G. Aiken. Letter to Presbyterian Outlook. August 28, 1953.

attractive, made any impression on him. He saw himself as uniquely suited for the University community and planned to live out his days in Chapel Hill. It was this conviction and the loyalty of his congregation, that would not allow him to take the Presbytery investigation seriously until it was too late. The fact that he would go on a sabbatical while under investigation shows how little he thought would come of the case. His fallacy was that he underestimated the determination of the Commission, who saw a problem and wished to have it removed. Jones was to them the problem. They wanted him out of Chapel Hill voluntarily if possible, but if not voluntarily then by action of Presbytery. It was these two opposing forces, Jones and the Commission, that could never communicate. Yet their clash is important for it changed the Presbyterian Church in two ways.

"First, it pricked the social conscience of Presbyterians. Historically, Presbyterians have always considered themselves open-minded and ready to experiment with new modes and ideas. Charles Jones called them to take seriously the race issue at an inopportune time. The year 1952-53 was not a good time to be talking about black-white relations in the southern pulpit. Yet a minister for not doing so was not attacked directly, but indirectly. Herein was Jones' weakness. Jones was a known social liberal, who had demonstrated his credentials for ten years in Chapel Hill, and as such was an embarrassment to the Presbytery leaders. Yet at no time was the race issue mentioned in public as the reason for the investigation, but it was always the chief unwritten agenda. In fact had Jones not been so socially active, it is hard to imagine the Presbytery appointing a Commission to investigate his ministry. Yet Jones was vulnerable. By his own admission he stated that there was a case against him, but the Commission had used the wrong case. The valid case against him was his failure to take the ordering of the church seriously. Jones did not properly encourage and administer the sacraments. He did not properly train and ordain his officers. He simply did not take as a great priority being a Presbyterian. He firmly believed the church was broad enough to take everyone in and its administration would take care of itself. It was this failure as an ecclesiastical administrator that allowed the Commission leverage to dismiss Jones without ever mentioning the unwritten agenda of race.

"The second change resulting from the case was an amendment to the Book of Church Order. Jones was dismissed under paragraph 76 which states that Presbytery may dismiss a minister 'where the interests of religion imperatively demand it.'[329] Following the Jones case and with the agitation of the Presbyterian Outlook the Book of Church Order was amended to read 'when it finds the interests of religion imperatively demand it, following a hearing which provides procedural safeguards as in cases of process.'[330] This amendment has one meaning as far as the Jones case is concerned. No Commission today can be empowered to dismiss a minister in the manner in which Jones was dismissed. The procedure used against Jones is now illegal.

---

[329] The Book of Church Order, 1952, p. 152.
[330] Ibid., 1972, p. 46.

"Charles Jones, the cause of so much bitterness, never left Chapel Hill. He started the Community Church and remained its pastor until his retirement. His influence at the University remained great, but the peak of his ministry had passed. When Jones left the Presbyterian Church, the Church lost one of its truly progressive voices, and Jones lost much of his ability to be heard beyond the confines of Chapel Hill. The Jones case is a human tragedy with no heroes."[331]

Rev. Johnston was right in much of what he said, but not entirely so. On a purely factual basis, Jones did not found the Community Church—he repeatedly made clear that he would be the minister of a new church only if the church was needed and could survive without him. But it is also untrue to say that Jones had passed the peak of his ministry. In some ways, the best was yet to come as he would soon turn his preaching for civil justice into direct action, leading marches, showing students the path of non-violence and walking it with them.

The Sanford Herald expressed it well in an editorial commenting on Jones' acceptance as a clergyman by the Eastern North Carolina Conference of Congregational Christian Churches.

"We are neither qualified nor of a disposition to weigh religious traditionalism against liberalism. The relative importance of dogma and brotherhood we will leave to others.

---

[331] Johnston, Rev. Edward. The Controversy Between Charles Miles Jones and Orange Presbytery, 1952-53. Thesis prepared for earning M.A. Degree, University of Virginia. 1973.

"But we are encouraged nevertheless to know that in the same geographical area of the Rev. Charles Jones dismissal there is an established agency of Christianity in which he is welcome to wear the cloth. We are pleased at the realization that in conducting the services and affairs of a newly organized interdenominational church at Chapel Hill, Mr. Jones will have the dignity and comfort of recognized ministerial status.

"The saga of Charlie Jones, we think, has come to a happy ending—and to a hopeful beginning."[332]

[332] Sanford Herald. October 23, 1953.

Chapter Ten

A Community Spirit

*"Now what I fear for you folk is not the kind of tradition-
alism Jesus condemned. Many of us see its errors—the looking for God in the wrong place, in the letter of an infallible
Scripture, in Creeds, in sacred organizations and institutions, in doctrinal systems. You will not be traditionalists of
this kind.*

*"What I fear for you is the shallow rejection of all that is
past. I fear that you will not know enough, ponder deeply
enough, nor commit yourself to the great tradition. It is only
as you do this that the Christian faith and way can become
not weighed down by the dead and heavy hand of the past,
but a life-giving reality and power in your lives." - CMJ.*

The first Sunday service of the Community Church was held on August
16, 1953, at the Congregational Christian Church of Chapel Hill. The
first church program carried this statement:

"[The Community Church is] a worshiping and working fellowship of
people from varied backgrounds and faiths, a church of open membership,

free from denominational limitations; a spiritual home wherein there is unity in Christian essentials, liberty in non-essentials, and charity in all things; a fellowship dedicated to the worship of God and to outgoing Christian service." It was the statement of purpose first read by Lee Brooks at the formation of the Community Church. The spirit of openness to all faiths, and freedom to differ in opinion, was demonstrated early on by Phillips Russell, the man who had brought Jones to Chapel Hill more than ten years earlier. He left Jones a copy of the church program, underlining the word 'Christian' in the statement of purpose and hand-writing this message: "Don't we rather emphasize one God or Father of all? Don't we welcome Jew and Moslem and Buddhist? This limitation is disturbing."[333] Russell's concerns did not result in any change in the Church's statement, but was indicative of the freedom of expression and idea-sharing that was the very essence of the new Church.

If Jones had worried that the Community Church would be grounded on a fierce, but temporary, anti-Presbyterian sentiment he must have soon been reassured. In the Fall of 1953 the Church moved to the University campus. The taking in of new religious groups was something of a tradition at the University, and class rooms were set side for Sunday School meetings and an auditorium provided for the congregation to meet for Sunday Services. The Community Church was given Hill Hall, which would be its home for six years. During the summers of those early years, though, many services were conducted in the Forest Theater. And in the first few months the Church's membership

---

[333] Russell, Phillips. Note to Charles Jones, September 1953.

more than doubled, increasing from 68 at the Church's conception, to approximately 200 by November.[334]

Jones and his family had moved into a manse on Tenney Circle, a quiet, wooded circle close to Franklin Street. The four-bedroom house was brand new and spacious for Charles, Dorcas and Ginnia. Soon after they moved in, Preacher's mother, known as Mama Jones, came to visit from Tennessee. Jones had not shared with his family the intricacies of the controversy that led to his leaving the Presbyterian Church. Except for his brother Dub, in Kingsport, they knew only that he was no longer a Presbyterian. This was extremely upsetting for Mama Jones, a Presbyterian through and through—it was not that she blamed her son exactly, she just did not understand how a member of her family, and a minister at that, could have rejected, or be rejected by, the Presbyterian faith. As she inspected the beautiful new Cape Cod-style house, she paced slowly up and down, walking and looking, walking and looking, tapping her cane on the wooden floor. Finally she looked up and announced: "Your floors are not level."[335]

The house was spacious enough that Preacher and Dorcas could, to some degree, continue their open house policy, taking in people who needed help or a place to stay for a while. In the past, Jones had taken an interest in several men who had suffered from alcoholism. One of these was before he left the Presbytery, a man named Canada. He had become involved after the newspaper had run a story about the man's drunken run-in with police. It was the slightly irreverent headline that piqued

---

[334] Report to members of Community Church. November 21, 1953.

[335] Interview with Dorcas Jones.

Jones' interest: "Police Can't Keep Canada Dry." Sadly, Canada was something of a lost cause. He would come to the Manse late of an evening, and would find a welcome and a plate of food offered every time, in the hope of keeping him out of the bars. One time, Jones was due to take Canada and some papers to the mental health hospital at Butner, but could not because he had to leave town on business. Instead, he made the mistake of leaving Canada five dollars for the bus fare. Soon after, Dorcas and long-time friend Joe Straley headed to Durham, knowing better than Preacher how that money was likely to be spent. They divided the town into two sections and began hunting. Finally, Dorcas found him in the lobby at the Melbourne Hotel on the corner of West Main and Roxboro Street. She brought him out to the front of the building and was waiting for Straley to come with the car when the Reverend Kelsey Regan, minister of Durham's main Presbyterian Church, strolled by. He spoke to Dorcas, but never at that time, nor later, mentioning the drunk she happened to be propping up.

Dorcas was also closely involved with helping another alcoholic. The man had been a pilot during World War Two, serving in Germany. He had come back from the war to Chapel Hill and had started drinking. A friend of his family, Charles Rush, was also a friend of Jones and knew Preacher was wont to help all kinds of people with all kinds of problems. So he took the man to him, and in 1955 he took up residence with the Jones Family on Tenney Circle. He lived there for almost a year, and because of the heavy workload Jones was under, much of his care and rehabilitation was left to Dorcas. She felt he was worth the effort though, being both a good and intelligent man. He began seeing a psychiatrist in an attempt to work through his problems, and sure enough with this treatment and Dorcas' kindness, attention and cleaning up after his occasional relapses, he slowly pulled himself together. He finally moved out into a small apartment in Chapel Hill and went to work for Orville Campbell, editor of the Chapel Hill Weekly. He eventually married again and had two children, and was even elected to the Board of the Community Church, serving as its chairman.

As well as his preaching and social action in Chapel Hill, Jones continued to travel throughout the South and speak at various groups and associations. On February 25, 1954, he returned to his home state of Tennessee as the keynote speaker at the opening of the Southern Mountain Workers conference in Gatlinburg. At that meeting Jones dealt with an issue that was close to his heart, and one that he had spent a year working to address: the educational and health needs of mountain children. However, he made some remarks in his speech that were picked up by the <u>New York Times</u>, which quoted him as saying:

"We can, in good conscience, no longer refrain from dealing with problems of justice and equality for the Negro in our mountains."[336] It was but one sentence from him, and a small story in total. But Jones' pedigree as a civil rights activist had been established and the controversy, which was referred to in the <u>Times</u> story, was obviously not forgotten. Jones received a letter as a result of the story from Winifred Speaks, who described herself as "a white woman, [and] an active member of the National Association for the Advancement of Colored People, in Connecticut."[337] She told Jones:

"I have traveled thru and visited in the deep South with my Negro friends, and I know how rare it is to find a white minister who dares, openly and unhesitatingly, to state and restate

---

[336] New York Times. February 26, 1954.
[337] Speaks, Winifred. Letter to Charles Jones. March 5, 1954.

his Christianity, in this matter of racial inequality. In fact, ministers here in New England are not much better.

"Again, I wish to express my admiration for your courage and integrity—for your simple Christianity—a quality rarely found in churches, North or South."[338]

Jones responded, thanking her for sending the clipping, and adding:

"We are just now experiencing a general reactionary trend in the South and it is with difficulty we are holding the gains we made in progress toward equality and fraternity during the war.

"It seems to me that the nation as a whole is being swept with a spirit of fear and it is good to know that throughout the country there are many folk in their own way putting in a blow here and there for the extension of democracy."[339]

Jones may have been right in his assessment of the existing political climate. That same month of March, reporter Roland Giduz, who had covered the Presbyterian controversy closely, wrote a long feature article entitled, "Parallels Obvious in BSU And Presbyterian 'Probes.'" The article appeared in the Durham Morning Herald, on Sunday March 21. The piece began as follows:

"Another line in a pattern that began forming several years ago was drawn here this week.

---

[338] Ibid.
[339] Jones, Charles M. Letter to Winifred Speaks. April 3, 1954.

"The pattern was the restricting noose of conservatism tightening around what many persons over the state felt was the bugaboo of 'liberalism' in Chapel Hill. The line was the decision that another popular, if controversial, minister in the University community is likely to be ousted because of an intangible quality about him that has made him eminently well-liked and successful among those with whom he works.

"Julius Caesar Herrin, chaplain to Baptist students at the University of North Carolina, is the second preacher in the town to find himself under fire for 'liberalism' in the past year. So far his case is a parallel to what happened in the instance of the Rev. Charles M. Jones who resigned under fire last summer as minister of the Chapel Hill Presbyterian Church."[340]

Giduz reported that both Jones and Herrin were attacked for their interest in social equality and for their lack of denominationalism. Giduz detailed the Jones controversy, drawing comparisons with the trouble Herrin was facing, and made it clear that these similar incidents of ecclesiastical persecution were neither isolated nor rare. As he put it: "Many of the events reviewed [in this article] might well be applied to other pastorates in Chapel Hill, and perhaps they will be. No doubt some of these preachers must right now be wondering if they'll be next."[341]

---

[340] Durham Morning Herald. March 21, 1954, p. 12.
[341] Ibid.

Meanwhile, Jones and the Community Church were flourishing. In April he wrote a letter to a friend, telling her that the Church had about 250 members, with Sunday congregations of up to 400 people, and a Sunday school catering to 135 children.[342] Still operating on the University campus, the Church had established a committee to both raise funds for a new Church building and to find a suitable site. However, the Church had been active in trying to carry out its mission of "outgoing Christian service," and by December of 1954 had established four committees that would try and further the goals of social justice and equality that would become the signature of the Community Church's work. These were the Memorial Hospital Committee, which organized accommodation for families visiting relatives in the hospital; the Public Welfare Assistance Committee, which gave financial support to unwed mothers, found temporary foster homes for children in need, and secured clothes, furniture and other essentials in the event of a sudden emergency; a Committee on Work in Corrective Institutions, which took reading material to inmates; and the Hislop College Committee, which collected books for the library of Hislop College in India, where a friend of some of the Community Church's members was head of the Sociology Department.[343] The one problem the church had was a shortage of finances, and while frequent requests were made to members to help out the officers knew that the lack of denominational support was a price worth paying for the Church's independence. And every now and again a little money would

---

[342] Jones, Charles M. Letter to Mrs. D.M. Wilson. April 4, 1954.

[343] Report on the First Year of the Community Church of Chapel Hill, NC. December, 1954.

come in from an unexpected source. In April 1955, Jones received a letter, and a donation, from a woman in New York. She wrote:

> "Enclosed please find a small contribution for your work. Actually we've owed you this for a little over 9 years now! You married Fred and I one April 6th, and knowing we were broke, you donated your most adequate services.

> "Faye Messick has written of your new work. I gather the financial end just plain stinks. However, having been exposed to your 'brand' of religion I know it will prosper. You use the same Book but through you it lives and works and comes alive especially to the student who needs religion to temper the blow dealt by the power inherent in material knowledge. I am sorry not for you but for the church that did not recognize your great strength, power, and ability. And tho' I am <u>very</u> active in that thar establishment at present, I feel the need to withdraw <u>some</u> of my meager financial support from it and pass it on to you. Let's face it—they don't need my nickels and dimes that much! And you don't need my foolish moral support—you need that nasty old almighty dollar."[344]

Jones' "new work" as Mrs. Morse had put it, was not too different from his old work. He had continued to work towards racial and social equality, and preached his inspirational sermons on these topics. He had begun 1955 with a sermon on the "gentle interlude" that the

---

[344] Morse, Mrs. Virginia M. Letter to Charles Jones. April 24, 1955.

Christmas period provided in a busy, confusing world. But he warned people not to confuse the Jesus of the Christmas stories with the Jesus they were in Church to worship. As Jesus grew from a babe in a manger, so must people grow and challenge the surrounding world.

> "It's apparent that he's grown a bit from that quiet babe to a disturbing man. From the very beginning of his adult life he astounded people, he disturbed them and he outraged them, so new and so disturbing was his message, so different was his method of meeting the crises of life that the question 'Why?' followed him just like a man's shadow follows him in the sun."[345]

Clearly the question "Why?" had followed Jones also, throughout much of his career. As far back as the 1940s when Jones was giving aid and comfort to inter-racial picnickers and to freedom bus riders, people were wondering why he needed to rock the boat, why he had to help people who were quite content living as second-class citizens in a supposedly free country.

But while he was just one of very few active in the 1940s, there were more and more people starting to speak out, and act, in favor of racial integration. Even the federal court system had recognized the problem, with the landmark Brown v Board of Education decision in 1954. Still, many in the South resisted, and in the late summer of 1955 Jones was called on to investigate an incident in the town of Tchula, Mississippi, that was symbolic of the tension, mistrust and downright hatred felt

---

[345] Jones, Charles M. Sermon. January 2, 1955.

towards anyone suspected of setting out to equalize relations between blacks and whites. The story, in fact, made national headlines, following closely on the heels of another incident in which 14-year-old black boy Emmett Till was kidnapped and murdered after wolf-whistling at a white woman. In this new incident, about 700 angry citizens of Holmes County, Mississippi held a mass meeting to "invite" two white men to leave their community because of alleged speeches for racial integration. The two men were Dr. David Minter, a general practitioner and described as something of a medical missionary in the rural area around the town of Tchula, and Gene Cox, who ran a 2,700 acre cooperative farm in the county where Minter and Cox were thought to have preached in favor of integration. The evidence was a two-hour tape that had been made of one black boy during the investigation of an unrelated incident. The Raleigh Times said:

> "The crowd heard a tape recording of a statement made by a Negro boy who was arrested last week and charged with making obscene remarks to a white woman. The recording said that Negroes and whites 'went swimming' together on the farm and that Minter and Cox preached racial mingling."[346]

There was subsequent debate about who had actually organized the meeting, but many believed it to have been called by the local Citizens Council, which State Representative J.T. Love described as an organization of "white males dedicated to preservation of segregation." One

---

[346] The Raleigh Times. September 29, 1955.

thing was not in doubt—the meeting was presided over by State Rep. Love. And he was not the only politician present that night. Fellow State Representative Ed White condemned Minter and Cox during the meeting, and said: "I don't call these gentlemen Communists but I do say they follow the Communist line."[347] The two men were given a chance to speak for themselves at the hearing, at which point they denied the allegations in the tape. Though they were heckled and mocked as they spoke there were apparently no signs of violent intent towards the men. The newspapers also reported that directly after the meeting, and in the few days afterwards, there had been no violence committed against either man, nor even any threats of violence. However, many people saw the incident as potentially dangerous, including H.L. Mitchell, the President of the National Agricultural Workers Union. He cabled Herbert Brownell, the US Attorney General, demanding an immediate investigation of the incident by the FBI. He wrote: "We fear for the safety of these men and their families and urge your department take action to protect them in their rights as American citizens. A.E. Cox is Secretary-Treasurer of our National Union."[348]

As a result of his past work with unions, Jones was contacted by the National Agricultural Workers Union and asked to go down to Tchula and investigate the incident. Mitchell wrote Jones before he left and explained the purpose of his mission.

---

[347] Ibid.

[348] Mitchell, H.L. Telegram to Herbert Brownell, Department of Justice, Washington DC. September 29, 1955.

"We are all concerned about the Cox and Minter families and want to know what we can do to help them, whether or not they are going to be forced out of the County and State, and if so, what's required in the way of finances, jobs, etc.

"A delegation from AFL&CIO called on the Department of Justice, Civil Rights Division chief Mr. Caldwell last Friday, who told us that until he could get a statement or an affidavit from someone who had personal knowledge that local or state officials were involved in this proposal to drive Cox and Minter away from their homes, he could not order the FBI to investigate. Normally, what was in the newspapers would be enough but it is a political matter and the Department under Attorney General Brownell is most sensitive to past criticism of their actions in having FBI make investigations of reports of denial of civil liberties. I am quite sure that in addition to the elected representative from Holmes County (Mr. Love who was chairman of the mass meeting) the Sheriff, some of his deputies were participants in that meeting. If a strong statement can be made to that effect then that should be enough to at least ensure FBI action in the County which in itself would provide some degree of protection to our friends."[349]

On October 10, Jones produced his report. He concluded that the lack of violence was encouraging, and as a result Cox was reluctant to

---

[349] Mitchell, H.L. Letter to Charles Jones. October 2, 1955.

ask the FBI to step in and investigate. However, Jones said that if necessary he could prove that at least two public officials were at the meeting, grounds sufficient to bring the FBI in if needed. He expressed his concern that although the situation was calm there at that time it could happen that Cox would not be able to get help in time, should he need it. "Things may develop so fast that he can't let us know if he needs help and we should keep a close watch on the situation…if necessary I could go down again on quick notice."[350]

Jones concluded his report as follows:

"Both Cox and Minter are uncertain about the future. They are agreed they should not let themselves be 'run out of the county.' Their intention is to see the present crisis through.

"However only the future will tell whether the animosities aroused will remain and make the Negroes fear to have anything to do with either Dr. Minter and his medical work or Cox and his farm and educational work. Both are agreed this may well come to pass.

"The wives and children of both men are under especial strain. If animosities remain or develop so that living in the community cannot be reasonably pleasant then they may have to move.

"Cox would like to find some similar situation where they can continue the kind of work he is now doing if it becomes necessary to leave. I did not see Minter to get his feelings to the kind

---

[350] Jones, Charles M. Report of an Investigation of the Holmes County Mass Meeting. October 10, 1955.

of work or the place of location he would want if they must move."[351]

Jones' unofficial letter to Mitchell, sent the day before the report was dated, gives another indication as to the mood in Mississippi at the time of Jones' arrival in Holmes County—and also documents an interesting coincidence that could have made the situation worse.

"Gene [Cox] suggested we spend the night in Jackson. Things were looking so bad then he feared my entrance in the county might upset things. It seems the local Presbyterian minister, Hayes Clark, formerly was in North Carolina and knows me. He preached a sermon against my racial and other views when I was under investigation by the Presbyterian denomination a couple of years ago.

"Thursday Gene and I spent in Jackson visiting the Catholic Monsignor in charge of the area, a rabbi who also serves a synagogue in Lexington, the county seat of Holmes County, two professors at Millsaps and several other ministers. They were given details of the situation and responded in varying degrees with offers to help. All of them were concerned, but I felt all of them were scared too.

"I do not know how much help to expect from the persons Gene and I visited when the going gets rough. It is a frightening

---

[351] Ibid.

atmosphere and the Citizens Councils have a way of 'unoffi-cially' acting. Pressure is terrific on these men."[352]

One light on the horizon for men like Cox and Minter, however, was the ever present eye of the media. As Jones had found out during his controversy with Orange Presbytery, even when the odds for immediate justice seem long, the media is there to highlight the existing injustices and provide hope that future crises will be resolved more fairly. The Mississippi incident was reported nationwide, turning some of the pressure exerted by the mass meeting back onto those who had voted to ask Minter and Cox to leave. Even the local newspapers spoke out on their behalf. The Delta Democrat-Times of Greenville, Mississippi, pulled no punches in an editorial.

> "This is just a reminder that Mississippi, including Holmes county, is still in the United States.

> "A number of Holmes countians—reportedly 700 to 1,000 strong—don't seem to know it. They are reported to have attempted to 'persuade' two citizens to leave the county because their ideas on race relations don't jibe with the majority's.

> "One thousand to two. It's a nice, safe ratio, and one-sided enough to scare most people.

> "So far, the two men…haven't left. We admire their guts. And we are sure they have been the victims of false witness, given by frightened Negroes.

---

[352] Jones, Charles M. Letter to H.L. Mitchell. October 9, 1955.

"But, we repeat, this is the United States. Those men are entitled to a basic American right. It is the right to disagree with any other American, openly and in security. To intimidate or punish anyone, whatever his opinions, his religion, his color or his lawful politics, is as un-American as any bestial idea that ever came out from behind the Iron Curtain."[353]

Jones was not called back to Mississippi, and the incident died down of its own accord. But there was one footnote that was of interest to Jones especially. A Presbyterian minister in Kosciusko, Mississippi, named March Calloway spoke out against the mass meeting, questioning the legality of using the tape-recorded interview as evidence against Cox and Minter. Two days later, Presbytery officials instructed the Rev. Calloway to voluntarily resign, which he did.[354]

The legal and ethical struggle over integration had been addressed the previous year in the Supreme Courts ruling against segregation in public schools. That was, for men like Jones, Minter, Cox and Calloway, a step in the right direction. But for a remarkable number of intelligent, educated men in the South, and elsewhere, the ruling was flawed—both in social and legal reasoning. Jones was invited to address some of these issues in early 1956, when he was extended an invitation to debate them at an event, labeled a 'town meeting', sponsored by the Institute of Religion of the United Church, in Raleigh.

The Chairman of the Institute, Mrs. Arnold E. Hoffman, explained the background and purpose of the debate to those who attended.

---

[353] The Delta Democrat-Times. September 30, 1955.
[354] Unidentified newspaper. October 8, 1955.

"For the past seventeen years, the [United] [C]hurch has sponsored the annual Institute of Religion, a series of six Monday night lectures and class sessions concerned with current problems. This unique community service has attracted national attention and has become known as a most distinguished forum in the South.

"The Church, Congregational-Christian and Quaker, feels that any problem which confronts the mind of modern man must be open to the light of ethical questioning and study. The Institute of Religion, with its emphasis on informed public opinion and its opportunity for open debate, is one implementation of this belief. Through the years the great and near-great—educators, statesmen, philosophers, theologians, leaders in many walks of public life—have come to our platform to inform, to stimulate, and to challenge us. We do not always agree with these speakers. Often they do not agree with each other. This has been, and still is, a free platform, where a person who has something to say is assured a hearing. In each annual series, based on a timely central theme, there is a thoughtful, vigorous survey of current opinion, with ample opportunity for questions and answers. The United Church feels that this is its truest contribution to the religious life of our town."[355]

---

[355] Transcript of debate sponsored by Institute of Religion. February 27, 1956., p. 1.

Sharing the platform with Jones that evening were: James Pou Bailey, a former FBI agent, World War Two veteran, State Senator, and prominent Raleigh attorney; Dr. W.C. George, former Head of the Department of Anatomy at the University of North Carolina at Chapel Hill; and R. Mayne Albright, North Carolina native who was director of the Raleigh Chamber of Commerce, a state Democratic Party leader and unsuccessful candidate for governor in 1948. Interestingly, Jones had been made aware, very pointedly, of the racial views of one of these men twelve years before. Dr. George was one of those who had written to Jones following the picnic incident in 1944, accusing Jones of stirring up racial trouble for political reasons, and telling him: "The white people of Chapel Hill desire to live in peace and harmony with the colored neighbors on a basis of mutual consideration and friendliness but social separateness. This basis is approved, I believe, by the majority of our sober colored people, and peace and harmony have prevailed."[356]

Jones spoke first at the meeting. He told the audience:

> "The Supreme Court decision calling for an end to racially
> segregated schools was a welcome one to Christian leaders in
> the South. Legal sanction to an unchristian practice was with-
> drawn. At last, life could be breathed into the Christian plati-
> tudes about brotherhood, human dignity and respect for man
> .... Jesus set forth a religion that was supra-national, supra-
> cultural, supra-class and supra-racial: Jesus believed in God,
> the Father of all Mankind. His early followers declared that

---

[356] George, W.C. Letter to Chapel Hill Weekly. July 25, 1944.

God showed no partiality. He made of one blood all the peoples of the Earth to dwell together on the face of the Earth.

"Christians have seen the damage that segregation does to human beings, for both the segregated and the segregator alike suffer. They have seen that this vicious practice for more than a century has thus twisted the moral judgments of Christians. Racial discrimination has distorted the mind and personality of the segregated, loaded down their inner-life with inarticulate resentments, a sense of inferiority and limitation, but it has also hurt the segregator too.

"The Christian Church welcomed the Supreme Court decision. Yet the stark fact confronts us now there has been no desegregation in North Carolina schools, nor does there seem to be any preparation for it as far as we can see. Quite the contrary, despite the word from the Supreme Court asking the state to proceed in good faith, with practical flexibility, and a prompt and reasonable start with deliberate speed, we have drifted to the serious point of talk about interposition*, and a special session to make tuition available to students to attend private schools.

"Why, with the support of Christian people at the first, have we drifted so far from that enthusiasm?"[357]

---

* The doctrine that a state, in the exercise of its sovereignty, may reject a mandate of the Federal Government. The doctrine denies Constitutional obligation of states to respect Supreme Court decisions with which they do not agree. Based on the 10th Amendment which reserves to states those powers not delegated to the Federal Government.

[357] Transcript of debate sponsored by Institute of Religion. February 27, 1956., pp. 6-8.

Jones gave four reasons and remedies to explain this situation. He claimed there was a lack of political leadership, and that the state and the nation faced a time of rule by anarchy or rule by law. Political leaders were needed, he said, to "state clearly that we intend to abide by law."[358] He then addressed one of his favorite subjects, education in the state.

> "I believe our political leaders would help us if they would state very clearly that they intend to preserve and fulfill our public school system. No democracy can long endure unless it provides an adequate education for all its children. It is now clear that there are elements in our state prepared to destroy public education rather than to permit us further progress along the lines the Constitution is sending us. Can we depend on political leadership to preserve the public school system?

> "Then too, it seems to me it might help if our leaders could draw into their counsel, the help of Negro leaders throughout the state. Those few Negroes that have been chosen have been hand-picked, chosen by virtue of the fact that they know them, and they have been in the employ of the state—and it has been unfair to them and to the Negro people.

> "This is not asking the political leaders to believe in segregation or to disbelieve in segregation. It is asking them to do the

---

[358] Ibid., p. 8.

simple thing of saying, 'We will abide by the law. We will preserve our public school system.'

"Now, just a word about the Church and educational institutions. The law can't do everything. It is very limited. We need to do a quick and good job at changing attitudes and minds. Our churches have made resolutions but done little else. We must confront church people with a clear teaching of the Bible. With these fine resolutions from a high level of leadership we must establish friendly channels of communication and association. We will have to unsegregate ourselves. The unanimous decision by the Supreme Court outlawing segregation in public schools has posed a national problem as fateful as any faced by free people. If we accept the challenge, democracy will live, and Christianity will bear its witness to brotherhood. If we hesitate or if we reject that challenge, democracy will suffer—it might well be destroyed. Christianity will be totally discredited at the hands of those who profess to love her most. James Russell Lowell in a similar kind of crisis declared:

"'Once to every man and nation comes the moment to decide,
In the strife of truth with falsehood,
For the good or evil side.
They must upward still, and onward,
Who would keep abreast of truth.
Lo, before us glean her campfires,
We ourselves must pilgrims be.

"'Launch our Mayflower, steer boldly through
The desperate Winter sea.

And not attempt the future's portal with
The past's blood-rusted key.'"[359]

Raleigh attorney and former State Senator James Bailey spoke next, telling the audience, "I don't have a slightly different viewpoint; I have probably a totally different viewpoint from Mr. Jones. Mr. Jones has spoken of Christianity; I am not going to attempt to answer his argument at all, except to say that this is not a problem of the Church, has not been, and is not likely to be."[360]

Bailey addressed the legal implications of the case, and saw the central issue as being whether the Supreme Court had over-stepped its jurisdiction by dictating education policy to the states.

> "So far as I know, this is the first time it has ever been held that the Federal Government has any power whatsoever over the administration of the internal educational affairs of a state. I have found no such provision in our Constitution. So far as I know, this is a novel doctrine—one that in its broad implications, if followed in other cases, will inevitably result in the elimination of all the rights of the states."[361]

Bailey then remarked that interposition was not a valid option for opposing the Supreme Court's decision, and of violence he said: "Let me dispose of the use of violence. I know of no serious person who advocates it."[362]

He closed his remarks by saying:

---

[359] Ibid., p.9.
[360] Ibid., p. 10.
[361] Ibid., p. 11.

"We cannot concede that any person may be forced against his will to associate with any other person. If there is a right to be educated with people of other races, there must be a corresponding right not to be so educated. Both rights should be protected. The prompt institution of a program of grants-in-aid out of the school fund to persons who desire to be educated only with persons of their own racial characteristics is a proper step, and, in my opinion, is legal. I know of no other solution that will protect the rights of all. I feel certain that if such grants are available to all with only the reservation that the recipient not attend a public school that there is not legal or moral barrier to the program.

"No person will be forced against his will to send his children to an integrated school. The very fact that such a program is in existence would be a strong force toward voluntary separation of the races; but if it is not to be voluntary, let us as citizens of this state see that we continue to educate the races separately, to deal with all races fairly. I don't think that any of us will concede that the Supreme Court of the United States has any legal right to force us against our will to run our school system in any other manner than that which we ourselves wish to run it."[363]

---

[362] Ibid., p. 12.

Next up was the Professor of Anatomy, and President of the Patriots of North Carolina, Dr. George. He began by saying that the Supreme Court decision was made in error, and would "almost surely bring tragic results in its train."[364] He went on:

"I became active in the race problem not because of any animosity towards Negroes, but because of my desire that five, ten generations from now we might have in this country a breed of people capable of maintaining our civilization. My attitude with regard to Negroes cannot be better stated than was done by Governor Charles B. Aycock in addressing an audience of Negroes here in Raleigh fifty-five years ago. He said: 'No thoughtful, conservative, and upright Southerner has for your race ought but the kindest feelings; and we are willing and anxious to see you grow into the highest citizenship of which you are capable. And we are willing to give our energies and best thoughts to aid you. But to do this, it is absolutely necessary that each race should remain distinct and have a society of its own. Inside your own race, you can grow as large and broad and high as God permits with the aid, the sympathy, and the encouragement of your white neighbors. If you can equal the white race in achievement, in scholarship, in literature, in art, in industry, and commerce, you will find no generous-minded white man who will stand in your way. But all of them in the

---

[363] Ibid., p.13.
[364] Ibid., p.14.

South will insist that you accomplish this high end without social inter-mingling. This is well for you, and it is well for us; and it is necessary for the peace of our section.'

"Under this philosophy, so well expressed by a wise governor, the South has made great progress in racial cooperation, in economic well-being, and in mutual respect between the races. Within quite recent years, that progress has been stopped and put in reverse as a result of the Supreme Court's decision and the events leading up to it."[365]

George continued, heavily criticizing the Supreme Court for threatening the nation with "revolutionary turmoil."[366]

"The court's decision seems to me to be devoid of wisdom or virtue, and destructive in effect. Wise and virtuous judgments involving the fates of peoples and nations must be based upon critical examination of the nature of the people and circumstances concerned and the probable consequences of any proposed action program. The judgment rendered by the Supreme Court had no such basis. Reaching general conclusions and making decisions on the assumption that factors and people are equal when they are not, introduces error that invalidates the decision and may lead to tragedy.

"Use of the words 'equal,' 'superior,' and 'inferior,' other than in a qualified sense, may be unwise. However, everyone knows that some breeds of plants and animals are superior to others

---

[365] Ibid., pp.14-15.
[366] Ibid., p. 15.

in some respects. Everyone knows also that some people are superior to others in various respects. Joe Louis, I am sure, is superior to me and to any of us, perhaps, in physical strength. It is likewise true, although unfashionable to recognize it, that some racial groups are superior to others in various respects. Whatever other virtues Negroes may have—and they have many—all of the evidence that I know about—and there is a lot of it—indicates that the Caucasian race is superior to the Negro race in the (LAUGHTER AND APPLAUSE) (this is my qualification) ... is superior to the Negro race in the creation and maintenance of what we call civilization (CALLS, LAUGHTER ETC.). Elaborate support of that statement would require more time than is available here."[367]

George finished his talk with the following remarks which received what the transcript denotes "tremendous applause."

"In my judgment the Supreme Court's decision is unrighteous because mixing our white and Negro children in the intimacies of school life until they are grown would speed up the mixing of the blood of the races. The result would be a hybrid race probably without the capacity to advance or maintain our civilization. It is unbelievable to me that we could adopt such a program as public policy."[368]

---

[367] Ibid., p. 16.

Last to speak was R. Mayne Albright, the Chamber of Commerce head and President of the Raleigh Little Theater. He began with a somewhat more conciliatory tone, making the audience laugh several times before setting out his thoughts on the Supreme Court's decision. He asked the question, "what points of general agreement can be reached as the basis for a workable solution? On what minimal program can we agree?"[369]

Though seeming to disagree with the Court's decision, he suggested five grounds as a basis for his "workable solution."

"First, even though to many sincere people this decision seems merely a nightmare that will be gone in the morning, we should recognize that it has now become the law of the land. (APPLAUSE) Whether the decision was legally sound, whether the decision is socially wise, whether the decision came too early or too late is not the issue. The decision is here, and it is here to stay …. We do not have to like it, we do have to live with it. (APPLAUSE).

"Second: we should recognize the fact that as good citizens we have no choice but to obey the law (APPLAUSE). And the state's position is clear on that point. In the words of Mr. Tom Pearsall speaking as chairman of the Governor's Advisory Committee—'North Carolina is not going to defy the Supreme Court's decision because, one, North Carolina is

---

[368] Ibid., p. 17.
[369] Ibid., p. 18.

made up of law-abiding citizens, and two, there is no way to avoid it. The court has too much power.'

"Third: we must resolve that this decision shall not destroy that which has been closest to the heart of all North Carolinians for half a century—our public schools .... Our real danger is what we can do to ourselves if we should ever decide to sacrifice our schools. We must not make that needless and useless sacrifice. We owe it to our past and to our future not only to preserve but to strengthen our public schools, and to maintain a statewide system of public education, free, public, and universal.

"How can we recognize this decision, comply with it, and still preserve our schools? As a fourth point, I suggest that we can, and must, move slowly .... And we can move slowly for these reasons: the Constitution, as Judge John J. Parker has said, does not require integration, it merely forbids discrimination; and even in eliminating discrimination the law requires only a prompt and reasonable beginning; not an immediate completion.

"Under these rules we can move slowly, but as a fifth and final point, we must move. North Carolina schools in the areas of Negro majority, cannot be made ready for integration in 1956. But, some areas in North Carolina appear to be ready to make a voluntary start in accepting a few well-qualified Negro pupils who apply. As evidence of a good-faith beginning in North Carolina, any such areas should be allowed to do so, as in fact, North Carolina law now permits them to do.

"In my opinion it comes down to this: if we throw open the school-house doors at this time, we may cause such a draft as to blow school appropriations out of the window and thus destroy the schools. If we lock and seal all school-house doors absolutely, we close the school itself to all the school children of North Carolina. But, if in good faith, we permit at least a crack in the door when and where local people are willing, we will in the next half-century be proud that North Carolina weathered this storm and fought for and preserved its public schools. (PROLONGED LOUD APPLAUSE)."[370]

The moderator, George Denny, then read to the four panelists questions that had been prepared by members of the audience. The first he directed at Bailey, asking him, "Just why is not a great moral and social question the concern of the churches?" Bailey responded by saying, "I think the church might well concern itself with religion as such. I think the church, so far, in my own estimation, has failed to meet that problem without trying to meet a lot of other problems along with it."[371]

Jones was given a chance to answer that, and said, "Religion, by nature of the word, as I understand it binds together man and his world and binds man to his fellow man, and man to God. It seems to me if you take religion in its root meaning, it includes all of those relationships— I suppose we disagree on that point, Mr. Bailey." To applause, Bailey answered, "We do."[372]

Other questions followed, dealing with genetics, the Supreme Court's role in interpreting the Constitution, and the cost of subsidizing private schools for all of North Carolina's children. Then Denny directed a question, penned by a student, directly to Dr. George: "As a sociology major in college here in Raleigh, I would like to know exactly where you

---

[370] Ibid., p. 21.
[371] Ibid., p. 21.
[372] Ibid., p. 22.

get your facts that the Caucasian race is superior. I have never come across such facts or any implication of such." Some in the audience applauded the question, and Dr. George replied as follows:

> "One might ... pick out the great achievements that have made up our civilization and he will find that they are all achievements of Caucasians, whether in science, literature, religion, or what-not."[373]

Again, there was applause from the audience. Then Jones was asked if he could give an example of Jesus taking a stand against racial segregation.

> "One of the chief charges against Jesus was that he ate with the Samaritans. The Samaritans were Jewish folk. When they had been captured and overrun at one time, part of the Jewish folk were taken away and part were left behind. The part who were left behind, did as usually happens make friends with the people who had conquered them and they intermarried; and there you had what you would probably call a half-breed situation, and it was in such a case that Jesus would not ostracize such persons and that was, as a matter of fact, what brought the ire of the purists down on him."[374]

Free from the constraints and requirements of Presbyterianism, Jones and the Community Church were realizing one of the chief ideals on which the Church had been founded: social activism. Some had thought that once Jones was away from the Presbyterian Church his influence in Chapel Hill would decline, but this was far from the truth,

---

[373] Ibid., p. 23.
[374] Ibid., p. 25.

as invitations to these kinds of debates proved. Likewise, fears that the Community Church was founded out of a sense of revenge or bitterness towards the Presbytery, and that as a result it would soon falter, were also groundless. The congregation continued to grow and Sunday morning services, of which there were now two, were packed. And as the nation began to face up to its own social problems, so Jones addressed them in his own church.

On February 10, 1957, Jones stood in his pulpit at Hill Hall, on the University's campus, and preached a sermon entitled, "A Realistic Look at Race Relations in Chapel Hill." The date and topic were significant, because that Sunday was Race Relations Sunday, and as he spoke that morning Jones' words were broadcast simultaneously on WCHL, Chapel Hill's radio station. The sermon itself is significant not just because of its wide audience, but for its content. Jones was, and always would be, an advocate for non-violence, for negotiated change, for peaceful change. But without doubt he wanted change. His words that day are a reflection of not just his hopes, but also his frustration, perhaps, and what was not being done to win equality and social justice for blacks. His words were, in some ways, a call to action: he recognized that Supreme Court decisions were important but would not themselves ensure the right kind of social change in the foreseeable future. Churches, communities, individuals, all had to be prepared to do instead of wait, to act and not just talk.

> "Sermons on occasions such as these tend to take an inspirational or hortatory turn. They are often abstract and emotional. Surely inspiration and exhortation are not to be scorned, but we need wisdom as well as goodwill and zeal. Jesus' counsel to his disciples was that they be 'Wise as serpents and harmless as doves.' Too often our thought on human relations deals with the necessity for gentleness, kindness, understanding, consideration and love in approaching our racial

conflicts and the necessity for hard realistic and concrete thinking goes unrecognized.

"So let's speak plainly about race relations in Chapel Hill. Under God's moral laws every person, irrespective of his color, OUGHT to have access to educational and cultural opportunities. Concretely this means that in Chapel Hill schools, libraries, restaurants, motion picture houses, playgrounds, swimming pools, golf courses, and buses OUGHT to have no racial restrictions. It should go without saying that Christian churches endeavoring to keep the claims of God before the people OUGHT to have no racial restrictions whatsoever in membership, privilege or opportunity.

"Christian church leadership, both Protestant and Catholic, has declared that racial segregation is sinful, a transgression of the moral law of God and OUGHT to be eliminated wherever it occurs. This declaration is no ideal we wishfully hope might come to pass but is a realistic judgment of God.

"We can be thankful we have no violence between the races in our community, but let us not be so deceived as to think it is because our relationships are good. We have no violence in our community (though there was a cross burned recently in our county), but it is not because all Negroes are satisfied or because our relations are fair, truthful, righteous and brotherly.

"All Negroes in Chapel Hill are not pleased. Mr. Martin Luther King has in an article in the Christian Century recently pointed out the revolutionary change that has taken place in the Negro's conception of himself. Once the Negro thought of himself as inferior and patently accepted injustice and exploitation. Those days are gone. There is a 'New Negro in the South.'

"The Negro of today is not the Negro of yesterday. Travel, service in the armed forces where democracy was better practiced than in civilian life, improvement in economic conditions, rise in education and other factors enabled him to revalue himself. 'He came to feel he was somebody.' Moreover, his religion told him that God loves all his children and the important thing about him was not his color but the quality of spirit.

"This new sense of respect and dignity on the part of the Negro has made him profoundly dissatisfied with his present relations and opportunities. Some of our Southern friends cannot understand why our formerly 'good' relationships are now so strained. They attribute the change to outside agitation. As a matter of fact it is due to inner agitation in the spirit of the Negro. The tension we are experiencing today is due to the revolutionary change in the Negro's evaluation of himself and his determination to struggle and sacrifice until rights and opportunities denied him in a segregated society are secured.

"Let us then in hard-headed, even though painful, fashion place what exists now in Chapel Hill alongside what ought to be and see wherein we lack. If you were a Negro in Chapel Hill you would be impressed with the fact that even though the Supreme Court declared racial segregation in public schools illegal you would have to have a son or daughter of college age to enjoy your legal rights. Negro students, under pressure to be sure, have almost full rights and privileges as students in our University community. They enroll for any classes and have been received without discrimination in student activities. They are welcomed to the swimming pool and dining hall without discrimination. It is the testimony of our Negro students that they have had fair, courteous and friendly acceptance by the administration, faculty and students. One deficiency still remains—Negro students are given rooms in one section of one floor in one building despite the willingness and desire of both white and Negro students to eliminate this kind of segregation.

"Yet despite the declared law of the land our elementary and high schools have indicated no willingness to offer unsegregated education. Procedure has been established to avoid compliance with the law in this regard.

"If you were a Negro and had a child who loved to read you would know the children's library in the white elementary school would not welcome him. You would know too, the Negro library, despite efforts of Negroes and others to maintain it, had mostly cast-off books donated by persons who no longer wanted them and many of these books were adult books and not children's books. If you were a Negro you would have no swimming facilities for your child despite the fact white children in our community have such advantages. If you were a Negro and wanted to see Tolstoy's War and Peace which played in one of our local theaters last week you would know the manager of the theater would have refused you entrance into the theater. If you were a Negro and became hungry between the bus station and Durham, you would stay hungry until you got to Durham if you did not just happen to try the one restaurant in town that would welcome your patronage.

"Realism demands we admit our race relations are not good. There is no violence in Chapel Hill, but the 'New Negro' is not satisfied. What EXISTS is in some cases illegal, and in many cases unfair when stacked up against what OUGHT to be.

"Realistic thinking demands we begin now to fan out into all areas of our community and to all people of our community to work together. Parent teacher associations should discuss the problem, teachers of both Negro and white children should discuss in their classrooms how they may go more than half way in meeting the demands of justice. Churches, civic clubs, the radio and the newspaper all have a responsibility in enabling our community to bring its fear and hopes, its doubts and its faiths to play in this problem.

"Assembly programs in Negro schools by students from white schools and programs in white schools by students from Negro schools would be helpful. Ministers of Chapel Hill and Carrboro have had an integrated Ministerial Association for several years. Our churches have had Community Thanksgiving and Brotherhood Day services. Last summer a Community Vacation Church School was held with nearly 140 students almost evenly divided between the races. These activities must be continued and expanded.

"In short, our present 'wait and see' attitude is not realistic if we want to have good race relations in Chapel Hill. We need not leave the problem of integration solely up to school administrators or hide it away in an advisory committee to await a crisis when a Negro makes application for unsegregated school privileges.

"In the 51st Psalm I read for our scripture this morning the writer prays, 'Lord, uphold me with a willing spirit.' One of the finest things in the Christian life is the voluntary giving of justice, mercy and love. Justice that is forced on us from the outside, mercy and love that come only out of expediency, deny the very essence of Christ's teachings.

"I believe we CAN have race relations that are morally and religiously sound, that make the finest in educational and cultural advantages available to all people. I believe we CAN rid ourselves of social customs that violate the dignity of the Negro. Let us pray with the Psalmist that God will uphold us with a willing spirit."[375]

Preacher's forceful words and powerful ministry had attracted many such willing spirits, but despite the large and active membership of the Church, it still lacked one thing: its own building. The committee established to locate an appropriate spot, however, eventually came up with a proposal for a site on twenty-four acres, near to the campus at the intersection of Mason Farm Road and Purefoy Road. In May of 1957, the Church's officers authorized the Property Development Committee to begin working closely with the architects in developing final plans. These would then be presented to all members of the Church for approval and building work would begin immediately thereafter. By June of 1957, pledges and gifts to the building fund had exceeded $63,000.

Once the congregation approved all plans, building was begun quickly as intended. The Community Church had never stated a long-term goal of physical development, but the idea now was to develop a

---

[375] Transcript of sermon broadcast on WCHL Radio Station, Chapel Hill. February 10, 1957.

multi-purpose building, one that could be used for Church services, social activities and group meetings—and the dream was realized in the Fall of 1959. On the occasion of the dedication of the building, Jones made this statement about its purpose.

"This house will become a church home when it is greatly used. This building will be a church home for us and the community when it has become tracked with the muddy feet of children, when walls show usage, when its doors are open wide and often to ourselves and strangers, our own groups and groups who have no home but stand in need of a place in which they may gather; when there is controversy within it; when these differences are not resented, not simply tolerated but prized and expressed in loving and creative controversy within our church family; also when it has controversy with the culture in which we live; when we are so bound to the common good and have such courage that we are lifted from conformity, custom and habit and are impelled to a creative maladjustment and controversy with 'normal' society."[376]

---

[376] Pamphlet describing the history of the Community Church. Issued by the Community Church.

Chapter Eleven

Leading the Way

"Authentic Christian conscience is used in inward, dynamic dealing with motives which prepare for decisions in such a way that rules may be broken at times while justice, mercy and faith are maintained." - CMJ.

The decade that was the 1950s ended quietly with regard to the civil rights movement. This was, however, no portent for the times to come—the 1960s, in Chapel Hill as elsewhere, would see revolutionary action and change. At the turn of the decade, the race problems in Chapel Hill mirrored the problems that existed most everywhere in the South. Despite being a relatively liberal community on account of the University, by the beginning of 1960 there had been few material gains for blacks. Some restaurants were still refusing to serve blacks, while others made them sit in special areas, and both of the town's white owned movie theaters refused admittance to blacks altogether. But there was something of a groundswell that indicated change might be on the way.

In fact, it was just sixty miles away, in Greensboro, that four freshmen decided to challenge segregation at a single establishment, a move that sparked a sit-in movement that blazed across the South. The young men, Ezell Blair, Franklin McCain, Joseph McNeil and David Richmond, entered C.L. Harris' Woolworth's during the last hour of business on February 1, 1960. They bought items from other areas of the store, keeping the receipts as evidence of the equal treatment received in those sections as opposed to in the whites-only eating area, and then positioned themselves at four stools at the counter. Their requests for service were refused, but they were not forced to move until Harris closed the store an hour later.[377] This one courageous act inspired other black men and women to take up the cause, and in a similar vein, and rapidly caught the attention of the media. A movement had been born.

And then, for a few days that same month, Chapel Hill's own racial problems became once again the focus of media attention, and once again Charlie Jones was in the thick of things.

On February 27, four students from the black Lincoln High School went to Long Meadow Dairy bar on West Franklin Street, where they bought food from the stand-up counter from which blacks were served—the booths on the premises were reserved for whites only—which they took to the segregated lunch room at the Chapel Hill bus station, where they sat down in the booths reserved for whites. The following night the group was larger, and this time headed to the Colonial

---

[377] Wolff, Miles. Lunch at the Five and ten. New York: Stein and Day. 1970.

Drugstore, a place that catered to blacks and whites at all counters, with the exception of the whites-only lunch facilities. The wife of a local bank president was taking coffee in one of the booths when she was unexpectedly joined by three members of the group.[378] Then on the third night, February 29, more than a hundred boys and girls of high school age were on Franklin Street, and tensions were running high. Jones would later credit the police with prompt and efficient action which prevented any outbreaks of violence.

The following evening Jones was returning from a meeting in Asheville, driving with three other people, one of whom was black.

> "We got hungry near Statesville and decided we would ask Howard Johnson's for service. We went in, the four of us. I said to the hostess, 'There are four of us please.' She looked twice, then smiled and took us to a booth and we were served politely with good food. Leaving a generous tip, we went on our way. Things are changing, I thought."[379]

However, the moment Jones arrived back in Chapel Hill he received a phone call asking him to come to the Hargraves Community Center, two blocks from Franklin Street.

> "I pointed out how late it was but if they would still like for me to come, I would come. They would still like, so I went. I arrived at the Community Center and it was full, boys and

---

[378] New York Herald Tribune. May 11, 1960., p. 20.

[379] Jones, Charles M. Sermon delivered at the Community Church. March 13, 1960.

girls standing around the edges of the room. Negro ministers and a few other Negro citizens were there."[380]

Jones said he was asked to say a few words, at which point he told them about stopping and being served at the Howard Johnson's that evening. He had read in a newspaper about the Lincoln High School students picketing the Franklin Street businesses. He told them: "What you are trying to do is right. It will take level-headed thinking, calm action, and cannot be done by explosion. But it's right."[381]

The discussion when he entered the room had been on what part adults should play in future action by the group. Some of the youngsters thought they needed adult advisors, while others thought they should not because they would then just dictate what the group could and could not do. This latter faction thought that if there were adults in the group, they should vote and work directly with them, and this view eventually prevailed. The group then elected an Executive Committee, which consisted of Jones, two black students from the University, two whites, two recent graduates from Lincoln High School and five black high school students. The group became known as the Chapel Hill Council on Racial Equality, or CORE,[382] and its Executive Committee elected Harold Foster, an eighteen year old high school senior, editor of the Lincoln High School student newspaper and a three-letter athlete, as its chairman. The Reverend J.R. Manley, the black minister of the First Baptist Church and a local school board member, declined to join the committee but offered to act as an advisor.

---

[380] Ibid.

[381] Ibid.

[382] Somewhat confusingly, CORE was also the acronym for the Congress of Racial Equality, a national organization.

Jones later talked about the development of the group in those first few days after that large gathering.

"After the mass meeting there was a meeting of the Executive Committee. It was apparent to me that these first two or three days were explosive ones. I am not sure it was apparent to the youngsters, I think it was. But we began to raise these kinds of questions: what would have happened had you gotten arrested? Would you have been legally in the right or in the wrong? How would you have gotten out of jail? As a result of this kind of questioning the Executive Committee had a University of North Carolina Law School Professor [Daniel Pollitt] spend two hours with them. He explained to them that the Constitution granted everyone freedom of speech and picketing was a way of talking; the only way sometimes that people could get their message spoken. And he explained to them that picketers, walking quietly and without blocking doorways, should receive police protection. From that discussion I felt a new strength coming into them.

"Still another problem confronted the Executive Committee. These young people had seen how easily people could lose tempers and how close violence came to Chapel Hill those first days. I had overheard two students talking together in the back of the room about what they would do if they got in that restaurant—'If he pushes me, I'll push him.' And we realized a need for an understanding of and an education in non-violent protest. So a young man who was deeply committed and experienced in non-violent action was secured to give us help. These kinds of things, non-violence, how necessary it was and its strength, the legal aspects of their protests, were each communicated to a mass meeting of students. Despite the deep snow, they have had no mass meeting with less than 75 to 100 youngsters."[383]

The members of Executive Committee were divided up into three sub-committees that would each deal with a specific issue: picketing, negotiation, and public relations. These groups held their first working sessions on March 1. Jones told his congregation about the work one of the sub-committees did.

"The Picket Committee, of which I am most familiar, came out with a proposal to the Executive Committee that two requirements be made of anyone who would picket. First, they must swear that under no circumstances would they return violence for violence, cursing for cursing, blow for blow—as we put it, even if someone spits on you, you swallow your own spit. The second requirement would be to go through picket school. The picket school does not last for a semester, it lasts for about two hours. We joke with each other and say when you get through you get a degree, M.P., Master of Picketing. There is training, what you group dynamics people call 'role-playing.' The students practice picketing. Somebody takes the role of a friendly white person and asks the picketer a question, and sees how he will respond. Somebody plays a role of an unfriendly person and jostles the picketer, and we see if he can step back and say, 'Excuse me.' We have had two picket classes, to date, and have 35 well-trained, self-disciplined persons of high school or college age who are ready for that work. You will know, of course, from the newspapers, that there was one hour of picketing. This committee sent to [Police] Chief [William] Blake a committee of Negroes who took with them

---

[383] Ibid.

a sheet called 'Pickets Wanted.' Chief Blake was, they said, very good to them—polite, friendly. He was impressed with their sheet and said if they abided by those things he would provide police protection. They have agreed to, and do, let Chief Blake know when any activity of a public nature is taking place. The effect of this training was shown by the contrast of their picketing activities last Monday with those first three days of confusion."[384]

The week that Jones spoke to his Church about the work of the Executive and sub-committees, the groups had decided to call off any public protests for a practical reason. As Jones had mentioned, the snow lay thick on the ground, and the youngsters were afraid that it would be too easy for people to bombard any protestors with snowballs—and possibly too easy for the protestors to justify throwing them back. But clearly their organization and tactics were having an effect—the chairman of the Chapel Hill Mayor's Committee on Human Relations, D.D. Carroll, had asked the group to cease picketing for a week to give the Mayor's Committee an opportunity to work towards some sort of resolution to the town's problems. The Executive Committee decided to agree to Carroll's request.

In his sermon, Jones gave his interpretation of the importance of the developments that year.

"The united activity of students here in Chapel Hill and throughout the South is not a follow-the-leader affair. Nor is it an adolescent rebellion against authority. The[ir] leaflet tells why they picket. Let me read from it: 'We do not picket just because we want to eat. We can eat at home or walking down

---

[384] Ibid.

the street. We do not picket just because students in other cities are picketing. We do not picket to express our anger or resentment at anyone, or to humiliate or put anyone out of business. We do picket to protest the lack of dignity and respect shown us as human beings, to enlist the support of all (whatever their color) in getting service to places of business that will grant us dignity and respect. We do picket to help the businessman make changes that will bring us closer to the Christian and democratic practices.' There is a big head of steam up among Negro students now. They are boiling, and this boiling comes out of a long, long hurt. Hurt not to the stomach but to the human spirit. It is difficult for white people to feel this. I have felt it dimly in the past ten days. I felt it by imagining what would have happened to me, had from childhood to adolescence, everywhere I turned, someone said, 'No, not here. Not good enough. For whites only.' That would build a fire under any self-respecting human being. Human dignity has been hurt and it can no longer stand this discrimination."[385]

Jones went on to praise the youngsters for their courage, their self-discipline and their willingness to work with adults, whites, or anyone who would help them achieve their goals non-violently. He also declared them as the new black leaders of the South, replacing the black leaders who had been put in charge by whites.

---

[385] Ibid.

"For a long time, white people have selected from among the Negro people, those with whom they would deal, and called them leaders. That day is gone. New leaders of the South are here and we must now deal with these people …. Far be it for me to call these boys and girls children, but it may be true, if we handle this crisis well with them, we can look back and say the high school students did indeed lead us into a path we long ought to have walked, and to goals we long ago took but to which we have moved too slowly or not at all."[386]

And he called upon his Church's members for a solidarity of purpose in helping, simply through judicious use of their own purchasing power and spending habits, to bring about the miracle of integration in Chapel Hill's stores and restaurants. And that meant, he said, not just giving one's business to those who serve blacks equally, but actively avoiding those places that refused to do so.

"[Businessmen] need to know that white people will not refuse to trade with them if they treat colored citizens with ordinary decency and equality. They are scared to death that if they serve a Negro in the ordinary fashion they will go broke. I don't believe it. Some restaurants now serve patrons without discrimination and they haven't gone out of business. It is my firm conviction, that if we could find a way for the white people of Chapel Hill to assure the merchants of their support in

---

[386] Ibid.

their efforts, almost a miracle could happen …. And if they won't change by persuasion and good will, they have to learn another way. There is something in that that kind of hurts me to do, I confess it, and yet I see no other way. The only thing that will move such people, and I suppose it is in keeping with human dignity, is to say if you cannot give fair treatment to all, I cannot cooperate with you in treating people unfairly."[387]

He ended his sermon with an exhortation for people to understand the importance of the new movement in Chapel Hill, and the importance for people to act in furthering the movement and gaining ground in the civil rights struggle.

"Finally, let's admit the seriousness of this crisis …. I firmly believe that this crisis is an opportunity, to use Martin Luther King's phrase, to 'make a stride toward freedom.' Not only for freedom for the Negro, but for us. In the light of these facts we each need to ask, 'What is my privilege and my responsibility to do such that the present crisis becomes an opportunity?'"[388]

The community in Chapel Hill responded to Jones' call for action, and responded to the actions of the young black students who launched the sit-in movement in Chapel Hill. In fact, the students planned the movement to last for ten weeks, and such was its success, particularly in the realm of non-violence, that the New York Herald Tribune ran a long

---

[387] Ibid.
[388] Ibid.

feature story entitled, 'How One City in Dixie Doused Race-Hate Fires.' The story appeared on May 10, and began as follows:

> "All the elements but one of the South's agony over its race problem came to the surface in this state university town of 15,000 during a two-and-a-half month campaign against seg-regated eating facilities that closed for the summer tonight with an interracial hot-dog roast.
>
> "The one missing element was violence. The others were the display of adamant feelings by the extremists on both sides of the question, the search for a moderate position, the influences of politics in religion, the changes of the Southern patterns of life and thought among both Negroes and whites, the influ-ence of Northerners seeking to lend a helping hand to the inte-grationists, and the ever-present danger of physical violence from the rural 'red-necks' who took exception to the high-faluting doings of the 'Chapel Hill crowd.'
>
> "Chapel Hill, although it lies almost in the center of this upper South state where all legal opposition to racial integration is sanctioned, if not officially urged, is not typical of the South."[389]

The newspaper then gave details of the various sit-ins and protests during the first few months of that year. The article ended as follows:

---

[389] New York Herald Tribune. May 11, 1960., p. 20.

"The protest movement ended today with the distribution to every household in town of a handbill explaining the actions of the Chapel Hill Council on Racial Equality. The handbill outlines the accomplishments of the last two-and-a-half months, claims the organization will remain intact, and urges action to end segregation in the movie theaters. Meanwhile the boycotts of Long Meadow and Colonial Drug continues although with no demonstrations.

"Tonight's hot-dog roast was conducted against the background of frustrations throughout the rest of the South."[390]

Though this particular sequence of protests had ended with a friendly picnic, this is not to suggest that any of the protesters were content to now sit back and wait for things to go their way. The sit-ins had provoked a great deal of debate around the town of Chapel Hill and on the University's campus. Many University students reproached those who supported or practiced segregation, calling it a moral evil, un-Christian, contradictory to the Constitution, and an "absurdity."[391] Others defended the store and restaurant owners' rights to choose their customers, praised them for taking a stand against pickets and boycotts, and attacked critics of the Southern way of life as "some punk[s] from the North [who] tell us how we should deal with our problems."[392] A poll taken in March revealed that although a majority of people were willing to patronize an establishment that served people of all races, of

---

[390] Ibid.

[391] Justice, John. Daily Tar Heel. March 13, 1960, p. 2.

[392] Rapfort, Thomas. Letter to the Daily Tar Heel. March 18, 1960, p. 2.

those who opposed desegregation, "one-third of the 'no's' were of the more emphatic 'Hell No!' variety."[393] Even if a minority, the segregationists were a defiant and vocal minority, angered and threatened by the challenge to their superiority and supported by the power of tradition. The resistance may have been restrained by the bounds of civility for now, but beneath the surface the town was "as steeped in prejudice as any Southern Hamlet."[394] But as support for desegregation grew, even the bounds of Chapel Hillian civility would be strained to breaking point.

While these first protests were noted for their peacefulness and organization, and were never likely to bring about the town's full integration, they were fundamental in establishing a movement in Chapel Hill that might one day be capable of taking on and destroying the existing, traditionalist power structure. And more than that, these civil protests and sit-ins created a tone that would be followed by subsequent activists in Chapel Hill, a tone of peace, decency, calm and determination, that would do more to earn the respect of on-lookers and opponents than any violent or aggressive manner could possibly hope to do.

As the handbill distributed by the Chapel Hill Council for Racial Equality indicated, the next target was the town's two movie theaters, the Carolina Theater and the Varsity, both of which sat along the main thoroughfare on Franklin Street beside the University's campus. The Varsity Theater was already well-known to Jones—on many a Saturday afternoon, he had taken Ginnia and Bettie Miles there to watch Roy

---

[393] Mayer, Henry. Daily Tar Heel. March 27, 1960, p. 1.

[394] "Our Doors are Open to All: All White People, That Is." Editorial. Daily Tar Heel. January 7, 1961.

Rogers and Gene Autry westerns. Though hardly the only institutions to discriminate, the theaters became a focus of attention simply because at the beginning of the 1960s there were simply no alternatives in Chapel Hill. Local blacks could find other places to eat in town, as many of the restaurants were already desegregated, but to enjoy a movie blacks in Chapel Hill were forced to travel to Durham to sit in the balcony of a segregated theater.[395]

The picketing of the Carolina Theater began in January of 1961, following the refusal of management to allow a teacher from a black elementary school to bring her students to a showing of <u>Porgy and Bess</u>, a film with an all black cast including Sydney Poitier. Black leaders asked the Ministerial Association for its assistance, and the clergy attempted to persuade the owner to offer a single afternoon integrated showing of the film as a compromise. The best counter-offer, though, was a single, late-night, segregated showing, and this in turn was rejected. In response to the impasse, four protesters began to picket the theater on January 6, led by Mary Mason, a native of Chapel Hill and a senior at North Carolina College. By the end of the next day, there were 54 picketers, including "several Carolina students and faculty members" who threatened to remain picketing the theater until it, and the Varsity, were integrated.[396] The first official meeting to organize these pickets was attended by 125 people, of which sixty per cent were black, and forty per cent were students, and with representatives from the Ministerial Association and the N.A.A.C.P. present.[397] Picketing was called off after

---

[395] Harris, Harvey. Robinson, Mike. Daily Tar Heel. January 15, 1961, p. 1.

[396] King, Wayne. Daily Tar Heel. January 7, 1961, p.1.

[397] Clotfelter, Jim. Daily Tar Heel. January 13, 1961, p. 1.

a week to allow for negotiation with the management of the two theaters, but resumed three weeks later under the control of the Committee of Open Movies (COM), with Preacher Jones acting as spokesman for the group. Picketing continued throughout March without interruption and with only one incident of violence (a white picketer was left with bruises after an attack outside the Varsity), but also without having changed the policies of either theater. At that point, Jones told the media the pickets would be called off "with no intention of resuming," in the belief that no positive action would come from continued efforts.[398] Even though some of the pickets failed to achieve their primary goals, that is, the integration of a particular establishment, they were by no means futile exercises. They remained constant reminders to the people of Chapel Hill that all was not well within their community, that injustice lived and there were people prepared to battle it. Moreover, the pickets fostered a sense of pride and dignity in those who took part, a restoration of the pride and dignity that each segregated place of business tried to whittle away. As one protestor said in an editorial column, "Shout me no shouts, and pat me no pats on the back. I am only trying to be a Man."[399] As Jones told the same newspaper, "I am not so sure the greatest value of the picketing is in the economic boycott, but in speaking to the conscience of the people."[400]

Despite the initial failure to get the movie houses to open their doors to all races, COM acknowledged the need for protest to provoke change, and consequently returned to picketing the Varsity and Carolina theaters

---

[398] Clotfelter, Jim. Daily Tar Heel. April 6, 1961, p. 1.

[399] McHaney, Tom. Daily Tar Heel. March 2, 1962, p. 2.

[400] Harris, Harvey. Robinson, Mike. Daily Tar Heel. January 15, 1961, p. 1.

in the fall of 1961. This time, after some months of frustration, negotiation and silent cooperation from the theaters, the Varsity Theater in October adopted an unannounced, unofficial policy of integration, and three months after that, under the threat of pickets, the Carolina Theater followed suit.

As the civil rights movement continued to foment throughout 1962, Jones spent much of his time that year putting together a three-day meeting, due to be held in Nashville on December 27. It was being staged by the Southern Regional Council and the Fellowship of Southern Churchmen, the latter an organization in which Jones had long been a member and was now Chairman. The event was, in fact, labeled a consultation instead of a conference, and it was hoped to keep the numbers of attendees down to below 150 so that more interaction could take place. It was called, 'A Consultation on the South: the Ethical Demands of Integration (Integrating a Desegregating South), and featured seven main speakers, the first of whom was Martin Luther King Jr. whose subject was, 'An Analysis of the Ethical Demands of Integration in the South.' Jones was the chairman of the event's planning group, of which King was also a member. Attendance to the consultation was by invitation, and sent out along with these were copies of the intended program which contained a statement that explained the need for the event.

> "Desegregation is only the first step on the road toward the good society. Desegregation removes the legal and physical barriers to the enjoyment and exercise of the rights and responsibilities of our common life. The process of desegregation, too slow in speed and too small in amount, must go on. Integration is the next step—the positive acceptance of desegregation and

the glad welcoming and full participation of Negroes into the total range of human activities."[401]

It was this topic that Jones tackled, and in doing so once again made headlines in the local newspapers, just two weeks before the Nashville Consultation. Jones spoke at the annual meeting of the North Carolina Council on Human Relations, when he urged members of the Council to move beyond desegregation of public facilities and concentrate on what he called real integration of social activities. The Durham Morning Herald covered the meeting and reported it as follows:

> "The Rev. Mr. Jones, pastor of Chapel Hill Community Church, said, 'Even among 'liberals' of the races, how little traffic goes on between us.' He said the races only meet through formal groups such as race relations councils and ministerial associations.
>
> "Real integration, he said, will only come with the growth of opportunities for 'human experience'—dinner parties, cocktail parties, Christmas sings and dances.
>
> "'Transformations of men are not by arguments, they are by experience and we need to offer the opportunities for human experience,' he concluded.

---

[401] Program for 'A Consultation on the South: the Ethical Demands of Integration.' December 27-29, 1962.

…."The turnout made the event the largest annual meeting in the group's history. The crowd filled the Carolina Inn ballroom.

"The Rev. Mr. Jones began his speech with a criticism of euphemisms used by groups working in the field of race relations. 'I don't know why we so studiously avoid using the word race,' he said, noting that the groups refer to 'human relations.'

"In assessing the progress of race relations, he said, 'The real danger is in looking at how far we have come instead of how far we ought to have come.'

"North Carolina, as a whole, has not really made progress in integration, he said. 'It would be more accurate to say a few people, mostly young Negroes, have made modest gains in desegregation.'

"'Unless we make this distinction between desegregation and integration, we shall be blinded to our goals,' he said. 'Desegregation without integration may leave us in a worse state than when we started.'"[402]

Martin Luther King echoed his words two weeks later at the Consultation Jones had organized in Nashville. He defined desegregation as a destructive thing, the breaking of barriers that have

---

[402] Durham Morning Herald. December 14, 1962.

made our society "prohibitive."[403] But integration, he said, was a creative process involving the positive acceptance of human beings by each other.

"The bells of history are tolling for segregation," he said, and he predicted that in less than ten years desegregation would be a reality throughout most of the South. "But the human relations dilemma of our nation will still be monumental unless we launch now the parallel thrust of the integration process."[404]

The Southern Patriot, published by the Southern Conference Educational Fund, covered the event and reported King as saying that it was important to have laws to protect blacks, but laws themselves were merely a good start:

"'The law cannot make a man love me, but it can keep him from lynching me, which I think is pretty important,' he said.

"His main point was that along with desegregation, which is 'enforceable by law,' there must be efforts to arouse in people, both Negro and white, the inner attitudes that will lead them to obey the 'unenforceable obligations' of integration."[405]

The article went on:

"Toward the close there was a general letting down of hair among those in attendance, and at the end, the Rev. Charles

---

[403] The Southern Patriot. January, Vol. 21. No. 1, 1963.
[404] Ibid.
[405] Ibid.

Jones, white minister from Chapel Hill, N.C., who heads the Fellowship of Southern Churchmen, commented: 'Now I think we are at the point where we could have a good consultation.'

"He articulated what everyone in attendance sensed: that even in a group like this—and it included probably some of the most enlightened people in the South, Negro and white, and some of those most eager to break through artificial barriers— there remain tremendous emotional blocks to mutual trust."[406]

The meeting, however, was not a great success for Jones. Despite his own gift for speaking, he was not a man who settled for appropriate speeches and lofty oratory. He wrote to a friend in April of 1963, telling him, "…the Nashville Consultation … was not really very successful in what it got done."[407] In the letter he went on to say that he was hoping to lead the Fellowship of Southern Churchman into a new, more active and effective era.

Jones' own gift for speaking landed him in hot water in February of 1963, though in reality it was a misinterpretation of his message that had segregationists and anti-integrationists scribbling their fury to Jones and their local newspapers alike. He had been speak-

---

[406] Ibid.
[407] Jones, Charles M. Letter to Mike Hoffman. April 30, 1963.

ing at the final session of the second annual Human Relations Institute in Greensboro, N.C. He was quoted as follows:

"We must move from desegregation to integration.

"We are afraid of intermarriage which is a human thing. People apologize and say it really won't happen but I say we cannot have the highest human relations without solving the problem of the races by inter-marriage.

"Let's not pussyfoot. Human relations between people means the right to belong to each other in church, family, club or school."[408]

The comments were picked up by the UPI and almost all of the major newspapers in North Carolina printed his words— but it was the headlines and reporters' text that fanned the flames of controversy this time, expanding on Jones' message with headlines like 'Minister Calls for Intermarriage'[409] and 'White Cleric Would Solve Bias With Intermarriage.'[410] The letters came thick and fast—thus far marriage had been one of the few human traditions unassailed by the integrationists and many saw Jones' words as a threat to this most precious, and pure, institution.

---

[408] Charlotte Observer. February 25, 1963.
[409] Ibid.
[410] Unidentified newspaper.

The newspapers themselves were the first to weigh in on Jones, saying:

"In or out of context [his] statement tends to inflame the half-hidden fears in many people that extension of full rights of citizenship to Negroes will bring on wholesale intermarriage.

"Many a southerner violently resists the extension of even basic rights to Negroes because of hazy but very real beliefs that someday the right to associate with, talk with or marry whom he wants, will be abridged by the law.

"Many people see dangers lurking at every turn, and the slightest hint of shadow sends them into paroxysms of real, earnest fear. Jones' Greensboro remarks do not contribute anything toward understanding."[411]

Jones was also criticized by Charlotte's Mayor, Stan Brookshire, who told the Charlotte News:

"The advocacy of racial intermarriage by the Rev. Charles M. Jones of Chapel Hill in Greensboro yesterday, which will no doubt be given wide circulation, is unfortunate and harmful to the intelligent efforts that are being made to improve race relations.

---

[411] Charlotte Observer. Editorial, 'Jones' Statement is Hindrance.' February 26, 1963.

"Extremist views tend only to antagonize and create antipathies that hinder sane and sensible progress. I believe the views held by the leadership of both races and most people in North Carolina are moderate and reasonable."[412]

Jones was sent a copy of the Mayor's comments and wrote him, enclosing a copy of a letter he was sending to the editors of the newspapers who had run the story. And with Mayor Brookshire, Jones continued his practice of extending the olive branch, never taking criticism personally and always hoping to come away from such misunderstandings on better terms with those who disagreed with him. He told the Mayor:

"You may still feel your statements are justified and that is all right with me if you do. In any event, please do not interpret this letter as an effort on my part to get a further public statement from you. I write merely to bring about a better understanding.

"Incidentally, I was associated with Mr. Nelson of the Douglas Aircraft Corporation in a consultation in Nashville, Tennessee, in December on 'Integrating a Desegregating South' and there he told of the progress that is being made in Charlotte in the area of employment and promotional opportunities without regard to race. From his report, much of the credit goes to you

---

[412] Charlotte News. February 26, 1963.

and those associated with you. When I came back to Chapel Hill I had intentions of writing you and expressing appreciation for the political leadership you gave, but as you know the intention was never followed through into a deed."[413]

The Mayor replied to Jones, still critical of his stand on intermarriage, saying:

"You are at least encouraging the Negroes to expect to be able to intermarry in the white race, holding this up as the ultimate in race solutions. In this position or inference I must take personal exception. I think that the preservation of the integrity of both races is highly important to both races and that they can live side by side, each contributing to the welfare of the other."[414]

Jones spoke in Greensboro a second time that week, this time at A&T College, addressing the same issue and trying to correct some of the impressions he thought audience members might have.

"I have never suggested that interracial marriages would solve our race problems. I doubt that marriage solves any problems, even when consummated within races."[415]

The letter that Jones sent to the newspapers explained his position more fully, and read as follows:

---

[413] Jones, Charles M. Letter to Mayor Stan R. Brookshire. March 1, 1963.

[414] Brookshire, Stan R. Letter to Charles Jones. March 7, 1963.

[415] Greensboro Daily News. February 27, 1963.

"Two talks made by me in Greensboro recently were reported by the press throughout the State. It was necessary (and I attach no blame to reporters) that only excerpts from the talk be made. It was also necessary for headline writers to do their job (I don't envy them) and the combination of quotes and the selection of headlines in some cases has caused a great deal of confusion. A friend said to me, 'I wonder what Jones did say?'

"Will you try to find space to print this summary of [my] talks which were an answer to this question: 'What do we want: Racial Relations or Human Relations?'

"Briefly put, I said: Improving racial relations serves primarily to ease tension and prevent violence but the ultimate solution of our racial problem is not 'improved race relations' but establishing 'good human relations.' The Judaic-Christian faith declares that God 'hath made of one blood all nations' and that 'God is no respecter of persons,' that we are all children of One God, one family under God, made to love Him and one another. This makes race irrelevant in the various relationships of the human family.

'I then tried to explore what a good 'human relationship' ought to be, saying that as human beings, to Negroes and whites, we would each and all grant to one another the right to have things like education, houses, the buying of food at eating places, swimming pools etc.; also conditions, like justice and respect. In the talks I attempted to evaluate the degree to which that exists in North Carolina.

"In addition to the 'right to have' which is a human and not a racial right, I mentioned the 'right to belong' saying that human beings, members of the family of God, belonged to one another. Discrimination destroys the human right to have and segregation destroys the human right to belong. Good human relation-ships would mean here what improved racial relationships would not mean:—the elimination of race as a criteria for 'belonging', for example to the D.A.R. [Daughters of the American Revolution]; the American Legion; the North Carolina Medical Association; Chambers of Commerce, churches etc. I spoke of the most sacred 'belonging relationship' that human beings have, i.e. marriage. Marriage is first and last a union of human beings who love one another and if we accepted one another as human beings, as children of God and not as members of races, intermarriage between the races would not be feared or deplored. Where men fear, deplore and con-demn the marriage of two people who happen to be of different color, God does not condemn but blesses such a union.

"I did not state that interracial marriages would solve the race problem, nor did I call for interracial marriages to solve the race problem. I did say if we could view one another as human beings then interracial intermarriages would no longer be a problem, they would be a part of the solution as we moved from having 'racial relationships' into good human relation-ships.

"Since I have received many letters and phone calls this state-ment may help to answer the question, 'What did Jones say?'"

The letters to which Jones referred were as strong in content as any he had received thus far in his career—with the subject of intermar-riage, he had really touched a nerve. One letter was sent to his P.O. Box, addressed to "God II." Many were sent anonymously, including the postcard from Columbia, South Carolina, that was addressed to: "Rev Chas Jones, Chapel Hill, NC" and which read in full:

"Of course that lousy filthy niggardly NAACP communist tirade of yours in Durham was not the first such filth coming out of Chapel Hill vice mongers."[416]

Another read, in part:

"How can you, then, as a minister of God, make such stupid utterances. The cause of the flood in Noah's Day was due to this very thing—marrying and giving in marriage in wanton and reckless disregard to God's Laws. You, sir, are a servant of the <u>Devil</u>. You will have your reward in Ghenna fire.

"Beware of 'false prophets' Jesus warned. He sure was <u>right</u>! Wolves in sheep's clothing."[417]

Jones received a second postcard, this one just addressed to "Rev. Charles Jones, Chapel Hill."

"This is to let you know how impressed I was by your 'Human Relationships' talk, as reported in the Sunday G.D.N. [Greensboro Daily News]. It impressed me by the calm, intelligent, human-spirited, Christian approach. Yes, and I'll add one more adjective: 'fearless.' Furthermore, these adjectives reflect my approval of you personally and through the years in your public stand on fundamental issues. It is an inspiration to know that you are in our community."[418]

[416] Anonymous postcard to Charles Jones. March 6, 1963.
[417] Anonymous letter to Charles Jones. Undated.
[418] MacKinney, Loren. Postcard to Charles Jones. April 22, 1963.

Two months later Charles Jones led the first mass demonstration in Chapel Hill's history; 35 students, professors, ministers and townspeople, marched from the St. Joseph's Christian Methodist Episcopal Church, pastored by the Rev. W.R. Foushee, toward the main shopping district of the town, Franklin Street. Before setting off, the marchers recited en masse the non-violent oath:

> "I promise I will participate in this march in the spirit of non-violence. I promise that if abusive language is directed at me, I will not answer in kind. I promise I will meet all situations with non-violent words and acts."[419]

In fact, there was no violence against the demonstrators, just a few cat-calls and booing from people on the sidewalks. The marchers, half of whom were black and half white, carried signs and sang freedom songs as they made their way into the center of town. They stopped at several eating establishments along the route to protest the policy of segregation practiced at many of the town's public accommodations. When the marchers reached the Town Hall, Jones addressed the group, the city of Chapel Hill, and Mayor Sandy McClamroch, who avoided a confrontation by listening from inside the building, apparently sitting on the clerk's desk, watching through a window.[420]

Jones stood on the steps of the town hall and spoke to the crowd, which had increased in number as the march had progressed. "Do you

---

[419] Chapel Hill Weekly. May 26, 1963.
[420] Ibid.

want your freedom?" he asked, and the marchers shouted back "YES!" Jones went on:

> "A lady called to me on the telephone last night and asked, 'Must these people march tomorrow?' I said 'Yes.'
>
> "Fifteen years ago the buses were supposed to be integrated but it was ten years before the bus station had just one room for us all. There was the 1954 Supreme Court decision, and now not all of that has been done. We had some students from Lincoln High School go into Colonial Drugstore, but that is still segregated. There is only one desegregation move in two years and that is nothing.
>
> "The reason we must protest is because there is no movement. We must protest with two words, two words ringing across the South. They are 'NOW' and 'ALL.'"[421]

Jones then listed the means by which complete desegregation could be achieved, and immediately, by the Board of Aldermen: to refuse to issue business licenses to segregated businesses.

The marchers then moved down West Rosemary Street, passing several more segregated businesses. As the march came to its final stop, Harold Foster, Chairman of the Chapel Hill Council for Racial Equality, announced the integration of two of the businesses the protestors had passed that morning. He also announced that demonstrations would be

---

[421] Ibid.

suspended for two days to allow the Mayor's Committee to negotiate the desegregation of the town's remaining businesses.

> "If nothing occurs during those two days, it will be necessary to begin action again. You can look forward to either an announcement for the end of demonstrations, or a call for more."[422]

The assembly concluded with the song that had become the anthem for civil rights protestors throughout the South, 'We Shall Overcome.' As Chapel Hill's first major demonstration broke up, it was clear a new priority had been set: establishing open public accommodations as the primary objective for civil rights activism in Chapel Hill.

Pressure for change grew in Chapel Hill, and marches and sit-ins were by now oft-used tools. The Chapel Hill Weekly recognized that "on experience, there is no real reason for Negroes to think that anything other than unceasing pressure will be successful."[423] But as the intensity of feeling and action in the town grew, so did some people's fears that things were getting out of hand. In fact, the Chapel Hill Weekly opposed demonstrations that would disrupt the entire town, saying protestors should concentrate on just those businesses that were segregated still and not interfere with the lives of ordinary citizens.[424] Even the liberal Governor Terry Sanford called for order—three days after a protest march of 200 people from St. Joseph's Church to Carswell's Colonial Drugstore, and after the conclusion of demonstrations in Greensboro,

---

[422] Ibid.

[423] Chapel Hill Weekly. May 22, 1963.

[424] Chapel Hill Weekly. June 9, 1963.

Sanford issued a "special message" to the state of North Carolina, calling for an end to demonstrations and a focus on negotiation by both sides in the conflict. He said: "Further mass demonstrations breed disorder, endanger lives, establish animosity, and serve no good purpose. I will take whatever steps necessary to preserve the peace."[425]

The proposed public ordinance, and the issue of free access to all public businesses and restaurants, had remained the focus of civil rights activists in Chapel Hill throughout the early part of the summer. A new group, led by Harold Foster, was formed to deal directly with this issue, the Committee for Open Business (COB), and the Mayor's Committee finally agreed that such an ordinance would go a long way to promoting desegregation. On June 11, the Committee recommended that the Board of Aldermen pass the ordinance at their next meeting.[426] The COB suspended all protest action pending the decision of the Aldermen.

The meeting of the Board of Aldermen took place on June 25 before a capacity crowd at the Town Hall. Statements were made both for and against the ordinance, including a period of audience discussion. Then a prepared statement by Alderman Paul Wager, one of the officers at the Chapel Hill Presbyterian Church when Jones had been there, laid out the path the community would follow. His words were a bitter disappointment to the civil rights crowd. Basing a proposal of "indefinite postponement" on the difficulty of the issues raised, and the fact that "there are no guidelines in North Carolina, we respectfully urge you not

[425] Chapel Hill Weekly. June 19, 1963.
[426] Chapel Hill Weekly. June 12, 1963.

to press us for immediate action."[427] This despite the urging of Alderman Adelaide Walters, who implored her fellow board members to find the courage to support the ordinance.

As a result of this decision, or lack of a decision, the COB saw no alternative but to continue its demonstrations—in spite of Governor Sanford's warnings and in spite of a message from the <u>Chapel Hill Weekly</u>:

> "In the event the Committee for Open Business refuses to call a halt, we ask the appropriate Town officials to take whatever steps necessary to end downtown marches. The convenience and safety of the public, we believe, now demand it."[428]

Despite the COB's determination not to give in, some of its members were recognizing that mass demonstrations were of limited value and might be counter-productive if they caused excessive disruption to innocent people, and if the police decided to take a firm stance against them. So on July 7, the group's executive committee announced that, in addition to continuing marches, boycotts and pickets, it would begin conducting workshops in non-violent civil disobedience. In a letter to the <u>Chapel Hill Weekly</u>, COB member Hubert Hawkins warned the community that "we shall call upon a higher law and break the public laws—here, soon, very soon."[429] And in the following month, numerous protestors were placed under arrest for trespassing, obstructing traffic and blocking sidewalks, refusing to move and having to be carried away,

---

[427] Chapel Hill Weekly. June 26, 1963.
[428] Chapel Hill Weekly. July 10, 1963.
[429] Hawkins, Hubert. Letter to the Chapel Hill Weekly. July 17, 1963.

limp-bodied, by police officers. While this particular spate of civil disobedience calmed down relatively quickly, the remainder of 1963 saw a continuation of pickets and demonstrations, and subsequent arrests, by members of COB and other civil rights organizations. And civil disobedience as a tactic in the civil rights struggle was being used more and more by protestors in Chapel Hill, the rest of North Carolina, and throughout the South. By the end of the year, hundreds of people had taken their seats and refused to move at major traffic intersections, in stores, and on sidewalks.

Preacher Jones remained active, on the streets of Chapel Hill and in the pulpit of the Community Church, where his ideas on race relations found their way into the hearts of his congregants and beyond. And his egalitarian principles were not just reserved for the ongoing struggle between the races. In the summer of 1963, Jones addressed an issue that would become an equal rights battleground a few years later. It was the unequal status of women that concerned him, and he preached a sermon on the subject following the North Carolina legislature's refusal to guarantee equal pay for women in the state.

> "The status and the rights of women is one of our continuing moral problems. It is ironic that in spite of our assumptions of the high level of democracy in the United States, Russia has outdone us in granting rights to women.

> "Our religious texts do not provide a clear call for equal rights for women …. The equality of women before the Lord, as is true also of the equality of the slave before the Lord, is a poor substitute for economic and domestic freedom. But equality before the Lord has served as a creative principle, which once set to work can either be leaven or dynamite depending on the speed with which it works."[430]

But the pressing problem of equal rights for blacks was never far from his mind. And he began in 1964 to directly address the new movement towards civil disobedience. He then repeated what he had said in a long article for the Daily Tar Heel. What follows are excerpts from that article.

"Civil disobedience is practiced on a grand scale in Chapel Hill. Within a month's time two hundred thirty-nine anti-segregation protestors have been arrested and charged with violating trespassing and other laws. It is a sad and serious situation. What can we do about it?

"Some are already doing something about it. In a grocery store which has a sign on the door 'Whites Only' protestors have had Clorox and ammonia poured on their bodies and sprinkled in their eyes. Some of them have required medical treatment before they could be jailed.

"…. Others are responding to the wave of civil disobedience in verbal anger. The words one hears most often are 'anarchists,' 'irresponsible students.'

"This morning I want to place some thoughts before you concerning our sad situation. They will be in the context of faith and worship. This does not mean you are asked to accept them simply because they are uttered by a minister from a pulpit in

---

[430] Jones, Charles M. Sermon taken from 'Quotes from Sermons by Charles M. Jones.' The Snuffbucket Draft. 1995.

the hour of worship on Sunday morning. They are offered only for your prayerful and thoughtful consideration.

".... If we, who are white, had been more aware of the deep hurt and the unspoken dissatisfaction of our Negro brethren we would have expected civil disobedience to become a part of the struggle against racial injustice. In 1958, Dr. Martin Luther King wrote in his book, 'A Stride Toward Freedom':

> "'We will take direct action against injustice without waiting for other agencies to act. We will not obey unjust laws or submit to unjust practices. We will do this peacefully, openly, cheerfully because our aim is to persuade. We adopt the means of non-violence because our end is a community at peace with itself. We will try to persuade with our words, but if our words fail, we will try to persuade with our acts.

> "'The way of non-violence means a willingness to suffer and sacrifice. It may mean going to jail. If such is the case the resister must be willing to fill the jail houses of the South. It may even mean physical death. But if physical death is the price a man must pay to free his children and his white brethren from a permanent death of the spirit, then nothing could be more redemptive.'

"Not all law-breakers are immoral according to the long teaching and practice of Protestant Christianity. Man's conscience does not belong to Caesar, it belongs to God. When men's laws violate God's laws, then man has not only the right but the duty to disobey them.

".... What are the laws of any time but the public expression of the minimum amount of justice the majority of citizens are willing to give each other? Laws must be supported by a majority of the people and seldom does a majority vote on anything raise anything to its greater height. Few of us would want to take our musical standards by the popular vote that produces the ten most popular tunes of the month. If a man will not foolishly submit his musical conscience to popular vote, then he will be equally sensible not to submit his moral conscience to the unchallenged domination of the state.

".... The law-breakers in our midst are troublesome to many of us because they are breaking the law to change the law and that, even though we are sympathetic to their cause, does not seem right. We know how dependent we are on law and respect for law to promote peace and tranquility, to establish justice, to promote the general welfare, to educate us and enable us to be civilized persons. It is because of an awareness of the inherent goodness in the state that many are saying, some simply sadly, 'It isn't right to break the law to change the law.'

"....When one holds a law to be unjust and openly disobeys it, asking for the penalty of the law to be placed on him, he is not an anarchist but is following [as philosopher of the law, Scott Buchanan said:] 'a natural and necessary part of the great due process of our law, that process of persuasion through which we govern ourselves. Civil disobedience is a kind of persuasion of the last resort, within the boundaries of law, sometimes the only kind available.

"To put forth the proposition that civil disobedience, the willful and persistent breaking of man's laws with a cheerful acceptance of the penalty for such violations as not being necessarily anarchistic or irresponsible, presents man with a frightening question and one that is expressed often: 'Then this means every man can decide to break the law.' [At which point you have to ask the] question: 'But are they justified at this time and in this place to break our laws?' And the answer for many will be: 'I cannot justify their acts. They are irresponsible.'

".... This is written, not to lift all the persons involved in the present wave of civil disobedience to the high status of sainthood, nor to imply there is nothing but religious and democratic purity in their motivation or action, but to put our situation in the perspective of religious and democratic tradition and practice that we might do more than react angrily with invective.

".... We are probably in for more, not less, conflict in Chapel Hill—conflict between those who practice civil disobedience and those who segregate, conflict even among those working for the end of segregation. But wherever we stand, whatever our judgment and conscience lead us to do or refuse to do, we must try to remember we are all fallible, erring, selfish and fearful human beings. One need not act with less conviction— he will need to act with more love; one need not act with less self-assurance—he will need to act with more humility and less angry judgment as regards his fellow man.

"To people in controversy, the Apostle Paul once wrote, 'Brethren, if a man be overtaken in a fault, ye who are spiritual restore such a one in the spirit of meekness, lest ye also fall.' He was never quite able to do that himself, but it never prevented him from keeping such a goal before him. The measure in which we are able to remember we are all human beings will to a large degree determine the quickness with which we emerge from this crisis and the genuine progress we make because of it."[431]

Over the next several weeks, many members of Jones' congregation came and spoke to him about the problems in Chapel Hill and his own stand, including his words on civil disobedience. Their concerns reflected the concerns throughout Chapel Hill—the demonstrations had begun to increase in number and frequency, resuming after a brief respite over the Christmas period.

One of the most serious incidents, and one that entered Chapel Hill civil rights lore, took place at Watts Grill and ended with the arrest of sixteen white and black demonstrators, including professors from Duke and Chapel Hill. Their arrests came after they were assaulted at the Grill for attempting to enter the place. Albert Amon, a North Carolina College psychology professor, was beaten with a broom handle, resulting in numerous cuts and bruises. The other demonstrators were sprayed with a garden hose as they sat in front of the restaurant waiting for the police to arrive. The incident achieved such notoriety because Mrs. Jeppie Watts, wife of owner Austin Watts, raised her skirts and urinated on the head of one demonstrator.[432]

---

[431] Jones, Charles M. 'A New Kind of Persuasion of the Last Resort.' Daily Tar Heel. January 11, 1964.

An editorial in the <u>Chapel Hill Weekly</u> praised the non-violent stance adhered to by the protestors, and strongly condemned the violence on the part of the business owners.

> "Possibly it won't happen again, but those in places of official responsibility should make it clear that such acts will not be condoned in Chapel Hill and will be dealt with as harshly as the law allows."[433]

Then, for the last half of January, further protests were suspended while Chapel Hill officials were given a chance to end segregation in the town. Following two weeks of fruitless meetings of the Mayor's Mediation Committee and limited protest activity, the date of the ultimatum laid down by CORE arrived, with no change in the status of segregation in town. As promised, Saturday February 1 brought a series of unprecedented demonstrations to the streets of the community. As they had ten months before, 350 people, men, women and children, black and white, marched from St. Joseph's C.M.E. Church to the Town Hall. Some of these marchers split off from the main group, carrying their protest signs into three intersections along Franklin Street, and after spacing themselves along the road, they sat down. Traffic was disrupted for thirty minutes as police pushed, pulled and carried them into the new paddywagon—a refurbished bread truck converted for just this purpose. Later that evening, fifty-three more were arrested for more conventional sit-ins at Brady's Restaurant and Carlton's Rock Pile.

---

[432] Bulkley, Joel. 'New Year Brings Race Violence to Chapel Hill.' Daily Tar Heel. January 7, 1964.

[433] Editorial. Chapel Hill Weekly. January 25, 1964.

Seventy-three more people were arrested during street sit-downs on the following Sunday and Monday.[434]

For the next month, Chapel Hill was littered with the stationary and limp bodies of civil rights protesters—street corners, intersections, restaurants. They even rode out on the main highways into and out of Chapel Hill and blocked these one day, the sentiment being expressed by some as 'No-one enters and no-one leaves Chapel Hill until it deals with its unfinished business.'

But Mayor Sandy McClamroch and his Board of Aldermen were decidedly unwilling to deal with this business, at least in the way the protesters wanted. At one of their meetings, in January, the aldermen were talking about the problems the police were having in dealing with so many pickets and demonstrations. One suggested solution was for an ordinance that would place a curfew on picketing, allowing it from 7am to 7pm. This was debated, and then voted on—a three-three vote that was broken in favor of the curfew by the Mayor.

A few days later, after hearing about the vote, Jones decided the curfew should be tested in the courts. He called his friend at the law school, Dan Pollitt, who assured him such a curfew was, indeed, unconstitutional. Jones and Pollitt then went to see the Mayor and told him that he could either withdraw the ordinance or see it challenged in the courts. McClamroch offered to get the time limit changed, to 9pm. Jones told him that would not do. Some time after, Jones said:

---

[434] 'Racial Roundup.' Chapel Hill Weekly. February 5, 1964.

"I phoned Chief Blake and told him we were going to be arrested that night and we could come to the Town Hall and picket there, in order to make it more convenient for him, and we could appear at any time he set. Chief Blake asked if he might call us back. I'm sure he didn't really want to arrest us."[435]

The evening ended without Jones and his three companions being arrested. However, Blake found the men before they went out to picket that night and told them that a state law required a town ordinance to be passed by a two-thirds vote or, failing that, be passed at the next meeting of the aldermen by a majority vote. Thus there was no picketing ordinance to be worried about. And in fact the issue of the ordinance was not taken up at the next meeting of the Board of Aldermen, so it was never passed into law.

In reaction to the vehemence and persistence of some of the protestors, one evening about 40 members of the Ku Klux Klan, along with over 100 other angry whites, made their way to Chapel Hill, where they found themselves confronted by an equally large group of blacks and whites who were protecting two young men on a public fast in the town, whom the Klansmen and their friends had come to "visit". But the strong and dedicated actions of the protestors began to grate on the town's less involved residents. Their extreme tactics did not seem to accomplish anything concrete, and just as the public was becoming tired of the inconveniences the demonstrators often foisted on them, the young people were themselves becoming battle weary.

---

[435] Ehle, John. 'The Free Men.' Harper &Row, New York. 1965., p.197.

And in March and April the loudest voices of the Chapel Hill movement were as good as silenced. Approximately 1,500 cases were to be tried concerning civil rights protests in Chapel Hill. Many received prison sentences, and this, combined with the exhaustion of the young demonstrators, did much to remove the wind from the sails of the Chapel Hill civil rights movement. But just as the local movement seemed to be faltering, the Federal Government breathed life into the hopes of African-Americans, in Chapel Hill and across the nation. By early July of 1964 a Federal Civil Rights Bill seemed inevitable. Charlie Jones and some others in Chapel Hill decided to be ready to test the law, to ensure local businesses were complying. They held a meeting at the Community Church and divided themselves into integrated teams that would go out on the morning of July 4. President Johnson signed the Bill on the evening of July 2, before Jones had expected, so on the night of July 3, an integrated group headed over to Brady's Restaurant. They were served. They then went to Watts Motel and Restaurant, where they were told to leave, and then assaulted.

The next morning, July 4, Jones and his teams went into the previously segregated restaurants, including Watts Restaurant, asked to be served, and were. Although Austin Watts arranged not to be present when the group arrived, and Jeppie Watts refused to wait on the group herself, by noon Jones and his teams could report that every restaurant in Chapel Hill was now integrated.[436]

Though the racial problem was now ostensibly more settled in Chapel Hill, the Civil Rights Act of 1964 was clearly only a beginning, and in many places in the rest of the state of North Carolina, attitudes towards blacks and integration were as firmly set as they had ever been.

---

[436] Ehle, John. 'The Free Men.' Harper &Row, New York. 1965.

Just a few weeks before the new law was passed, a situation erupted in Elm City, North Carolina, a small town of 729 people,[437] about two hours drive directly east of Chapel Hill. The incident contained all the worst elements of small town racism—a community trying to improve a small black church, threats, arson, and the Ku Klux Klan. Jones was one of the first people to head to Elm City in response to the crisis, and after the event he compiled a report of the incident.

> "The Synod of Catawba (Negro), United Presbyterian Church, in cooperation with a Pittsburgh United Presbyterian Church scheduled a high school work camp in Elm City, N.C., to begin the latter part of June. Soon after arrival they were visited by 250 Ku Klux Klansmen and their Grand Dragon (State head officer) who, according to his own account, told them 'if they wanted to integrate with those niggers, they should take them back to Pennsylvania with them.'

> "The United Press interviewed Grand Dragon Jones who said he did them a 'favor' by advising the group to leave Elm City. The group left.

> "The Mayor of Elm City issued a statement of regret at the intimidation but at the same time expressed a hope that no attempt would be made to bring in a group to replace the one that left. Already the Synod of Catawba had asked the Board of

---

[437] Greensboro Daily News. July 15, 1964.

National Missions of the United Presbyterian Church to put their full resources behind any project which may be similarly threatened or endangered.

"Widespread comment by newspapers of the state expressed alarm over the forced cancellation of this church project. Not all commentators believed the Klan should be defied by the coming of another project however.

"It was at this time it appeared to me we should look into what was happening and if possible lend some help. Being acquainted with a few white Presbyterian ministers I called Tom Miller, Associate Student Chaplain in the Presbyterian Church of Chapel Hill and he also knew some ministers in Rocky Mount, the closest large town to Elm City. Charles Webster also came into our conversations and he was born and reared in the county in which Elm City sits. So the three of us met with some half dozen white Presbyterian ministers, with Jim Costen, the local Negro pastor whose church was being painted, his assistant, a young student from Union Seminary New York (he, a native of Durham) and another Negro minister from Wilson, a nearby town. The Chairman of the Rocky Mount Good Neighbor Committee, a white businessman, also attended.

"The white ministers, while concerned, had not contacted Jim Costen and this meeting turned out to be useful in giving them this opportunity to find out real facts beyond newspaper accounts. They were also, with the exception of the Good Neighbor Council Chairman and perhaps one minister, of the opinion that plans of the Catawba Synod and the United Presbyterian Mission Board to send in a work camp of ministers, students and lay people to replace the one which left, was a necessary one, though it might be unwelcome by the general populace and the Klan."[438]

That, then, was the first half of the story. What happened next was that Jones and an interracial group headed to Elm City to complete the painting job for which Pastor Costen had first requested help. But such were tensions in the town, and such were fears for the safety of the incoming workers, that five highway patrolmen stood guard while the work was being done at the church, and 25 more were kept on stand-by in case of trouble. Moreover, Governor Terry Sanford issued a stern warning to the Klan:

> "Let it be clearly understood that the Ku Klux Klan is not going to run North Carolina and, furthermore, is not going to take over any part of law enforcement.
>
> "...Local law enforcement, backed up by state forces, will supply all of the protection needed by any citizens who are threatened.
>
> "The people of Elm City are decent and honorable people. They do not want their fine town turned into a battlefield. We are going to give them all of the protection they need. The painting of the church is a private project of the United Presbyterian Church, and whether people think it is an act of wisdom is not for us to judge.

---

[438] Jones, Charles M. 'Report on Elm City Situation.' July, 1964.

"It is true the KKK cannot be responsible for protecting Elm City, but we can, and we will do everything necessary and possible to see that groups promoting violence do not take us over."[439]

Despite the governor's warning and the police presence, attempts were still made to burn down the church, two attempts in two nights, in fact. The second evening though, two youths were caught red-handed by police, and the painting of the church was completed without major incident.

Jones returned to Chapel Hill, to a town quieter and more settled than he had known in years. And it was, too, changed. Twenty years before he had begun his ministry in a college town that was considered by many to be the liberal bastion of North Carolina, but a town where in reality segregation and other forms of racism, subtle and overt, were an established and accepted part of life. The Chapel Hill that welcomed him now was still recovering from the battles that had been fought on its streets, in its stores and in its restaurants. To be sure, there was yet tension in the air, but the scars and social divisions were now of a more temporary nature. The deeper wound caused by social and institutional racism was healing. The crisis in Elm City was one of the last sparks in the ferocious fire that had consumed North Carolina for ten years—a fire that had been fuelled by the convictions, the words, and the deeds of

---

[439] Sanford, Governor Terry. 'A Warning to the KKK.' Chapel Hill Weekly. July 16, 1964.

Preacher Jones so that its flames might consume the evil of racism, and its light might be seen by all.

Chapter Twelve

Journey's End

"We are thankful for those who in the mystery of life could find their path; those who in darkness lighted a lamp for other men to see by; those who could bring to utterance the sacred insights of the spirit; who have made plain life's nobler way." - CMJ.

With the success and then the waning of the civil rights movement in Chapel Hill, Jones turned his attention squarely to activities at the Community Church. The Church had, under his stewardship, come to be a respected and important member of Chapel Hill's religious community. Membership was high, funds were coming in, and it seemed as though the greatest challenges there belonged to the past. But it was to the past that Jones was now looking to launch the next phase in his life.

And so in August of 1966, Jones made the decision to retire. He wrote to the Board of Officers at the Community Church and tried to fully explain his decision.

"I will have completed 35 years of work as an ordained minister in May 1967, 26 of these years in Chapel Hill and the last fourteen as minister in the Community Church. Work throughout has been satisfying and stimulating but especially challenging and enjoyable has been the fourteen years in the Community Church. It is still so and the future probably holds more of the same.

"Nevertheless, several factors have led me to a firm decision to retire from the ministry and ask the Community Church to seek a successor.

"One of these is a self-regarding one. In the span of threescore years and ten allotted man, the major part of adulthood is consumed in making a living, rearing children and seeing them on their way to doing the same. One is fortunate indeed when he can choose the means of earning a livelihood and thereby receive the further satisfactions of joy and creativity. This has been my lot and for it I am grateful.

"Yet however happily we may be joined to our work there often remains a portion of ourselves, interests, skills and abilities, which necessarily have been denied expression by limitations placed on us in our chosen profession. So one is even more fortunate if while there is yet five to ten years of intellectual and physical strength he can and will make a change in his occupation to give release to these supposed, but as yet unrealized, potentials. He can thus have a second period of creative and satisfying activity. At the age of 61, I now have that opportunity and the desire to take it has contributed greatly toward making this decision.

"There are other factors also: the present stage of accomplishment, the present needs and the promise of future usefulness and growth of our Church.

"The Community Church was a venture of faith. Less then 100 persons envisioned the church as:

"'A worshipping and working fellowship of people from varied backgrounds and faiths, a church of open membership; a spiritual home wherein there is unity in Christian essentials, liberty in non-essentials, and charity in all things; a fellowship dedicated to the worship of God and to outgoing Christian service.'

"Without assurance that these purposes (which later were adopted as the basis for membership) would attract sufficient members to support operational or future building expense; without certainty that the life and work of this kind of church would be useful or welcomed in the community, the Community Church was organized and a minister engaged.

"Now after thirteen years these things are assured. Over 700 persons have become members of the Church during this time. Due to the mobile nature of Chapel Hill residents many have moved away but an official membership of 300 together with a sizeable number of families supporting the church and working in it has proved there are enough individuals who need and want this Church to ensure human and financial resources for its continuance.

"At the end of thirteen years financial support has been forthcoming not only to carry on operating and program costs but to purchase 24 acres of land ($22,000), build and furnish the all-purpose building we are now using ($106,000), erect and partially furnish an adequate and beautiful home for the minister ($26,000) and do paving for roads, parking and recreational use. With the exception of approximately $1,200 for paving the Church has no indebtedness.

"For several years an item of $6,400 was carried in the annual budget for the retirement of loans for building. Those loans being paid, this amount continues in the budget, being added to a bequest for a building fund. In February, 1968, this fund will amount to approximately $30,000.

"In these thirteen years the Church has taken its place with other churches in the community as it has worked with them meeting community needs. It is now accepted, respected and called upon for help.

"Today the present needs and the promise of future usefulness challenge the Church. During this year a Church Needs Committee laid before us not only our buildings needs but opportunities in the field of education and other areas of church and community life. During the same time a Religious Education Committee worked painstakingly to develop information from which we are now ready to select a curriculum and do a more comprehensive and intensive work with the children and young people of the Church and the community. As a result of the Church Needs Committee report, the Property Development Committee was instructed to study our needs, investigate the availability of architects, and take steps to move us closer toward the building of much needed worship, education and recreation facilities.

"Along with the strengths of the Church and the opportunities confronting it the length of the present pastorate has played a large part in my decision. Every human being has special aptitudes, strengths and weaknesses, likes and dislikes, in his work and consequently some work he does well, some less well, and some very poorly. Long established denominations, recognizing this, either force, encourage or make possible the movement of ministers in order that varied needs and opportunities of a church may be met over the years. I believe a too-long pastorate, while desirable in some respects, does tend to leave undeveloped many needs and areas of growth in a church. Mine has been a long pastorate (for some of you 26 years) and it has, in my reckoning, been a fruitful one. I believe the present needs and future promise of the church can be served better with suitable fresh, imaginative and younger leadership. Some of you may disagree, but this I believe to be true and it has contributed to this decision.

"No one of these factors by itself, except perhaps the last one stated, would justify this decision. It is putting them together;—my present age and the desire to have a second period of creative and satisfying work of a different kind, and the present strength of the Church, which opens a great opportunity for new leadership which will give the Church a second period of satisfying and creative life within itself and the community, that makes for a confident decision.

"While the decision is a long and carefully considered one which I make with confidence, I am not so confident as to the time element involved in implementing it.

"The first thought was that once such a decision was made its implementation ought to be within a relatively short time, two to four months. If we were denominationally connected even less time would be wise. After giving this more thought it seems to me the Church ought to have sufficient time both to form in its mind the qualities of leadership it needs and to find the person who most nearly meets this need. I am therefore making my request in a way that will permit flexibility as to time.

"Will you please accept my resignation as of September 1, 1967, or as of any date prior to that time when a successor is found and it seems wise that the change be made?

"Whatever the time span, be it months or a year, I shall look forward to our working together in getting a good start toward the building program, the improvement of the educational work and the other activities we engage in."[440]

The board and members of the Church were deeply saddened by his decision. This was reflected in the statement board members issued when they met and voted on his resignation request in September.

"Because we owe it to him to respect his considered decision, we accept the resignation of Charles Jones—but only with the greatest reluctance and the most profound regret. His pastorate spans the life of the Church. Without him the Church would not have come into existence; and he has, to this day, been its inspiration, the foundation of its strength, and the heart of its work. For this, as well as for what he has meant to us as individuals, we are forever in his debt.

---

[440] Jones, Charles M. Letter of resignation to Board of Officers, Community Church. August 15, 1966.

"We assure him of our continued friendship, love, affection, admiration, respect and gratitude. We assure him also that we realize that we will have failed him—and will have deprived his work of some of the permanent value it deserves—if we do not ensure that the Church will grow in strength and in influence. Therefore, as a token of our love and gratitude, we rededicate ourselves to the ideals and mission of the Church. And we pray that, so long as he lives, the Church will have his interest and counsel."[441]

The announcement of Jones' retirement, of course, could not escape the notice of the newspapers. The article that appeared in the <u>Chapel Hill Weekly</u> must have been one of the least controversial pieces that ever appeared about Charles Jones. It was almost certainly the most unashamedly favorable, beginning this way:

"The end of an era, or at least the beginning of a significant new era, was marked in the community life of Chapel Hill this past week.

"Occasion was the announcement by the Rev. Charles Jones of the Community Church of his plans to retire at some convenient time during the next year.

"The Church members have known for some time that the 61-year-old preacher would be stepping down. But his departure

---

[441] Board of Officers, Community Church of Chapel Hill. Letter to Charles Jones. September 13, 1966.

will be a bit different than that of the minister of most churches, for the Community Church was founded as an institution almost wholly based on Charlie Jones himself."[442]

The real praises, however, were yet to be sung. Jones stepped out of the pulpit for the last time the following July, and on October 30, 1967, a dinner was held in his honor at the Ranch House restaurant in Chapel Hill. The main speaker for the evening was Henry Brandis, a former Dean of the University of North Carolina's Law School. He gave a wonderfully eloquent, and accurate, tribute to the man he described as the "best preacher I've ever heard."[443] He began as follows:

"At some point in his life—I do not know just when, because it was before I met him—Charlie Jones made peace with himself on terms which few other people I have known would have accepted and no one else I have known could have honored. He alone knows their full extent, but a reasonably perceptive observer, in a thoroughly astonished way, may identify some of these terms.

"He put aside not only anger, but also irascibility; he eschewed 'can't,' egocentric pride, pomposity, and sanctimony; he agreed to take seriously the most disturbingly difficult precepts of Jesus of Nazareth; and he embraced for the span of his life the fundamental simplicity of common decency. In consequence, he has radiated a moral influence which glows, if sometimes

---

[442] Giduz, Roland. 'Preacher's Retirement Ends Era.' Chapel Hill Weekly. September 28, 1966.

[443] Brandis, Henry. 'Best Preacher I've Ever Heard.' Chapel Hill Weekly. November 5, 1967.

fitfully, in the lives of those within his circle and, through them, passes, somewhat diminished because of resistance in the conductor, into the lives of others."[444]

Brandis went on, saying the laudatory things that people had long thought about Jones, and ended his tribute by referring to the unifying threads that ran through all of his careers. For it was in the very place that they were eating that night, the Ranch House Steak House, that Jones had begun his new career—and reentered the restaurant business.

The Ranch House, on Airport Road, had been owned by Ted Danziger, a member of the Community Church. Danziger had been the one who found the site for the Church back in 1958, and had played a major role in establishing the Church there. His father, known as 'Papa D', had owned a Viennese coffee shop on Franklin Street in the late 1940s and early 1950s. One time, though, knowing of Jones' restaurant days and love of cooking, Papa D asked him to make some chili that he could sell from his store. Jones did so, and it sold so well and so quickly that Papa D realized he was onto a good thing. He and Ted dug out the basement of his store, and there Ted opened a new restaurant, which he called the Rathskeller.

Papa D's son, Ted, also turned to Jones for help, but during the years Jones was preaching it would be more for advice than culinary expertise. He would visit Charles and Dorcas at the Manse on Purefoy Road, pacing up and down the length of the house with a glass of milk in his hand, throwing questions out at Jones about new ideas he had for one

---

[444] Ibid.

of his restaurants, listening as Jones advised him on how to deal with personnel problems.

In 1965, two years before Jones retired, Ted Danziger died after fighting a losing battle with cancer. At that point, Dorcas went to work at the Ranch House with Danziger's wife, Bibi, helping her in the office, setting up a system of control to try and monitor more closely the consumption (authorized and unauthorized) of the restaurant's stock. So in 1967 Preacher Jones also began at the Ranch House, working full-time on site doing as he had been doing informally while still preaching—advising, dealing with staff and generally helping in the office. These were good times for Jones, and for Dorcas, they enjoyed their work immensely, Preacher reliving his days at the Jones Café in Texas, only on a somewhat grander scale.

Dorcas retired in 1972, at which point Charlie decided to go part-time—opening up and running the restaurant for the lunch crowd. He retired for good himself two years later, in 1974.

It was also in 1974 that Charles and Dorcas moved to Williams Circle, into the house that would become their last home in Chapel Hill. They lived there like any other retired couple, enjoying many of the same pursuits. Every winter, for the next four years, though, they headed for Palo Alto, California, to spend time with Janet Jenkins, their former baby-sitter and now close friend, who had contracted cancer. They rented an apartment in her building and spent the winter keeping each other company, shopping and cooking for her when she was too tired to do so herself. Sometimes Dorcas would be there alone with Janet, and they would take trips out, to concerts. One year they went to San Francisco and saw the tenor, Dorcas' favorite, Luciano Pavarotti. Another year they saw the violinist Yitzhak Perlmann. When Charles was there also, the entertainment could occasionally be less sophisticated—debates over whether his tapioca was better than Janet's.

In 1977, the year before Janet died, Charles and Dorcas bought a small cabin in the North Carolina mountains, near Pensacola. They had never lost their love of the wilds, and the tiny cabin was evidence of that.

During his retirement, Charlie Jones was honored for his work in civil rights many times, collecting awards and plaques from grateful organizations who were keen to recognize his bravery and foresight in the early days of the civil rights movement. Since 1993 the Chapel Hill-Carrboro Chapter of the American Civil Liberties Union has presented the Charles M. and Dorcas Jones Award to local citizens who have contributed significantly to the civil liberties effort at the local level. And in 1980, an area of land behind the Community Church was dedicated as a park, and named Jones Park.

After a long illness, Charlie Jones died on April 6, 1993, at the age of 87, at home in his own bed, and surrounded by his family. Newspapers across the state paid tribute to Preacher Jones. One such tribute came from veteran newspaperman Jim Shumaker, who wrote in the Charlotte Observer, and commented on Jones' own view of death:

> "If Heaven turns out to be racially segregated when Charlie Jones gets there, assuming he is still on the way, there's going to be Hell to pay, as sure as God made little green apples.

> "His ideas on predestination were at odds with Presbyterian dogma and Heaven and Hell held for him neither fear nor awe. 'I have faith in immortality,' he said, 'but in what manner or body I am not sure. This has come to be a great mystery to me. The storied conceptions of Heaven and Hell hold no attraction for me.'

"There might be another Charlie Jones around here some-where, but if there is he has escaped notice so far."[445]

Charlie Jones went on to the great mystery in the sky leaving behind a wife, three children, 10 grandchildren, and 10 great-grandchildren.

*　　　　　*　　　　　*

"The more thoughtful a man is, the more of a riddle life is. Beginning with birth where a single cell carries over an amazing weight of inherited possibility from the race behind. Until death, when this mysteriously physically compounded organism dissolves into its elements—what an enigma death is! And in between birth and death, loveliness and tragedy walk hand in hand.

"Finally, in the face of most riddles, we are not completely ignorant. There is enough truth to live by." — CMJ.

---

[445] Shumaker, Jim. 'The Preacher who Raised Hell.' Charlotte Observer. April 18, 1993.

Postlude

The civil rights movement of which Charles Jones was a part was more than just one movement. It was a swell of dissatisfaction that began in the South many years before Preacher ever took to the pulpit. It was a movement that grew thanks to the many courageous men and women who pushed up against the profound weight of the status quo so that those beneath and around them might share the light, that same light that shone solely upon the white majority in America. Many of those pushing hardest in the early years of the civil rights movement were white, men like Preacher Jones who used their positions in the community and their education to help those who were not always in a position to help themselves. Herein lay their courage and decency: men fighting not for themselves, for they already had privilege and status, but fighting instead for their fellow man, risking their reputations, their careers and their lives to help others achieve what so many of their white brethren took for granted and fought to preserve exclusively for themselves. Their courage was in seeing through the fear of a difficult present, an unknown future, to a time where blacks and white were equal. And their courage was in pursuing that dream with all their powers. In the 1940s and 1950s Jones was one of few men in the South able and prepared to shoulder this responsibility. Later, as the civil rights movement gained momentum and rolled through the Southern states, as the black community found its own leaders and the press, police and politicians began to turn their attentions to these men, white leaders like Charlie Jones continued to fight for what they believed was right, even while their names were replaced in the headlines by those now more commonly associated with the civil rights movement. This was perhaps a natural evolution, with blacks taking over the reins of the civil rights movement, insisting on winning their freedom rather than having it won for them by their white friends and colleagues. But whether led by black or white, the force of the movement came from the South, where change was most needed and where despite the segregation and overt racism in so many communities there were pockets of men and women, black and white, who lived and worked for equality, who fought for justice hand in hand knowing that the day would come when their South recognized and acknowledged in all men the same civil rights and human dignity, regardless of color.

To say that the work of Charlie Jones lived on after his death would be a profound understatement. Following in his footsteps, and often using his name, numerous people have worked to bring to life the principles he championed. One of the most notable, and successful, of these efforts was the establishment of an adult day care center serving Chapel Hill, Carrboro, and Orange County. Called The Charles House, it was founded by Preacher's daughter Bettie Miles and her husband Roy Bradford.

Charles and Dorcas had been living on Williams Circle, in Chapel Hill, with Bettie Miles and Roy, both of whom were working. As time took its toll on Preacher's mental and physical abilities, his family found it increasingly difficult to fill his days with interesting and challenging things to do, and also found it difficult to provide him with the near constant companionship he needed. Realizing that there must be many families facing similar problems, Bettie Miles turned to Jones' old friends and admirers to help her start a non-profit adult day care center. The goal was to establish a center that could provide a program of supervised activities in a safe, homelike setting where Preacher, and others like him, could spend time, allowing their families to work or rest on weekdays, resuming the role of caregiver in the evenings and on weekends.

Bettie Miles sent out a hundred letters to friends, asking if they would provide support should the venture go ahead. Ninety-nine responded positively—the one who did not had passed away. In 1984, Charles House was incorporated, and by 1987 Bettie had raised enough money to purchase suitable property. Construction began in 1989, and that same year Bettie quit her job and became the first executive director of Charles House. Much of the money for the building, and indeed many subsequent donations, came from a group of people who had remained close to Charlie Jones for three and four decades, the Snuffbuckets.

Charles House opened in June of 1990, and Charlie Jones and three others became its first participants. In the twelve years since, Charles House has grown to be able to accommodate eighteen people daily—and it is still the only adult day care center in Orange County. And it almost goes without saying that serving the needs of men and women of all races, colors, and creeds has been an integral part of Charles House's mission. As with so many things that Preacher Jones touched and inspired, his legacy lives on even there—the day-to-day running of Charles House is founded on the belief that every individual has worth and should be treated accordingly.

Since his death, the spirit and memory of Charlie Jones have inspired the Snuffbuckets to do more than help found The Charles House.

In April 1999 the Snuffbuckets gathered in Chapel Hill to establish the Charles M. Jones Fellowship for Human Rights. The organization's stated purpose is "to encourage the creative continuation of human rights initiatives in the spirit of Charles Jones through lectures, discussions, recognition of projects in progress, publications, and information about and promotion of human rights."[446]

The keynote speaker at the gathering was Professor John Hope Franklin, who played an instrumental advisory role with NAACP

---

[446] Announcement of First Presentation of Charles M. Jones Fellowship for Human Rights. April 18, 1999.

attorneys in preparing the Supreme Court brief in <u>Brown v. Board of Education</u>. Franklin, a Fulbright professor in Australia and professor emeritus at Duke University School of Law, also served on the boards of the National Humanities Center and the National Council on the Humanities, and in 1996, President Clinton awarded him the Presidential Medal of Freedom, the highest honor a civilian can receive. His credentials, and willingness to speak at the founding of the Fellowship, reflect the importance of the new mission to be carried on in Preacher's name, and reflect also the strength of spirit that Jones had made a permanent part of those who had known him—the spirit that brought the Snuffbuckets together in the 1940s, and held them together for more than half a century.

For a 1973 reunion in Chapel Hill, Snuffbucket Jack Anderson wrote a poem which showed the power of this spirit.

> "Gathering
> From the continental Dispersion
> Like leaves in whirlwind
> Or raindrops on highways
> Or grains of wheat
> (Or chaff, or snuff)
> We came back
> To that invisible womb
> (Or bucket)
> Whence we were untimely plucked—
> Driven, as from Eden,
> Away from the nourishing warmth
> Of that village haven
> And inner circle
> Where we talked

Danced
Touched
Cried
Sang—
Where we groped
Joked
Worshipped
And played God.

"Converging now
On that eccentric meadowed common
Near the hub
Yes, nearer the Hub
Than the hub itself –
By auto, train, jet
And on that one wing
(With or without a prayer)
Which brought that intrepid pair
Whose laughing smiles were,
If not a sermon,
At least a benediction.

"We heard the clash
Of verbal battle
As tired knights
Charged yet one more mill
And sought

In the confusion of tongues
To make one thing perfectly clear –
How to stop the computered slaughter of war,
How to halt the spiraling spew of babes,
How to recycle some shred of paper
Some scrap of steel
Some crumb of earth's dwindled store.

"We heard the harpsichord's
Ancient tintibulation,
And the piping note
Of the recording angel,
And the soaring song
Of that rich voice
Which fills the air
Where'er you walk
And, tho passing by,
Is ever with you still."[447]

---

[447] Anderson, Jack. Hubbub Near the Hub. April 1973.

After more than 30 years ministering in Chapel Hill, it is no surprise that the Snuffbuckets were not the only ones to honor and remember Preacher Jones. In 1974 he became Minister Emeritus of the Community Church, the honor being bestowed as "a simple reminder of a good time in his long, prophetic, and gentle ministry to the people of Chapel Hill." In 1976 he was presented with the Frank Porter Graham Civil Liberties Award, "for achievements in defending and advancing civil liberties in North Carolina." That same year, he was given a plaque in recognition of his service to the Orange and Chatham Counties Health Services, by that organization's board of directors. Two years later, Chapel Hill's radio station, WCHL 1360 honored him during the celebration of its 25th anniversary with a Leadership Award. In 1980, the town of Chapel Hill dedicated a piece of land beside the Community Church, naming it the Charles Jones Park. Its entrance is marked by a large granite boulder bearing a bronze plaque, donated from gifts made in memory of scientist, UNC professor, and Community Church member Oscar Rice. In 1986, the South Orange Black Caucus presented Jones with their Martin Luther King Award, at the organization's annual MLK banquet. It was "in recognition of his courage and services rendered in the Chapel Hill and Carrboro Civil Rights movement." He was also awarded the MLK Jr. Citizenship Award, posthumously, in recognition of his "great legacy and contribution to the community in civic and religious affairs."

One final thought from the author:

In 1993, the Chapel Hill/Carrboro chapter of the American Civil Liberties Union created the Charles M. and Dorcas Jones Award. It is presented annually in recognition of local citizens who have contributed significantly to the civil liberties effort at the community level. This is perhaps the most significant of his awards. Not least because it recognizes the one other person who made so many of his great deeds possible, the one person who helped Charles Jones become the great man and inspirational leader he was—his wife Dorcas. The award is

396 / Faith, Grace and Heresy

also significant because while recognizing Charles and Dorcas, it shifts the spotlight onto others who have worked for the betterment of their community. Charles and Dorcas were ever humble in their achievements, modest about their successes. And the greatest of those successes was the legacy of inspiration that encouraged so many others to do the right thing. Having an eye on the bigger picture while keeping both hands busy in the community was their way of working, and the award in their name, given to others, acknowledges this and tells us much of what we should know about Preacher and Dorcas Jones.

Glossary of Presbyterian Terms and Hierarchy

Deacon: church members elected by congregation to minister to its members who are in need, e.g., by visiting the sick and comforting mourners.

Elder: elected by a congregation to oversee running of a church and its congregation, and like deacons take an active role in congregants' lives. They also have authority equal to the minister in representing their church in the courts of the Presbyterian Church.

Clerk: keeps minutes of all proceedings and all businesses transacted by an individual church.

Minister: the pastor or preacher responsible for a particular church, and moderator of the Session.

Session: directs and runs an individual church, and is made up of a church's minister and its elders. It has the power to receive members into the church, instruct and ordain elders and deacons, report conduct of a minister that goes against Presbyterian teachings, to supervise and develop church programs, and to petition the Presbytery to take action that furthers their church's religious mission.

Presbytery: regional court or governing body made up of several churches. A Presbytery has the power to organize, receive, dismiss and dissolve churches, to establish or dissolve a pastoral relationship, to condemn erroneous opinion which injure the Church, and to appoint representatives to the Synod and the General Assembly.

Synod: regional 'governing bodies' made up of several presbyteries. The Synod can hear and decide issues and complaints raised by presbyteries, and take action relating to presbyteries, sessions and churches that furthers the mission of the Presbyterian Church.

General Assembly: the highest court of the Presbyterian Church. Has the power to decide all controversies, appeals and complaints brought from below.

Commissions:: any church court, Presbytery, Synod or the General Assembly, may convene a commission. A commission can have either administrative or judicial function. Hearings and church visits, followed by a report to its governing body, is a commission's usual method of conducting business.

0-595-21718-4